RELIGION AMONG
WE THE PEOPLE

RELIGION AMONG WE THE PEOPLE

*Conversations on Democracy
and the Divine Good*

FRANKLIN I. GAMWELL

STATE UNIVERSITY OF NEW YORK PRESS

Published by
STATE UNIVERSITY OF NEW YORK PRESS, ALBANY

© 2015 State University of New York

All rights reserved

Printed in the United States of America

No part of this book may be used or reproduced in any manner whatsoever without written permission. No part of this book may be stored in a retrieval system or transmitted in any form or by any means including electronic, electrostatic, magnetic tape, mechanical, photocopying, recording, or otherwise without the prior permission in writing of the publisher.

For information, contact
State University of New York Press, Albany, NY
www.sunypress.edu

Production, Laurie D. Searl
Marketing, Anne M. Valentine

Library of Congress Cataloging-in-Publication Data

Gamwell, Franklin I.
 Religion among we the people : conversations on democracy and the divine good / Franklin I. Gamwell.
         pages cm
 Includes bibliographical references and index.
 ISBN 978-1-4384-5807-6 (hardcover : alk. paper)
 ISBN 978-1-4384-5808-3 (pbk. : alk. paper)
 ISBN 978-1-4384-5809-0 (e-book)
 1. United States—Religion. 2. Democracy—Moral and ethical aspects.
 3. Religion and politics—United States. I. Title.
 BL2525.G364 2015
 322'.10973—dc23   2014044287

10 9 8 7 6 5 4 3 2 1

For
Elizabeth J. McCormack

CONTENTS

PREFACE ix

CHAPTER ONE
Consent to Religious Freedom: The Legacy of Thomas Jefferson 1
    The Present Question 1
    Jefferson's Answers 5
    Refining the Question 15
    Reason's Tribunal 20
    Jefferson's Legacy 28

CHAPTER TWO
On Constitutional Authority: A Conversation with David Strauss 31
    The Living Constitution 31
    Jefferson's Question: Hermeneutical and Normative 37
    The Tradition of Popular Sovereignty 41
    Advancing the Tradition 52

CHAPTER THREE
Democracy and Nature's God: The Legacy of Abraham Lincoln 61
    Lincoln's Political Sentiments 61
    The Declaration's Laws of Nature 68
    The Almighty's Purposes 76
    The House Divided 80
    Lincoln's Legacy 86

CHAPTER FOUR
On Religion in the Public Sphere: A Conversation with
Jürgen Habermas 91
    The Institutional Proviso 93
    Habermas's Proposal: A Critique 100
    Habermas and Rawls: The Basic Problem 105
    The Better Solution 109
    The Attachment to Democracy 115

CHAPTER FIVE
On the Humanitarian Ideal: The Promise of Neoclassical Metaphysics — 121
    Kantian and Post-Enlightenment Challenges — 124
    Metaphysics and Human Purpose — 132
    Making the Humanitarian Ideal Explicit — 143

CHAPTER SIX
Reinhold Niebuhr's Theistic Ethic: The Law of Love — 147
    Niebuhr's Systematic Project — 147
    Niebuhr's Ethic: Harmony and Sacrificial Love — 151
    Niebuhr's Ethic: A Critique — 161
    Niebuhr's Intentions Revisited — 172

CHAPTER SEVEN
On the Loss of Theism: A Conversation with Iris Murdoch — 179
    Emphatic Moral Realism — 179
    Good without God — 183
    The Loss of Worth — 185
    The Necessity of God — 189

Conclusion — 195

Notes — 201

Works Cited — 225

Index — 231

PREFACE

The following essays ask about the moral principle by which good politics is authorized and how, given that principle, democracy in the United States should be understood. The divine good, I argue, defines the moral law and thus the ultimate terms in which democratic politics should be explicated and assessed. At the same time, a political community in which "we the people" are sovereign requires religious freedom, which legitimizes any conviction about the ultimate terms of political evaluation any citizen finds convincing. Accordingly, governmental activity is constitutionally required to remain neutral to all such convictions and, thereby, is prohibited from teaching that any given such conviction is either true or false. How democratic politics can depend on God's purpose and yet be constitutionally neutral to both affirmation and denial of a divine reality is, then, one of the central issues to be pursued here. Moreover, the very consistency of democracy with religious freedom might be doubted. Given that forms of government are forms of political activity, democracy itself cannot be morally authorized except by the ultimate terms or principles of justice. Hence, a form of government neutral toward all possible beliefs about those terms may seem impossible.

Taken as a whole, the essays here defend the coherence of democracy with religious freedom and its moral dependence on metaphysical theism. I seek to show that democratic politics can prescribe relevant governmental neutrality toward all religious convictions if the political constitution establishes nothing other than a full and free political discourse about the ultimate terms of justice and their application to decisions of the state. Discourse or argument is explicitly neutral to whatever differing assertions it seeks to validate or invalidate; hence the constitutional conditions of political discourse can be explicitly neutral to the diversity of legitimate religious convictions. Moreover, democratic politics can itself be morally authorized because a democratic constitution may imply but not explicitly assert or stipulate the ultimate principles of justice "we the people" in their discourse seek to clarify and apply. Those terms, I argue, presuppose metaphysical theism, which does, indeed, authorize a democratic form of government. The conclusion is that politics in accord with the divine purpose is a belief that belongs politically only within the full and free political discussion and debate, where it alone can be validated and, given its validity, ought to inform decisions about the state's activities.

A word about how "metaphysics" is used in the following essays may be useful. On my accounting, the term has two systematically related senses. In its strict sense, metaphysics is critical thought that seeks to explicate the character of reality or existence as such or, with that meaning, the character of ultimate reality. In its broad sense, metaphysics is critical thought that seeks to explicate the character of existence with understanding or subjectivity as such and, insofar, the character of all distinctively human existence. Also on my accounting, metaphysics in the strict sense is included in, although it does not exhaust, metaphysics in the broad sense; that is, the character of ultimate reality is an aspect of the character of all subjectivity. Existence with understanding as such is a specification of existence as such, a specific kind of existence.

As will become apparent, the following essays, and especially chapter 5, are indebted to and seek to defend what I call neoclassical metaphysics, which, in its complete sense, is a metaphysical proposal in both the broad and strict senses. In order to minimize misunderstanding, however, I will in the following essays reserve "metaphysics," unless otherwise noted (as occurs, for instance, in chapter 7), for use in its strict sense, that is, the attempt to explicate ultimate reality—and accordingly, will use other terms, such as "subjectivity," to designate existence with understanding. In speaking of thinkers who reject metaphysics, then, I mean, unless otherwise noted (as occurs, for instance, in chapter 5), those for whom knowledge of reality as such is impossible. Also, I will sometimes use "metaphysical" to designate the characteristics or features of ultimate reality that metaphysics seeks to explicate.

Roughly speaking, the following discussions are divided into two sets, the first attending more to the meaning of democracy with religious freedom and the second to the ultimate principles of evaluation and thus the divine good—but both concerns are present throughout. There is, I believe, minimal repetition from essay to essay; still, some is unavoidable because a constructive project is present throughout, and further, I intend each essay to be readable on its own, without familiarity with any of the others.

Each of these inquiries, with one possible exception, also pursues its point in conversation with another thinker whose achievement is important to the book's focus. Thomas Jefferson, who stands in national memory as the principal mind and voice responsible for religious freedom in the United States, is my conversation partner in chapter 1, where the question is whether democracy with religious freedom, which legitimizes political disagreement at the most fundamental level of evaluation, is a coherent form of political community. Jefferson clearly thought so and, moreover, offered at least two differing arguments for that coherence. I seek to show how both are echoed in contemporary responses to this question and why both are problematic—and then how his thought provides the basis for a convincing approach, all too ignored in the contemporary discussion, that we should critically appropriate.

Chapter 2 asks how the US Constitution is authoritative for US politics and pursues an answer through conversation with Professor David Strauss. On my reading, Strauss's 2010 book, *The Living Constitution*, provides a telling argument against so-called originalism in constitutional interpretation and a compelling argument for a common law constitution in addition to the document of 1787 and its formal amendments. Still, his own proposal, as far as I can see, does not include any abiding constitutional meaning by virtue of which US politics as such is a political tradition to be distinguished from others. Accordingly, I offer a friendly amendment. Notwithstanding the living character of our Constitution, I argue, the provision for popular sovereignty in the United States defines our political tradition—and does so because the Constitution derives its authority from, in the phrase used by some eighteenth-century patriots, the "promise of the Revolution" as expressed in the Declaration of Independence. For this reason, religious freedom, understood to mean the sovereignty of each citizen over her or his conviction about the ultimate terms of political evaluation, is of the essence of our Constitution's authoritative definition.

Chapter 3 attends to Abraham Lincoln's religious sensibilities. If Jefferson provides or implies an account through which to understand religious freedom, Lincoln was, I argue, preeminent among US presidents in conceiving and articulating democracy's relation to a divine order—and this is another inheritance we should embrace. The chapter is, then, a conversation with Lincoln, and its reading of him is developed in part through attention to John Burt's analysis of the Lincoln–Douglas debates in Burt's recent and continually instructive volume, *Lincoln's Tragic Pragmatism* (2013). Although I appreciate Burt's studied conclusions regarding the complexity of Lincoln's intentions with respect to slavery and political equality, Burt's reliance on the political thought of John Rawls threatens to ignore Lincoln's elemental commitment to the universal moral order asserted in the Declaration of Independence. Thereby, one cannot do justice to Lincoln's theistic convictions, which are, I argue, especially well represented in his use of the "house divided" metaphor.

A conversation with Rawls is also present, to a greater or lesser extent, within each of the essays of this first set and most notably in chapter 4, which expresses a debt to Jürgen Habermas, especially to his explication of democracy as politics by the way of discourse, that is, through assessing the validity of contested political claims by the giving of reasons. Habermas proposes a corrective to his understanding of Rawls's treatment of religion, and the chapter attends to the similarities and differences between the two thinkers. The corrective notwithstanding, Habermas's discussion of how religious convictions relate to democratic discourse is, on my reasoning, compromised by what he calls a postmetaphysical understanding of democracy, an account informed by his overarching theory of modernity. As far as I can see, that account requires a constitutional stipulation prohibiting reasons for political decision dependent on metaphysical affirmations—and, thereby, a constitution that contradicts its own provision for religious freedom. Accordingly, I will argue, his revision of Rawls fails to address the more basic problem: neither thinker avoids an express constitutional denial of at least some beliefs that religious freedom legitimizes. In conclusion, this essay seeks to state the better solution.

The second set of essays, then, is principally focused on the ultimate moral principle and thus the divine purpose I take to be implied by the earlier discussions of democracy. Chapter 5, "On the Humanitarian Ideal: The Promise of Neoclassical Metaphysics," presents a straightforward constructive statement. Accordingly, it might be considered an exception to essays having major conversation partners. Still, this chapter defends, against both Kantian and post-Enlightenment alternatives, the argument for metaphysical necessity advanced by Alfred North Whitehead many decades ago in *Adventures of Ideas*. His analysis followed the humanitarian ideal as it developed in Western civilization, and I seek to extend his point in response to our contemporary need for an ideal sufficient to our global context. As the term "neoclassical metaphysics" may suggest, my own philosophical convictions take their bearings from Whitehead and from others who have taken their philosophical bearings from him—and in that sense, the chapter is especially in conversation with Whitehead. In any event, chapter 5 attempts to explicate the moral law, to articulate its prescription of democracy with religious freedom, and to show why morals and politics depend on metaphysical theism.

The final two chapters engage the achievements of two other thinkers without whose legacies our own thought about democracy and religion would be impoverished. Chapter 6 seeks critically to appropriate Reinhold Niebuhr's theistic ethic. In the nearly half century since his death, I judge, Niebuhr has not been surpassed in relating politics to theism, and his sustained systematic thought has abiding significance. He developed his Christian theology in contrast to what he called classical and modern (where the latter is, for Niebuhr, equivalent to secularistic) understandings of the human condition, and he is, I believe, convincing in his critique of those alternatives. Insofar, he gives the best of reasons to affirm a divine source for the meaning of history and politics. Still, his norm of human existence is compromised by implications that are, in his terms, classical in character. The essay seeks to explain how and why this compromise occurs and to outline how his theistic ethic and thus the ground of his political realism may be more coherently formulated.

Chapter 7 is a conversation with Iris Murdoch, whom I call a "reserved friend" to theists. Although not herself one of them, theists have every reason to applaud her argument for the metaphysical ground of religion and thus against alternatives so often persuasive in the recent philosophical context. With appreciation for her friendship, I contend that her nontheistic account is problematic because she takes it and the traditional conception of a completely eternal God to exhaust the metaphysical options, neglecting the possibility of understanding the divine reality—with Whitehead and, especially, Charles Hartshorne—as the eminently temporal individual.

Some or all of these essays have been read by several people who have given me the benefit of their critical and thoughtful responses, and for this I am grateful to Philip Devenish, Larry L. Greenfield, Schubert M. Ogden, Richard A. Rosengarten, David Tracy, Alex Vishio, and two anonymous readers for SUNY Press. I am also grateful to the Visiting Committee of the Divinity School of the University of Chicago for its discussion of remarks I offered on Abraham Lincoln and Thomas Jefferson in 2009 and 2010 respectively; to the Center for Process Studies for three different conferences on neoclassical metaphysics and political thought, held between 2007 and 2011 (the last also sponsored by the Divinity School and its Martin E. Marty Center), in which I was privileged to participate; and to The Divinity School of the University of Chicago for its 1994 conference on the thought of Iris Murdoch, orchestrated by Maria Antonnacio and William Schweiker, at which the essay here in conversation with Ms. Murdoch was originally presented. My discussions of religious freedom have benefited from the work of students in the course on that subject I have taught over the years, and similarly, the essay here on Reinhold Niebuhr has been thoroughly aided by students in the class on his theology I have regularly offered. Mistakes that remain are my own.

I take the liberty of dedicating this book, as an expression of my admiration and affection, to Elizabeth J. McCormack, whose wisdom, in private and in public, has long exemplified how incisive thought makes a difference.

I express thanks for permission to make use of the following previous publications: Chapter 7, in conversation with Iris Murdoch, republishes, now with minor revisions, my essay "On the Loss of Theism," in *Iris Murdoch and the Search for Human Goodness*, ed. by Maria Antonnacio and William Schweiker (Chicago and London: The University of Chicago Press [© 1996 by the University of Chicago. All rights reserved]), 171–89. Chapter 6, in conversation with Reinhold Niebuhr, is a greatly extended adaptation of my essay "Reinhold Niebuhr's Theistic Ethic, in *The Journal of Religion* 54:4 (October, 1974 [© 1974 by the University of Chicago. All rights reserved]): 387–408. That essay was also republished in *The Legacy of Reinhold Niebuhr*, ed. by Nathan A. Scott, Jr. (Chicago: The University of Chicago Press [© 1975 by The University of Chicago. All rights reserved]), 63–84. Chapter 4, in conversation with Jürgen Habermas, draws on some paragraphs in my review of his book, *Between Naturalism and Religion*, in the *International Journal of Philosophy of Religion* 70:2 (October, 2013): 179–83.

CHAPTER ONE

CONSENT TO RELIGIOUS FREEDOM

The Legacy of Thomas Jefferson

Recent discussions of religious freedom and US politics have typically pursued whether and, if so, in what way citizens who are also religious adherents may properly rely on their religious beliefs in making or publicly advocating political decisions (see Greenawalt; Rawls, 440–90; Audi and Wolterstorff; Eberle; Stout; Habermas 2008, 114–47). In response to this question, debates have largely occurred within the unquestioned assumption that all citizens, whether religious believers or not, are or can be committed to a democratic political process and thus a democratic constitution. This assumption, in other words, is typically present notwithstanding the differing views on what restraints, if any, religious adherents should observe in relating their activity as citizens to their religious convictions. Whether a theory simply privatizes religion, or allows political appeal to religious beliefs only in certain circumstances, or imposes a "proviso" on any political conclusions advanced on religious grounds, or permits without qualification political recourse to religious backing, or in some other way defines how religious believers properly participate politically, the context of common consent to a democratic constitution is typically taken for granted.

THE PRESENT QUESTION

This essay is focused on whether the democratic assumption is itself consistent with religious freedom. To help mark that question, it should be distinguished from another, namely, whether democracy with religious freedom is morally good or right—an answer to which requires a more or less complete moral theory and its political application. On my reading, the recent discussions of US politics mentioned above have typically taken for granted not only the self-consistency of democracy with religious freedom but also its moral permissibility. Intending to ask about the former, I, too, will posit the moral authorization of a democratic constitution—although only on condition that politics with religious freedom is coherent. Hence the question for discussion is this: if the constitution legitimizes any religious understanding a citizen might believe, is principled common consent to democratic politics itself possible?[1]

Notwithstanding how widely a positive answer is assumed, its validity is not immediately apparent, for the following reason: the differing religions at least may include differing beliefs about the ultimate context and encompassing purpose or ultimate orientation of human life, the most fundamental principle or principles of both individual and communal activity. Why, then, should an open-ended plurality of such beliefs result in the common allegiance a democratic constitution requires? I will here seek an answer through a conversation with Thomas Jefferson, who, I am persuaded, appreciated the question. Although he finally failed, I am also persuaded, explicitly to offer a convincing response, a coherent account is, I will argue, implied by his abiding commitment to reasoned inquiry, so that we today may endorse religious freedom in profound continuity with him.

Among the founders of our republic, Jefferson stands in national memory as the principal mind and voice responsible for religious freedom, surpassing even James Madison, Jefferson's close and enduring personal and political friend. Some may argue for Madison's greater significance, especially given his role in congressional approval of the First Amendment to the United States Constitution in 1788. But Jefferson's leadership on religious freedom was already secure when Madison entered politics, largely because Jefferson authored in 1777 the Bill for Establishing Religious Freedom— finally enacted by the Virginia legislature, through Madison's leadership, in 1786. "The Virginia event," one historian writes, "was the most decisive element in the epochal shift in the Western world's approach to relations between civil and religious spheres of life after fourteen centuries" (Marty, 1). Also, Jefferson's superior gift for eloquent expression has impressed itself on our history. No sentence in our political legacy, I venture, more captures his stature on religious freedom than his confession of 1800: "I have sworn upon the altar of god, eternal hostility against every form of tyranny over the mind of man" (letter of September 23, 1800; Jefferson, 29).*

For Jefferson, religious freedom is a natural right and thus a prior constraint on all proper governmental power. To be sure, his Virginia Bill

---

*All references to Jefferson in this chapter are to Jefferson 1999.

was proposed as statutory law. But he clearly affirmed what he subsequently confirmed in protesting the absence of a bill of rights, including the right to freedom of religion, in the proposed 1787 Constitution (see letter of December 20, 1787; Jefferson, 360–61), namely, that religious freedom is properly a constitutional principle. Jefferson's proposed constitution for Virginia, drafted in 1776, included the provision: "All persons shall have full and free liberty of religious opinion; nor shall any be compelled to frequent and maintain any religious institution" (http//avalon.law.yale.edu/subject_menus/jeffpap.asp). The statutory Bill became necessary when the provision for religious liberty was not adopted, in part because Jefferson's draft constitution, sent from Philadelphia during his presence in the Continental Congress, arrived in Williamsburg too late for extensive consideration. Moreover, the Bill's final paragraph announced the properly constitutional character of the rights therein protected: "we [the legislators] . . . do declare, that the rights hereby asserted are of the natural rights of mankind, and that if any act shall be hereafter passed to repeal the present or to narrow its operations, such act will be an infringement of natural right" (Jefferson, 391–92).

But precisely how Jefferson conceived and defended political recognition of this natural right is not transparent. The opening phrases of his Virginia Bill as drafted cite a theistic justification:

> Well aware . . . that Almighty God hath created the mind free . . . ; that all attempts to influence it by temporal punishments, or burthens, or by civil incapacitations, tend only to beget habits of hypocrisy and meanness, and are a departure from the plan of the Holy author of our religion, who being lord of both body and mind, yet chose not to propagate it by coercions on either, as was his Almighty power to do, (Jefferson, 390)

One might well wonder whether Jefferson should thereby be charged with inconsistency: if religious freedom is justified by a certain theistic conception, does the political function of this principle depend, against its own provision, on all citizens commonly professing a certain religious belief?

Let me seek to clarify why such dependence yields an apparent contradiction. If religious freedom is a prior constraint on all proper governmental power, it is properly a constitutional principle because a constitution, on my understanding, establishes the political process as such and thus the form for proper determinations of the state's activities. Constitutional provisions, therefore, must be adhered to by all people who are actual or potential participants in the political process, rather as participation in a meeting requires adherence to Robert's Rules of Order. In republican or democratic politics, as no founder of the United States asserted more decisively than Jefferson, "the whole people" (although, for him, this excluded African Americans,

Native Americans, and women) confers political authority: "Independence can be trusted nowhere but with the people in mass" (letter of July 12, 1816; Jefferson, 217; letter of September 6, 1819; Jefferson, 379). Governments, as he wrote in the Declaration of Independence, derive "their just powers from the consent of the governed" (Jefferson, 97). Accordingly, consent to the constitution—by which I here mean adherence to, that is, acting in accord with, the constitution—defines the ethics of citizenship or is required of all citizens, as Jefferson, who never doubted that republican self-government requires a virtuous citizenry, agreed: the people are "inherently independent of all but the moral law" (letter of September 6, 1819; Jefferson, 379; see Gaustad, 120).[2]

But "the whole people" are precisely those for whom the constitution provides religious freedom. Here, then, is the political problem: because adherence to the constitution must be shared by all, notwithstanding the legitimacy of open-ended religious plurality, consent to democracy with religious freedom must itself be religiously free, that is, neutral to all religious differences. If that consent depends on belief in "Almighty God," is this not a particular religious belief that must also be professed by "the people in mass"? If so, this belief, one might conclude, should itself be stipulated by the constitution, so that government may ensure through its own teaching the common adherence to democratic practice. But, then, the democratic constitution seems at odds with itself—providing for freedom of religion even while stipulating a religious belief required of all citizens.

In his subsequent autobiography, Jefferson glossed the Bill as "meant to comprehend, within the mantle of its protection, the Jew and Gentile, the Christian and Mahomatan, the Hindoo, *and infidel of every denomination*" (cited in Alley, 62, n. 7, emphasis added)—whereby he denied, at least by implication, that common consent to religious freedom requires shared profession of a theistic belief. In view of this, some may read the Virginia Bill's opening theistic appeal as solely strategic: arguments from God's purpose were included to help persuade a legislature many of whose members were for religious reasons initially resistant to the desired outcome. Others may note that belief in God in some or other sense was universal, or virtually so, in the American colonies and newborn states of the eighteenth century; hence, theism could be taken for granted in making a case for religious freedom—although pervasive theism does not entail that Jefferson's conception of the divine was itself pervasively affirmed. In any event, these historical comments, whatever their merit, still leave unanswered the question of principle: absent a common theistic profession, is consent of the governed to religious freedom possible? To all appearances, Jefferson appreciated this question. However the opening appeal in his Virginia Bill should be understood, his larger legacy includes two themes, each of which might be meant to show how consent or adherence to a democratic constitution, the ethics of citizenship, is indeed religiously neutral.

JEFFERSON'S ANSWERS

On one theme, the common allegiance is taught by all religions, whatever their differences. "Reading, reflection and time have convinced me," Jefferson wrote in 1809, "that the interests of society require the observation of those moral precepts only in which all religions agree . . . and that we should not intermeddle with the dogmas in which religions differ, and which are totally unconnected with morality" (letter of September 27, 1809; Jefferson, 281). In 1800, as part of his eloquent defense of republican government delivered during his First Inaugural as president, he spoke of the country being "enlightened by a benign religion, professed, indeed, and practiced in various forms, yet all of them including honesty, truth, temperance, gratitude, and the love of man; acknowledging and adoring an overruling Providence, which by all its dispensations proves that it delights in the happiness of man here and his greater happiness hereafter" (Jefferson, 174–75). In 1816, he bemoaned the "quarreling, fighting, burning and torturing" occasioned "from the beginning of the world to this day" by "the dogmas of religions *as distinguished from moral principles*" (letter of November 11, 1816; Jefferson, 401, emphasis added). And in 1781–82, he directed attention to "our sister states of Pennsylvania and New York," where "religion is . . . of various kinds indeed, but all good enough, all sufficient to preserve peace and order" (Jefferson, 395)—implying agreement among the various religions on moral principles essential to republican government. "They [those states] have made the happy discovery, that the way to silence religious disputes, is to take no notice of them" (Jefferson, 396).

In speaking of "all religions," Jefferson may typically have meant differing opinions about, in Madison's words, a person's "duty . . . to render to the Creator such homage and such only as he believes to be acceptable to him" (Alley, 56)—so that all religions include belief in the deity, even if conceptions of God differed. More broadly, Jefferson may have intended something like what we today call the world religions, recognizing within each the possibility of contention about how that religion is properly represented—as Christianity, for instance, has embraced contention among sects and denominations. On this designation, "all religions" meant or, at least, included differing opinions about a person's proper relation to some reality beyond the contingently existing things of this world, and thereby each religion affirms for humans an ultimate orientation to or encompassing purpose given by some transcendent reality. A religion, Jefferson also likely recognized, typically inculcates the given opinion and orientation or purpose in or through a particular community and its defining representations, including representative practices, for instance, ritual practices.

In the first two sections of the present essay, I use "religion" in this Jeffersonian sense, that is, to include belief in some transcendent reality, whereby religious beliefs are distinguished from those of infidels or, as we today might say, from secularistic orientations. If, in this sense, all religious orientations were, for Jefferson, "good enough," perhaps he sought the ethics of citizenship in what Benjamin Franklin called "the essentials of every religion," in distinction from what Franklin called the "other articles" or inessentials by which religions differed from each other and that "serv'd principally to divide us" (cited in Mead, 64).

That Jefferson indeed considered such differences inessential is supported by his attempts to eliminate unnecessary dogma in his own, principally private reformulation of the Christian religion. A "syllabus, or outline . . . of the comparative merits of Christianity" (letter of April 21, 1803; Jefferson, 267; see 267–70) soon became "The Philosophy of Jesus of Nazareth," both written during Jefferson's first term as president (and the latter subsequently lost to history [see Gaustad, 118]). Years later, a longer work, "The Life and Morals of Jesus," retrieved from the synoptic gospels what Jefferson believed to be the simple message of Jesus by excising what Jefferson saw as the metaphysical or supernatural mysteries subsequently added by priests and theologians. "My opinion is that there would never have been an infidel, if there had never been a priest" (letter of August 6, 1816; Jefferson, 399).

On this answer to our central question, in any case, religious differences are irrelevant to consent of the governed because the ethics of citizenship and thus democratic politics is backed by religions generally. Something like the force of supposed religious essentials has led several twentieth-century thinkers to discover in US history and endorse for the country a national religion in distinction from the disestablished religious communities that nonetheless enjoy free exercise. Robert Bellah argued for a "civil religion"; Phillip Hammond found a "religion *behind* the constitution"; and Sidney E. Mead advocated a "Religion of the Republic" (see Bellah; Hammond; Mead).³ Summarily, the view these proposals have in common might be called the "religionist" account of religious freedom. If, for Jefferson, common adherence to republican government is consistent with religious freedom because the ethics of citizenship depends on something one might call religious essentials, then he, too, offers a religionist account.

In response, we should ask how any such account prevents a constitutional stipulation of religious essentials and thus is consistent with protection for, as Jefferson later insisted, the "infidel of every denomination" (cited in Alley, 62, n. 7). Here, as Mead has suggested, Jefferson perhaps relied on the widespread presence during the eighteenth-century of belief in God or, at least, in a transcendent reality. Given that all disestablished religions were "good enough," because they all taught the essentials, he could then assume widespread republican morality without religious establishment because infidels were relatively few. As Mead also notes, however, this assumption is precarious. If the refusal of all religion—or, as we may say, the presence of secularistic beliefs—were to extend significantly among the citizenry, the consent of the governed could not, on this religionist account, be assured (see Mead, 65). Given this possibility, a need for shared belief in religious essentials seems to entail a constitutional provision giving the government both the right and the duty to stipulate its religious backing if and when the disestablished religions are not "good enough," for instance, if and when nonreligious views of human life as such become sufficiently widespread to threaten common adherence to democracy.

Indeed, if democracy depends on religious essentials, a constitutional provision in which their content is stipulated seems urgent quite apart from a significant secularistic presence. The religionist proposal requires agreement among all religions *that* there are these essentials and *what* they are, and both may be controversial among the diverse religions (see Mead, 65–66). That certain supposed truths are potentially included in the teaching of all religious communities does not entail that they actually teach those truths. The needed agreement, in other words, appears to have as its object a quite specific religious belief or set of beliefs—as Jefferson's own view of "an ordering and overruling Providence" and "the simple message of Jesus" suggests. Some will object to this critique, insisting that a religionist can avoid contradiction with religious freedom by stipulating constitutionally solely the dependence of democracy on religion as such. Let us call this the minimal religionist account: consent to democracy does not depend on any specific religious belief; the essential is solely some or other affirmation of a transcendent reality as the proper object of ultimate orientation or ground of encompassing purpose. Accordingly, religious freedom is preserved because any conviction about the character of that reality is legitimate.

Something like that appears to be the classic proposal of John Courtney Murray, who asserts belief in "the sovereignty of God" as the first item of our American consensus and thus essential to our politics (Murray, 44). If I understand him rightly, Murray does not mean the Christian God or any other specific conception of a transcendent reality; rather "God" in the American consensus designates only something not of this world that is sovereign over it. The affirmation that all human life is ruled by or accountable to an eternal spiritual ground must, Murray argues, be constitutive of the political order as such. Only if all citizens acknowledge that spiritual questions concern human life in relation to eternity can politics be properly limited to nonspiritual or, as he says, temporal purposes and, thereby, occur democratically. For Murray, in other words, the distinction between questions about temporal affairs, answers to which depend on the natural law reason can know, and ultimate or spiritual questions, answers to which transcend what reason can know, must be shared by all democratic citizens. With that common belief, a political community can be "locked together in argument" (Murray, 6); politics may proceed by discussion and debate about the natural law and its application. But absent common affirmation of the eternal ground, some citizens will be secularists; appeal to reason, they will assume, can determine what it cannot determine, namely, the true answer to all questions, and politics by way of democratic reason and persuasion will become impossible. Thus, government should explicitly support religion as such in contrast to secularistic understandings—so that democracy implies religious freedom but does not imply governmental neutrality toward the difference between religious and secularistic beliefs.

As far as I can see, however, Murray's proposal is inconsistent with freedom for the differing affirmations of a transcendent reality. If common assent to the sovereignty of God—where "God" designates a reality otherwise undefined—is necessary and sufficient for common consent to democracy, the differences among understandings of this God make no difference to politics. But Murray thereby asserts something with which at least some of the religious affirmations thereby included may disagree. On some religious beliefs, perhaps, no political adherence could be a proper one unless based on the *true* understanding of God, which the religion in question is taken to represent. Indeed, any given belief in a transcendent reality as the proper object of our ultimate orientation seems to imply the dependence of all proper political activities on belief in the God thereby affirmed. Hence, any such religious understanding would be expressly denied by the first item in Murray's American consensus; stipulating that democracy depends on common assent without content to a transcendent reality contradicts at least some of those assents. Accordingly and against Murray's intent, his proposal becomes one among the many religious beliefs that religious freedom legitimizes and implies the constitutional provision of a specific religious belief, which the government is bound to inculcate.[4] In other words, an established religion is required. Given that even the minimal religionist account has this implication, moreover, the same will be so with any more substantial view of religious "essentials" as the basis for democratic consent—including Jefferson's, if indeed his solution was religionist.

But a second theme in Jefferson's writings may imply that he never relied on a religious belief. While he likely took certain essential moral principles to be common among all religions, perhaps those principles were, for him, independent of whether theism or any other orientation to a transcendent reality is true. On this proposal, consent to republican government can occur through a moral sense characteristic of human nature. In what measure so-called moral sense theory—represented by, for instance, Thomas Hutcheson and David Hume—influenced Jefferson's understandings is controversial among students of his thought (see White; Wills; Staloff; Gaustad). But his attraction to that theory is clear, and Jefferson could regularly speak of a "moral instinct" (e.g., letter of June 13, 1814; Jefferson, 287) or what Hume called a "sentiment of . . . humanity" (Hume, 235).

For Jefferson, it also seems clear, our moral sense is given by a divine creator. "The Creator," he wrote in 1814, "would indeed have been a bungling artist, had he intended man for a social animal, without planting in him social dispositions." As far as republican morality is concerned, however, Jefferson may have considered this a private opinion. In the same letter, he praised "the care of the Creator in making the moral principle so much a part of our constitution as that no errors of reasoning or of speculation might lead us astray from its observance in practice," a premise necessary, he says, in order to explain "whence arises the morality of the Atheist" (letter of June 13, 1814; Jefferson, 287, 285, 286). This reading of him, moreover, is perhaps reinforced by his lifelong reticence, notwithstanding his abiding focus on articulating political principles, to speak publicly about his own religious beliefs. "Jefferson kept his beliefs to himself," writes one biographer; "all his life, he was reluctant to reveal his views on religion to anyone except his closest friends" (Bernstein, 42). All such beliefs are nonpolitical, on this reading, because discernment by the moral sense was, for Jefferson, separated from any religious affirmation or denial. Asking what morality requires of a citizen is one thing; asking whether a transcendent reality exists is an independent question. If our moral instinct in this sense is the court of appeal before which moral disagreements can be brought, perhaps Jefferson intends an ethics of citizenship that is not religionist and thus purports to be neutral not only to all religious differences but also to the difference between religious believers and infidels.

On moral sense theory, roughly speaking, the faculty in question responds to its objects in a manner something like how other forms of perception sense their objects. The former perceives certain kinds of actions as right or good and others as wrong or bad in a way analogous, say, to how our sense of touch perceives certain things as smooth and others as rough. Such a theory might be thought to authorize a self-consistent account of religious freedom if discernment by this moral faculty is sufficient to validate the difference between moral and immoral actions. In that event, doubt or disagreement about supposed precepts of right or good can be resolved by appeal to our moral instinct. This does not mean that understanding must be absent from moral discernment, as if the moral sense were noncognitive.

The defining point is, rather, that reason or argument is not needed to validate proposed differences between virtuous and vicious action. Hence, what alone remains for reasoned deliberation to add is counsel about the proper means to ends defined by moral sense.

Some of Jefferson's statements may be read to advance this view. His tortured and torturing treatment of slavery in *Notes on the State of Virginia* catalogues what he reckons as the scientifically demonstrable disparities between blacks and whites, including a difference in rational capacity, from which he infers tentatively a conclusion of racial inferiority and superiority. But he finds blacks equal with respect to the moral sense: "Whether further observation will or will not verify the conjecture, that nature has been less bountiful to them in endowments of the head, I believe that in those of the heart she will be found to have done them justice" (Jefferson, 479). Even more to the point is his long 1786 letter to Mrs. Maria Conway, his friend and possible intimate while ambassador to France, in which he relates a "dialogue . . . between my Head & my Heart." In the extended conclusion, the heart instructs the head: "Respect for myself now obliges me to recall you into the proper limits of your office. When nature assigned us the same habitation, she gave us over it a divided empire. To you she allotted the field of science; to me that of morals. . . . In denying to you the feelings of sympathy, of benevolence, of gratitude, of justice, of love, of friendship, she has excluded you from . . . our moral direction" (letter of October 12, 1786; Jefferson, 10, 17–18).

Even recognition of the "want or imperfection of the moral sense in some men," Jefferson argued in 1814, no more denies its presence as "a general characteristic of the species" than does "the want or imperfection of the senses of sight or hearing" in some people denies them as general human capacities. Further, he defended the discernment of moral sense against what might seem a convincing critique, namely, "if nature had given us such a sense, impelling us to virtuous actions, and warning us against those which are vicious, . . . then nature would also have designated, by some particular ear-marks, the two sets of actions . . . Whereas, we find, in fact, that the same actions are deemed virtuous in one country and vicious in another." He then indicts the indictment, in a response reminiscent of Hume, for failing sufficiently to generalize: "The answer is, that nature has constituted *utility* to man, the standard and test of virtue. Men living in different countries, under different circumstances, different habits and regimens, have different utilities" (letter of June 13, 1814; Jefferson, 287–88).

Let us call this dependence on moral sense one form of a "separationist" account of religious freedom, where theories of this type warrant republican morality or consent to democracy by virtue of its independence from whether any religious understanding of human life is true. If this reading permits an ethics of citizenship without a common religious belief, a problem nonetheless remains, namely, the need for explicit agreement on this separation of morality from the truth or falsity of any religious belief. On the proposal we are now considering, relevantly neutral or religiously free commitment to the constitution is possible because the ethics of citizenship and thus democratic politics is based on our moral sense without explicitly or implicitly taking sides for or against any religious orientation. But moral sense theory is itself a general account of morality, and there is no reason to assume that diverse religions legitimized by religious freedom will include agreement on the supposed sufficiency of moral sense. Indeed, if religions include differing beliefs about the ultimate context and encompassing purpose of human life, one should expect extensive disagreement with the supposed independent force of the moral sense. Accordingly, that independence could provide the required common consent only if this theory is itself stipulated constitutionally—whereby the constitution now requires, in place of a religious belief, a provision about the separation of morality from whether human life relates to a transcendent reality. We may not call this an establishment of religion, but that provision stipulates, nonetheless, that religious conviction is not free: at least some religions are not constitutionally legitimate, namely, those that deny the separated sufficiency of moral sense.

The potential for this denial is confirmed when other students of Jefferson's thought question whether the independent veracity of a moral sense captures even his view. On Morton White's interpretation, the evidence from Jefferson's later life is inconclusive: "Moral sense, utility, revelation, intuitive reason—all of these are offered at one time or another as avenues to moral truth, but no one of them is clearly given the sort of preference that intuitive reason was given by Locke, utility by Bentham, and the moral sense by Hutcheson" (White, 127). In contrast, White argues, Jefferson's mind on this issue during the 1770s is transparent. He was then persuaded by the reconciliation of "rationalism and . . . moral sense" (White, 107-08) found in the Italian jurist Jean Jacques Burlamaqui. On White's account, Burlamaqui "held that reason verifies what the moral sense first brings to our attention"—and Jefferson as a younger man also thought "that the moral sense was *subordinate* to reason" (White, 111, 114).

For this reading of the younger man, White argues, the absence of any "appeal to the moral sense in the Declaration [of Independence]" is convincing (White, 114). "We hold these truths to be self-evident: that all men are created equal; that they are endowed by their creator with certain inherent and inalienable rights; that among these are life, liberty, & the pursuit of happiness" (Jefferson's draft; Jefferson, 97). Although Jefferson's initial term was not "self-evident" but, rather, "undeniable," both meant truths whose apprehension depends on rational intuition (see White, 72–78)—and while the reality of a moral sense is not denied in the Declaration, the appeal to truth discerned by reason implies that "reason verifies" what the moral sense proposes. Assuming that White's reading is essentially correct, we should recall that Jefferson's Virginia Bill was also written during the 1770s and thus during a period when, for him, the discernment of moral sense required validation by reason. At least when this Bill was drafted, then, he could not have considered the moral sense sufficient to separate morality from whether any religious understanding is true.

To be sure, religious establishment might still be avoided if the common consent is possible because moral *reason*—or, at least, reasoning about justice—is separated from any religious affirmation or denial. Something like this second form of the separationist account has become the favored view of religious freedom in recent decades. Differing theories, some of them indebted to Kant, have been advanced to support this account, and all such theories are supposed to show how reason, without explicitly or implicitly taking sides for or against any religious belief, validates moral or, at least, political principles (see, e.g., Apel 1979; Habermas 2008, 114–47). More than any other, perhaps, the massively influential thought of John Rawls, especially as presented in his later *Political Liberalism* (2005) has come to exemplify this view. Indeed, on my reading, his proposal there differs from his earlier *A Theory of Justice* (1971) precisely because, on his own assessment, the earlier work failed to answer the question to which the present essay is addressed—namely, how to have common adherence to democracy consistent with a plurality of what Rawls calls "comprehensive doctrines" (Rawls 2005, 12). Rawls's answer is separationist because it advocates "freestanding" (Rawls 2005, 10) principles of justice. An ethics of citizenship can be common, religious freedom notwithstanding, because the appeal of public reason in deciding "constitutional essentials and issues of basic justice" (Rawls 2005, 224) stands free from the affirmation and denial of any given religious or nonreligious comprehensive doctrine—and the plurality of reasonable comprehensive doctrines participate in an "overlapping consensus" (Rawls 2005, 134) affirming principles of justice as freestanding.[5]

I doubt that Jefferson shared this form of separationism. The self-evident rights of "all men" affirmed in his Declaration of Independence are said to be endowed by "their creator," such that political independence is something to which people of colonial America are entitled by "the laws of nature and of nature's God" (Jefferson, 96). I take this to assert not simply a private religious belief but, rather, his conviction at the time that moral and political principles are rationally inseparable from theism. But even if he did anticipate a separationism of reason, that view shares with the separationism of moral sense the same problem: while the appeal may be to reason rather than to the moral sense, we still have a theory about morality, and there is no basis for assuming that diverse religions legitimized by religious freedom will include agreement on this theory. Indeed, if religions include differing beliefs about the ultimate context and encompassing purpose of human life, one should expect extensive disagreement with the supposed separation or freestanding status of any principles for the political order. Accordingly, that separation could provide the required common consent only if this theory is itself stipulated constitutionally. The constitution still requires, in place of a theistic belief, a provision that delegitimizes at least some religious beliefs—namely, those that deny the separation of moral or political reasoning from whether any religious belief is true.

In sum, then, both religionist and separationist accounts of religious freedom are problematic. The first is troubled because it requires consent by all citizens to a given religious belief, even while religious freedom legitimizes their dissent from that same belief, and the second is troubled because it requires consent by all citizens to a theory about morality, even while religious freedom legitimizes dissent from that same theory. If neither account can explicate a coherent constitution, it is now important to focus on another theme central to Jefferson's Virginia Bill. As suggested by his apparent appeal to reason in asserting the laws of nature and of nature's God, he was confident that religious truth, including whether there is any, is open to rational discernment. At least within Virginia's 1786 legislature, which enacted the Bill, the most controversial aspect of Jefferson's theism was likely his conviction that God's character and our duty to God are accessible to natural reason. The legislators deleted from Jefferson's draft those phrases in his opening appeal that expressed this conviction. Here is the beginning and conclusion of that appeal as drafted, with the deleted phrases emphasized:

> *Well aware that the opinions and belief of men depend not on their own will but follow involuntarily the evidence proposed to their minds;* that . . . the holy author of our religion, who being lord of both body and mind, yet choose not to propagate it by coercions on either, as was in his Almighty power to do, *but to exalt it by its influence on reason alone;* (Jefferson, 390, emphasis added)

Jefferson's bedrock affirmation of enlightened reason is underscored by all of his biographers and, with respect to religion, is stated summarily in his 1787 letter to his nephew: "Fix reason firmly in her seat, and call to her tribunal every fact, every opinion . . . Your own reason is the only oracle given you by heaven, and you are answerable not for the rightness but uprightness of the decision" (letter of August 10, 1787; Jefferson, 254,

255). Consistently, Jefferson's counsel continues: "Question with boldness even the existence of a god; because, if there be one, he must more approve of the homage of reason, than that of blindfolded fear" (letter of August 10, 1787; Jefferson, 254). But nowhere is Jefferson's rationalism more apparent, or expressed with eloquence and force not found in Madison or any other founder, than when the preface to the Virginia Bill justifies its enactment with this final authorization: "and finally, that truth is great and will prevail if left to herself; that she is the proper and sufficient antagonist to error, and has nothing to fear from the conflict unless by human interposition disarmed of her natural weapons, free argument and debate, errors ceasing to be dangerous when it is permitted freely to contradict them." Accordingly, the Bill stipulates "that all men shall be free to profess, and by argument to maintain, their opinion in matters of religion" (Jefferson, 391).

Perhaps, then, Jefferson answered the question of common adherence to the constitution as follows: democracy with religious freedom is possible because the differences among religions—and, indeed, whether any religion is true—can be adjudicated before the tribunal of reason. "Reason and free inquiry are the only effectual agents against error. Give a loose to them, they will support the true religion by bringing every false one to their tribunal, to the test of their investigation" (Jefferson, 394). Still, it is not clear what importance Jefferson attached to rational inquiry about religious claims. Perhaps he saw the tribunal as consistent with reliance on religious essentials or, alternatively, on the moral sense as sufficient for an ethics of citizenship. On that accounting, the tribunal was nonpolitical. The point of reasoned discussion was simply to purge religions of the "quarreling, fighting, burning and torturing" occasioned "from the beginning of the world to this day" by "the dogmas of religion as distinguished from moral principles" (letter of November 11, 1816; Jefferson, 401)—and Jefferson's own attempt to purge Christianity of mystery and superstition exemplified the triumph of reason over divisions caused by religious inessentials, the "other articles" that, according to Franklin, "serv'd principally to divide us" (cited in Mead, 64). The force of reason would hasten religious harmony in society—and later in life Jefferson predicted that "Unitarianism . . . will, ere long, be the religion of the majority from North to South" (letter of November 2, 1822; Jefferson, 406).

But if, instead, Jefferson saw rational assessment of religious beliefs as another way to explain consent of the governed, he failed to show how the two are related. Adherence to democracy is required of all citizens notwithstanding the freedom of each to believe any religion she or he finds convincing. Even if reason and free inquiry will distinguish religious error and truth, what must be common cannot depend on the true religious beliefs (e.g., on the theism, if it is true, expressed at the outset of Jefferson's Virginia Bill) because consent of the governed must be present even while the constitution legitimizes both true and false religions. On what, we must still ask, does adherence to democracy with religious freedom depend?

Notwithstanding this additional theme in Jefferson's accounting, then, he did not, as far as I can see, provide clarity on how common consent to the democratic constitution can be consistent with the religious freedom he relentlessly advocated—or, to say the same thing, how an ethics of citizenship can itself be religiously free. Nothing he explicitly says avoids constitutional stipulation of either a religious belief or a belief about the ethics of citizenship that will delegitimize some possible religions. Still, I wish to argue for a critical appropriation of Jefferson's legacy, on which democracy requires neither constitutive agreement on religious essentials and thus an established religion nor a constitutional separation of morality from whether any religion is true. Moreover, the critical reinterpretation necessary to reach a coherent account is, I believe, sufficiently minimal to credit his stature in national memory as the principal author of our religious freedom.

REFINING THE QUESTION

Among the reasons for religious freedom cited in its preamble, Jefferson's Virginia Bill includes the following: "to suffer the civil magistrate to intrude his powers into the field of opinion and to restrain the profession or propagation of principles on supposition of their ill tendency is a dangerous falacy . . . [and] it is time enough for the rightful purposes of civil government, for its officers to interfere when principles break out into overt acts against peace and good order" (Jefferson, 391). Perhaps the acts properly subject to governmental interference could be more clearly defined, but restricting legal intrusion to actions in distinction from opinions is, I think, correct at least in this respect: civil government should not interfere with a citizen's opinion about whether the laws are good or right. In a democratic political community, any law is subject to legitimate contestation by any citizen thereof—because the government is authorized by "we the people," and any law, constitutional or statutory, is subject to alteration or repeal by those same people through the constituted political process.

If democracy is the "sovereignty of the people," to reformulate the point, every democratic citizen is sovereign over her or his assessment of every political claim; that is, the state may not stipulate any citizen's assessment of any claim for the justice of any actual or proposed law or policy or for the validity of any norm or principle in terms of which political activities are evaluated. Together as equals, the people are the final ruling power, and they can be sovereign only if each citizen is free from any governmental authority in evaluating the activities or possible activities of all governmental authorities. "A government is republican," Jefferson wrote, "in proportion as every member composing it has his equal voice in the direction of its concerns" (letter of July 12, 1816; Jefferson, 211).

Popular sovereignty is also one way to interpret the importance of religious freedom. Naturally, any such interpretation depends on how religion or religious activity, in distinction from other human expressions or activities, is understood. For Jefferson, as we have seen, a religious opinion or conviction affirms some or other ultimate human orientation to a deity or, more broadly, some transcendent reality. That opinion, he likely thought, is typically inculcated in or through the defining representations of a particular community, and perhaps we should take such particular communities to be, at least typically, constituted by an originating person or event, for which claims to decisive disclosure are made. Still, these latter claims are not what connect religious freedom to popular sovereignty. The political importance of a religion is, rather, the understanding of human life that is represented or said to be disclosed. Inclusive of certain beliefs about the ultimate context and orientation of human life, each religion also affirms a conviction about the ultimate terms of political evaluation. A religion is politically pertinent, let us say, because it includes terms for evaluating politics as such. Thus, religious establishment stipulates to all citizens a given set of such terms, and a citizen cannot be sovereign over her or his assessment of every political claim without religious freedom.

Still, if popular sovereignty entails religious freedom, does religious freedom entail popular sovereignty, that is, the sovereignty of every citizen, religious (in Jefferson's sense) or nonreligious, over her or his conviction about the terms for evaluating politics as such?[26] For some, perhaps, religious freedom seems to legitimize only religious adherence, in distinction from not being a religious adherent, and thus is consistent with a constitutional stipulation that citizens should have some or other religious belief; on this account, the constitution requires the belief that human life's ultimate orientation is properly defined by a transcendent reality and leaves undefined and thus open to free decision what religious conception a citizen affirms. But this view is simply the minimal religionist account discussed earlier, for which I reviewed John Courtney Murray's proposal as exemplary. On that minimal view, religious freedom is consistent with democratic consent because all religions teach the allegiance all citizens should have, and thus government should support religion generally in distinction from secularism. The critique of this account, also offered above, argued that it requires the establishment of a specific religious belief.

If the critique is successful, it follows that provision for religious freedom implies the freedom also to affirm a nonreligious orientation in human life and corresponding terms for evaluating politics as such. In his own way,

Jefferson asserted this implication. Later in life, as noted earlier, he glossed the Virginia Bill as "meant to comprehend, within the mantle of its protection, the Jew and the Gentile, the Christian and the Mahomatan, the Hindoo, *and infidel of every denomination*" (cited in Alley, 62, n. 7; emphasis added)—thereby extending the relevant freedom to religious and nonreligious alike. Having recognized Jefferson's commitment to reasoned inquiry as sufficient to discern religious truth and error, we might interpret this gloss to assert the following: the mind is not truly free to assess diverse religions if it cannot require sound reasons for religious rather than nonreligious belief, and thus, by implication, citizens must be free to refuse all religions. As he counseled his nephew: "Question with boldness even the existence of a god; because, if there be one, he must more approve of the homage of reason, than that of blindfolded fear" (letter of August 10, 1787; Jefferson, 254).

Assuming that religious freedom and popular sovereignty do entail each other, we might nonetheless understand why, given his context, Jefferson used *"religious* liberty" to include, by implication, an equal right to nonreligious belief—that is, he might permissibly speak of religious freedom because, in Virginia and the emerging nation at his time, citizens overwhelmingly agreed on the reality of a deity or, more generally, of something transcendent to the world. At least given a situation where denial of all religious convictions has become more prevalent, however, one might doubt that a democratic constitution is especially well formulated when the right to affirm nonreligious terms for evaluating politics as such is provided only by implication. If the relevant democratic freedom concerns the sovereignty of every citizen, it seems needlessly complex explicitly to protect specifically religious grounds for political evaluation and include protection for nonreligious grounds as somehow implied thereby. Here, we might cite the words Jefferson, while ambassador to France, wrote to Madison in 1787 urging that a bill of rights be added to the draft US Constitution: "a bill of rights is what people are entitled to against every government on earth . . . & what no just government should refuse or *rest on inference*" (letter of December 20, 1787; Jefferson, 361, emphasis added).

Accordingly, the following account may be salutary for our contemporary understanding: "religious" in "religious freedom" has a more extended meaning than Jefferson's apparent intention. With him, religious opinions are politically pertinent because they include some or other belief about the orientation of human life as such; in contrast to Jefferson, this extended meaning designates as religious any explicit belief about the ultimate terms of political evaluation and, at least by implication, how these terms are authorized or grounded—whether or not this authorization is said to require a deity or a transcendent reality.[7] Thereby, the express meaning of religious freedom is protection for the sovereignty of every citizen over her or his terms for evaluating politics as such, so that every citizen can be sovereign over her or his evaluation of every political claim, and thus "we the people" are the final ruling power.

All things considered, I take the extended meanings of "religious" and, similarly, "religion" to provide, at least in our contemporary understanding, the best interpretation of religious freedom and, specifically, the religion clauses of the First Amendment to the US Constitution—and unless otherwise noted, I will in this discussion henceforth use these words with those extended meanings. At the same time, our public discourse so pervasively uses these words, with Jefferson, to designate beliefs or communities in which a transcendent reality is affirmed—that is, uses them in what I will now call the conventional sense—that such extended uses may seem inappropriately artificial. For this reason, I will, more often than not, substitute the phrase "comprehensive assessment," intending this as synonymous with what I take religious freedom properly to protect. A comprehensive assessment, as a religious affirmation in the extended sense, is an explicit conviction about the ultimate terms of political evaluation and, at least by implication, how those terms are authorized or grounded. Accordingly, I propose, we should now interpret religious freedom, in the conventional sense of religious, as representative of a more inclusive legitimization. For understandable historical reasons, in other words, "religious freedom" was the eighteenth-century term for the right of every citizen to affirm any comprehensive assessment she or he finds convincing.[8]

If the constitutional provision for religious freedom so understood is a coherent form of political community, it follows that statutory laws and policies enacted democratically should never include an express statement about the ultimate terms of political evaluation. An official governmental activity that explicitly affirms or denies any comprehensive assessment would stipulate the terms (or something about the terms) in which all citizens should evaluate all political claims. For the same reason, statutory laws and policies should never stipulate how any activity of the state should be evaluated—for instance, should not prohibit criticism of the current regime—because doing so would violate the right of every citizen to decide for ultimate terms in which she or he evaluates all political claims. This is simply to repeat that citizens cannot be sovereign unless each is free from any political authority in evaluating the activities of all political authorities—and thus to repeat, with Jefferson, that government's relation to religion is a constitutional matter.[9]

But whether religious freedom and principled common consent to the constitution are coherent is the basic issue here, and we can now return to that vexing question. To the best of my reading, Jefferson's steadfast defense of religious freedom nonetheless left uncertain how adherence to the constitution can itself be religiously free or properly neutral to the diversity of religions—and thus whether a democratic constitution must provide, in order to help ensure action in accord with the ethics of citizenship, a belief that contradicts religious freedom. His two most apparent proposals seem to advance, on the one hand, a religionist view, on which certain supposed essentials of all religions in the conventional sense will be commonly affirmed, and on the other, a separationist view, on which common consent is possible because republican morality is independent of whether any conventional religion is true. In either case, to repeat once more the conclusion argued earlier, democracy requires a constitutional stipulation on which at least some possible religions in the conventional sense are delegitimized.

If we take religious freedom to protect any comprehensive assessment, the point may be restated: both the religionist and separationist accounts are themselves comprehensive assessments—or, at least, define some specific class of comprehensive assessments, in which case those excluded from that class are explicitly delegitimized. Whether democratic adherence is said to depend on essentials common to all conventional religions or, alternatively, on a common agreement that republican morality neither affirms nor denies, explicitly or implicitly, any conventional religious belief, the required constitutional stipulation expressly contradicts some possible comprehensive assessments. Neither proposal, in other words, can provide a relevantly neutral ethics of citizenship. But if so, how can consent to the constitution be, in principle, common?

The apparent dilemma may be generalized by underscoring that a democratic constitution constitutes the political community, prescribing the practice in accord with which activities of the state should be determined and to which all citizens as political participants should adhere, and thereby itself makes a political claim. By definition, every political claim implies some ultimate terms of political evaluation by which it is taken to be authorized. Accordingly, citizens cannot, it seems, share a principled adherence to the constitution unless they share a comprehensive assessment.[10] Because an ethics of citizenship is indispensable to democratic politics, this logic concludes, the constitution must stipulate its implied comprehensive assessment, and that constitutional stipulation contradicts religious freedom.

In the end, I believe, this argument is not convincing. Still, it has transparent force and makes a point about political evaluation that a coherent account of religious freedom cannot ignore, namely, that every political claim is a claim to validity and thus implies ultimate terms by which it is taken to be validated. As an important consequence, one cannot fully argue for religious freedom itself without explicating and redeeming a comprehensive assessment. If popular sovereignty, in distinction from forms of political community in which some religious conviction or comprehensive assessment is established, is good or right, one can fully validate this conclusion only by way of defending terms for evaluating politics as such. Doing so is far more than this essay can achieve, and for this reason, as noted at the outset, I will not seek here to defend democracy itself. The present issue, also noted at the outset, is solely the following: given that some ultimate terms of political evaluation are implied by a political constitution, are religious freedom and thus the sovereignty of every citizen over her or his comprehensive assessment consistent with principled common consent to a democratic political community?

REASON'S TRIBUNAL

We may approach a positive answer by recalling again Jefferson's allegiance to reason as sufficient to distinguish religious truth and error. To the best of my reading, he did not explain how rational validation and invalidation of religious beliefs explains consent to the constitution. Clearly, the ethics of citizenship cannot wait on agreement about religious truth, even if, in principle, this can be reached by appeal to the tribunal of free inquiry. But is there some other way in which the powers of reason permit democratic union among diverse comprehensive assessments? Here, I believe, is the coherent alternative: given popular sovereignty, consent to the democratic process is present whatever political disagreement may occur because making any political claim at all *is* commitment to validate and invalidate contested political claims by the way of reason. Reason does not secure the required common adherence only subsequent to its discernment of religious truth; to the contrary, the tribunal to which Jefferson gave unsurpassed expression is the democratic way to which every sovereign citizen already commits herself or himself simply by making a claim for some political assessment.

On this proposal, one's claim to validity for a political evaluation claims to be authorized by the true comprehensive assessment—and the claim is made in the context of popular sovereignty, that is, the context in which every citizen is sovereign over her or his assessment of every political claim and government is determined by "we the people." Other citizens cannot be politically sovereign unless each may contest the comprehensive assessment and thus, if necessary, the evaluation for which validity has been claimed. In making any political claim, therefore, one issues the pledge that, if the claim is contested, its validity can be validated or redeemed by the giving of reasons—or, we may say, by argument that commands the assent of all citizens. Given popular sovereignty, in other words, every political participant commits herself or himself, whenever she or he makes a political claim that is contested, to its validation or invalidation by democratic reasoning.

This account, some may say, begs the question because it assumes popular sovereignty. But the issue at stake here is solely that of consistency between politics and religious freedom. Thus, the argument for it has every right to assume the context religious freedom creates, namely, one in which each who is ruled is sovereign over her or his conviction about the ultimate terms of political evaluation. The consistency is then present, I propose, because the ethics of citizenship stipulated by a democratic constitution imposes nothing on any citizen that is not self-imposed or pledged in making any political claim to validity.[11] Moreover, this pledge is itself religiously free—and that because it is *explicitly* neutral to whatever political claims might be made. Commitment to the practice of political discourse, to testing contested claims by way of argument, is, we might say, a meta-ethical feature of all democratic political claims—or, perhaps better, a pragmatic feature of the act of claiming, in distinction from whatever semantic or propositional content for which the act makes a claim to validity. Democratic consent does not require explicit belief in a given comprehensive assessment because the obligation to have contested claims validated or invalidated by the way of reason is self-imposed by a democratic citizen in making any political claim at all. In this respect, making such a claim is similar to making a promise: whatever content the promise may have, the promiser pledges to keep it, and this pragmatic commitment is explicitly neutral to whatever is promised.

In both cases, one participates in a social practice, that is, a pattern of interaction having reciprocal rights and responsibilities defined by a norm. In the one case, the practice is that of promise making, defined by the norm that a promiser ought to keep her or his promise to the promisee; in the other case, the practice is that of making political claims, defined by the norm that claims, if contested, should be validated or invalidated by the giving of reasons or by argument. Accordingly, the act of participation commits one to the norm and, in that sense, the norm is self-legislated. A democratic ethics of citizenship, then, is consistent with religious freedom because full and free political discourse is a form of politics to which every citizen commits herself or himself whenever she or he acts as a member of "we the people" and, thereby, exercises her or his sovereignty over the ultimate terms of political evaluation.

Perhaps this argument still seems tendentious. On this further objection, religious believers, even as citizens in the context of popular sovereignty, do not necessarily pledge themselves to politics by way of discussion and debate because, at least in some cases, the religions in question claim to express a truth reason cannot validate. If democracy is politics through full and free discourse, this objection continues, its constitution must stipulate adherence to the way of reason, and this provision contradicts religious freedom because religions on which the ultimate context of evaluation can be validated only by some special revelation or by faith in a specific disclosure are delegitimized. As far as I can see, this objection has merit only if any religious adherent who so believes has thereby a true belief, that is, only if true comprehensive assessments *cannot* be validated by reason. If, to the contrary, the question to which differing religions or comprehensive assessments are so many differing answers is, in truth, a rational question, making a claim for some religious understanding *is* a pledge to validation by the way of reason—and this is so even if the religious understanding includes a denial of such validation.

The similarity to making a promise is again instructive. Even if one's promise cannot be kept (i.e., one promises to do something one is incapable of doing), making the promise remains a commitment to keep it—because that commitment is given in the act or, to say the same, is defined by the practice in which one chooses to participate. If keeping the promise is impossible, the promiser engages in a pragmatic self-contradiction, denying in the content promised what she or he affirms in the act of promising. Given that comprehensive assessments can be validated or invalidated by reason, democratic citizens who claim truth for their religious beliefs are thereby committed to democratic discourse—and if one's religion claims to transcend what reason can validate, the religious adherent engages in a pragmatic self-contradiction.

Nonetheless, the objection cited here is correct in this respect: the political constitution cannot consistently provide for religious freedom unless the religious question is a rational one. If, to the contrary, answers to this question are immune to argumentative assessment, democracy with religious freedom becomes an alien imposition on at least some convictions the constitution purports to legitimize, namely, those for which the true character of justice as such depends on a suprarational ground, a ground reason cannot discover. Indeed, religious freedom is then expressly inconsistent with not only some but also all claims about the character of justice as such—because all citizens are constitutionally required to participate in a practice inconsistent with the way in which justice is discerned. On the contrary premise, then, politics could include a discussion and debate only if all participants explicitly accept some nonrational terms of all political evaluation—and thus those terms must be constitutionally stipulated. If the religious question is not rational, in other words, politics can include a discourse only if the discussion and debate is not *full*, that is, cannot include possible contestation and assessment of every political claim. To the issue addressed in this essay—namely, whether common consent to religious freedom is possible—the solution implied in Jefferson's legacy is this: yes, the First Amendment and thus democracy itself are self-consistent principles *because and only because* "reason and free inquiry . . . will support the true religion [in the extended sense] by bringing every false one to their tribunal" (Jefferson, 394).

In both the academy and the wider public, on my reading, our contemporary debates about politics with religious freedom are profoundly troubled by the virtually unanimous refusal of this legacy. Religious freedom is generally affirmed, but the differing accounts debated all assume—indeed, often take for granted—that at least conventional religious convictions cannot be validated or invalidated in public discourse. As a consequence, a common political consent becomes possible only if the view in question is either religionist (here using "religion" in the conventional sense) or separationist, the two alternatives Jefferson explored—and in either case, I argued earlier, the constitution stipulates a comprehensive assessment.

As far as I can see, the assertion that true religious claims cannot be validated by reason—or even that true religious claims *possibly* cannot be validated by reason—is itself a statement that cannot be validated by reason, and thus it cannot be the premise for a convincing objection to popular sovereignty. Whether religious beliefs or comprehensive assessments can be tested by Jefferson's tribunal cannot be given a negative answer except by explicit or implicit appeal to the authority of some given religious belief. Only the positive answer can itself be validated by argument—namely, by a sound argument for some comprehensive assessment. This is, I hold, sufficient to establish that the question itself implies the positive answer. But I will not here further argue the point. In what follows, I will presuppose, with Jefferson, that religious claims are properly included in "free argument and debate." Given that democracy depends on this presupposition, perhaps our widespread commitment to government by "we the people" as not only possible but also, wherever enabling conditions exist, prescribed will give pause to some who might otherwise deny Jefferson's tribunal.

On some readings, perhaps, Jefferson confined reasoning to empirical inquiry. For him, one of his biographers argues, reason "referred to the operation of the mind upon data, with the result sifted through the senses," and thus reason "was not *a priori* but, rather, *a posteriori*" (Gaustad, 27). Although the latter distinction means differing things to differing people, Jefferson clearly was dedicated to a posteriori reasoning in the sense of modern empirical science. He once called Bacon, Locke, and Newton "my trinity of the three greatest men . . . the world had ever produced" (cited in Bernstein, 95). But he also spoke, in the Declaration of Independence, of "self-evident" or "undeniable" truths, and on Morton White's analysis, as noted above, both terms meant truths whose apprehension depends on rational intuition (see White, 72–78). Whether or not these truths should be called a priori, the suggestion remains that, for Jefferson, reason's capacities stretched beyond what is validated by data "sifted through the senses."

I am persuaded, in any event, that politics with religious freedom requires certain undeniable truths. These are indispensable precisely because comprehensive assessments must themselves be objects of argumentative validation and invalidation. Given that condition, the ultimate terms of political evaluation must be defensible without the mere positing of some prior belief—and, as far as I can see, differences among comprehensive assessments can finally be rationally adjudicated only because some principle of evaluation is undeniable. This is not to say that clarity about that principle and whatever it implies is easy to achieve. To the contrary, I believe, explicating and defending what is undeniable is a common enterprise in which those who pursue it depend on discourse with each other, through which errors may be discovered and corrected (see Mead, 82–83). As this formulation suggests, however, affirmation of Jefferson's tribunal of reason does not require us to identify undeniable truths in terms of rational intuition, at least not in the sense that no argument for them is possible. Such truths, I believe, can be explicated and defended in terms of their pragmatic self-evidence.

A qualified illustration of such self-evidence was briefly mentioned earlier in defending an explicitly neutral ethics of citizenship. Given the social practice of popular sovereignty, the act of making any political claim is a pledge that, if the claim is contested, its validity can be redeemed by reasons that command the assent of all citizens. In that sense, commitment to democratic discourse cannot be denied by political participants. We may now speak in the following way of truths undeniable without qualification or undeniable by subjects as such, and I will call such truths pragmatically necessary: a statement is pragmatically necessary when the content asserted is implied by every possible act of understanding, that is, any subjective act or, we may also say, any participation in the practice of existence with understanding.

Accordingly, such statements designate conditions necessary to being a subject at all, and every act of denying a pragmatically necessary statement implies what is denied and thereby is pragmatically self-contradictory. Moreover, I mean to assert that a pragmatically necessary moral principle is understood in the dim background of all human consciousness. In the deepest reaches of her or his understanding, every person is inchoately aware of her or his inescapable moral obligation, if only because, absent that understanding, a moral principle would not be a necessary condition of subjectivity. This is one meaning of "ought implies can." Commonly taken to assert that a prescribed act must be among alternatives for choice, the dictum also means that a subject cannot be obligated to choose as prescribed unless she or he *can* choose as prescribed because (for the reason that) she or he ought to do so. Thus all subjects must understand a pragmatically necessary moral principle, and every denial of it is a pragmatic self-contradiction because the subject in question simultaneously affirms what she or he denies.

On this account, we should note, the phrases "ultimate terms of political evaluation" and "comprehensive assessment" are systematically ambiguous. They designate, on the one hand, some or other undeniable principle of moral evaluation and, on the other, some or other principle for evaluating specifically political decisions as such—where the latter implies the former. I here argue that what is validly designated in the first sense, that is, the pragmatically necessary principle, is what makes a full political discourse possible.[12] Still, that conclusion neither implies nor allows a constitutional stipulation that democratic discourse seeks to identify this necessary principle. What counts as convincing reasons for the validity of a comprehensive assessment is itself something to be determined only by discourse—and the argument here for undeniable terms of assessment is itself intended only as a contribution to the discourse whose coherence it seeks to explicate.[13]

Nothing in this analysis, we should also make clear, denies what seems to render religious freedom a vexing political provision: a democratic constitution is itself a political claim or prescribes a political practice and, therefore, the ethics of democratic citizenship implies some ultimate terms of political evaluation. But *what is implied by* a democratic constitution and *what it explicitly asserts* are two different things.[14] Democracy purports to imply the true character of justice as such, even while citizens explicitly agree on religious freedom and thus disagree about what comprehensive assessment is true. Their agreement, therefore, requires no shared commitment save to the ethics each legislates for herself or himself in the making of any political claim, whereby each pledges to seek through discourse the valid comprehensive assessment and its application to activities of the state.

Some may still find commitment to discourse inconsistent with religious freedom because a given religion might include affirmation of some nondemocratic—for instance, monarchical or aristocratic—form of government. A democratic constitution, this objection contends, is itself an explicit political prescription that delegitimizes any such comprehensive assessment. But this objection fails to take in full measure the commitment to resolve disagreements by argument: it is the one commitment explicitly neutral to all possible political disagreements and thus to all possible religious differences, including differences about the proper form of government. This is the case, moreover, notwithstanding that, as I have assumed, politics with religious freedom is, given its self-consistency, morally authorized. Comprehensive assessments on which aristocracy or monarchy is prescribed can be false and still be legitimate because the constitution, which stipulates politics as a full and free discourse, is explicitly neutral even to dissent from democracy itself. Given popular sovereignty, then, making a political claim for some nondemocratic form of government itself pledges that its prescription can be redeemed by reasons commanding assent from all citizens and thus pledges to pursue politics, even advocacy aimed at changing where sovereignty is assigned, by the way of reason.

Accordingly, what should be said is this: the ethics of democratic citizenship does not require a citizen to profess or assent to democratic politics, but it does require that she or he adhere to this ethics, that is, act in accord with it—because doing so is self-legislated in any action as member of "we the people." In this way, a properly democratic constitution is explicitly neutral even to contestation of its own claim to be morally authorized. "If there be any among us who would wish to dissolve this Union or to change its republican form," Jefferson prescribed in his First Inaugural, "let them stand undisturbed as monuments of the safety with which error of opinion may be tolerated where reason is left free to combat it" (Jefferson, 174).[15]

For all that, some may still object to including comprehensive assessments in public discourse, however subject in principle they may be to Jefferson's tribunal, because doing so ignores how intransigent and nonnegotiable such convictions are in fact. On that objection, disagreement at this fundamental level of evaluation does not, our political experience teaches, yield to civil discourse, and if that disagreement is allowed into the political process, the practical consequence will be political paralysis or instability. Accordingly, some other basis for democratic decision—for instance, an overlapping consensus—must be found. In response to this point, we may well affirm that wide agreements on political norms and values less general than ultimate terms of political evaluation is sometimes—although not always—salutary for a democratic community, and citizens are often wise to seek common political purpose with others who disagree with them religiously. Further, we can affirm that debate about comprehensive assessments themselves will typically occur in the more informal public discourse pursued through educational institutions and certain media and not in formal political settings, such as legislatures or political campaigns.

But this essay seeks to address a question of political principle: can one have a coherent theory of politics with religious freedom? To this question, I have argued, nothing less than the implication of Jefferson's legacy can provide a convincing answer. However salutary an overlapping consensus may be politically, it can be properly affirmed not because it provides a coherent theory of religious freedom but only because it is authorized by the way of reason.[16] Moreover, the point of principle has practical significance: recognition of what makes government by the people a possibility militates against recourse to mere conflict or withdrawal from civil respect when, for whatever reasons, differences among religious convictions or comprehensive assessments become important within "we the people"—as may occur, say, when some find the norms and values endorsed by an otherwise widespread overlapping consensus to be, at least in some respects, unjust.

One further objection should be addressed: some may consider democracy by the way of reason hopelessly idealistic; by implication, it seems to expect an incredible form of politics in which humans so transcend their self-interests as commonly to rely on sound arguments for a determination of their life together. In fact, we will be told, reason can be and is used as a resource for and rationalization of narrow purposes—and, accordingly, politics in our republic is largely a conflict of interests strategically pursued, where results are largely consequent on bargaining affected by inequalities of money or other forms of strategic power. On some occasions, perhaps, such power is sufficiently combined with limited forms of moral commitment to achieve a rough justice. But the process often gives state sanction to needless injustice, and what passes for discussion and debate is deceptive rhetoric or systematically distorted communication. "Man's capacity for justice makes democracy possible," Reinhold Niebuhr famously wrote, "but man's inclination to injustice makes democracy necessary" (Niebuhr 1944, xiii)—and in this aphorism, he expressed his own Christian account of politics: "In principle, the Christian faith holds that human nature contains both self-regarding and social impulses and that the former is stronger than the latter. This assumption is the basis of Christian realism" (Niebuhr 1965, 39).

In response to this political hermeneutics of suspicion, one may recall how the 1787 Constitutional Convention in America was profoundly sensible of political corruption and sought to control it insofar as possible by institutionalizing complicated decision-making procedures through which the political process determines activities of the state. Whatever the faults of that 1787 Constitution, its detailed provisions regarding the selection of officers and the separation of powers are attempts to minimize the measure in which strategic pursuit of narrow interests would debase political outcomes. Using Niebuhr's term, we might call this the realism of our Constitution. As Niebuhr taught, however, realism alone is a counsel about the pursuit of good politics, not a definition of it—and democratic realism is vacuous in the absence of some democratic ideal. The Constitution expresses that ideal in giving final power to "we the people" and thus in the principle of religious freedom. Moreover, the measure in which realism is properly recognized cannot render the idealism hopeless. Unless the exercise of democratic rights includes some significant adherence to the way of reason, that is, pursuit of truth as distinct from narrow interests, no decision-making procedure, whatever its protections, can prevent its exploitation by strategic power. If the second half of Niebuhr's aphorism—"man's inclination to injustice makes democracy necessary"—gives warrant for our Constitution's realism, the first half—"man's capacity for justice makes democracy possible"—gives warrant for religious freedom. In the end, government by the people depends entirely on the people.

JEFFERSON'S LEGACY

Assuming that full and free political discourse consistently explicates consent to religious freedom, we might now critically appropriate the apparent proposals for that common democratic commitment that are included within Jefferson's legacy. Given his use of "religion" in the conventional sense, the belief that republican morality can be found in the "essentials" of all religions is not convincing. But taking "religious" in the extended sense, whereby it designates any explicit belief about the ultimate terms of political evaluation, we can affirm a pragmatic "essential" common to the diverse religious convictions democracy legitimizes—namely, the commitment to discourse among "we the people" entailed in a political claim to truth for any comprehensive assessment. In its own way, moreover, the present account may provide meaning to the endorsement of a moral sense given with human nature. This cannot be a matter of the "heart" divorced from the "head"—or validation and invalidation of moral claims independently of reason. Still, we may use the term "moral sense" to designate our inescapable understanding of the principle by which all decision with understanding is morally obligated and which all comprehensive assessments claim to articulate in terms for evaluating politics as such. Given that democratic discourse is possible only because common human experience includes that awareness, we can say that reason validates what our original moral sense proposes.

Attending to democracy with religious freedom, however, we repair to Jefferson above all as the founder committed to the rational assessment of religious claims. "Truth is great and will prevail if left to herself; . . . she is the proper and sufficient antagonist to error, and has nothing to fear from the conflict unless by human interposition disarmed of her natural weapons, free argument and debate; errors ceasing to be dangerous when it is permitted freely to contradict them" (Jefferson, 391). If coherence has been achieved by the present account, this consequence has merely followed the implications of Jefferson's insight—and thereby gives us sufficient cause to call him the principal mind and voice responsible for our nation's commitment to religious freedom.

Finally, we may turn to Jefferson's theism: nature is divinely created and encompassed by a divine providence, and republican government specifies "the laws of nature and of nature's God." Formulated within the appropriation outlined here, the laws of nature's God are said to define the pragmatically necessary principle on which ultimate terms of political evaluation depend, such that this principle authorizes democracy. Only in the discourse among "we the people," this essay has argued, can that religious conviction be explicitly presented and assessed—even while that conviction claims to be convincing and thus claims to be the terms by which all political decisions ought to be informed. Before the political tribunal of reason, in other words, Jefferson's theism asserts a common human experience of the divine reality as our ultimate context, so that our relation to God can be explicated as pragmatically necessary. I will not here pursue such an argument for theism, although I do hold that moral validity depends on a divine purpose by which democracy is, wherever enabling conditions exist, prescribed. If that is so, Jefferson all the more deserves his stature as author of our religious freedom because, for him, the way of reason he, more than any other founder, marked for our approbation was authorized finally by the reality of God.

CHAPTER TWO

ON CONSTITUTIONAL AUTHORITY

A Conversation with David Strauss

The US Constitution constitutes our political community and is, therefore, a set of fundamental laws or provisions that frames the process through which political disagreements are engaged and the activities of the state determined. Still, just what those provisions are or mean is itself contested. As a modest contribution to this discussion, I seek here to make a general point about the Constitution's authority for US politics, and I will pursue this through a conversation with David Strauss's 2010 book, *The Living Constitution.**

Professor Strauss defends a constitution open to change in contrast to so-called originalism as a theory of constitutional law. For advocates of the latter, it alone prevents manipulation of constitutional meanings in whatever ways contemporary readings desire, whereby, in effect, "anything goes" (31). To the contrary, Strauss argues, a tradition of constitutional common law is, when taken along with the written text, a more adequate constraint on manipulation and, moreover, a more adequate accounting of "what we actually do" (44). I will propose an amendment to Strauss's proposal—a friendly one, I think, at least with respect to the contrast between originalism and a living Constitution.

THE LIVING CONSTITUTION

Originalism in what Strauss calls its "rigorous form" (11)—the sense I will intend unless noted otherwise—is the view or theory on which the meaning

---

*Subsequent references to this book will be by page number or numbers alone.

of constitutional stipulations is the meaning intended by those who drafted and/or ratified the Constitution's written text. Where the written document speaks in more general terms, originalism includes in this meaning the understandings with which the drafters and/or ratifiers did or would have applied the general stipulations. On this view, for instance, the Eighth Amendment's prohibition of "cruel and unusual punishment" is properly interpreted to permit the death penalty because the relevant eighteenth-century Americans did not consider it cruel and unusual (see 11). Similarly, the 1954 Supreme Court decision in *Brown v. Board of Education* is finally indefensible (although few originalists are sufficiently rigorous to admit this) because, on "the consensus view," the prohibition of school segregation is "flatly inconsistent" with the original understandings of the Fourteenth Amendment (78).

"When it comes to difficult, controversial constitutional issues," Strauss continues, "originalism is a totally inadequate approach" (4). On its reading, he notes, several things now generally assumed to be constitutionally prohibited would be, in truth, permitted—for instance, racial segregation in public schools, violation of the principle "one person, one vote," and governmental discrimination against women—and many federal, labor, environmental, and consumer protection laws would be unconstitutional (see 12–17). These conclusions would be required by the original understandings of the written text, the document of 1787 and its formal amendments. That such readings are inconsistent with our Constitution is now beyond serious dissent and makes clear the need for another theory of constitutional law.

In any event, originalism has three basic problems. First, it requires judges to be sophisticated historians of thought and practice in the eighteenth century or, say, the immediate post-Civil War period, a task for which judges "have no apparent qualifications" (20). Moreover, "it is often impossible to uncover" (18) the relevant original understandings, and in some cases, those open to us reveal a division of opinion. Second, "and more important" (20), constitutional interpretation requires translating prescriptions from former centuries in relation to sometimes radically changed circumstances, and one cannot look to the original understandings for this translation because neither drafters nor ratifiers of the written text anticipated the differing situation. Let us assume, for instance, that original understandings of the Second Amendment included the right of individuals to possess guns. The social situation was then largely rural, and weapons were relatively primitive. Had the founders envisioned the twenty-first century, with its largely urban society and its massively sophisticated weapons, might they have permitted significant regulation of firearms? Every answer is sheer speculation (see 21–22). Or, again, how is the clause granting Congress power to regulate "Commerce . . . among the several states" (cited, 22) properly understood today when, given an institutional complexity in our modern economy far beyond what could be anticipated in the eighteenth century, a wide range of intrastate conduct has significant effect on interstate commerce (see 22–23)?

Third, and most telling, originalism has no plausible answer to what Strauss calls "Jefferson's Problem" (24). Jefferson wrote to Madison in 1789: "The earth belongs . . . to the living . . . By the law of nature, one generation is to another as one independent nation is to another" (cited, 24; Jefferson 1999, 596). Why, then, is the contemporary generation responsible to political conditions stipulated by eighteenth-century people? "It would be bizarre to suggest that we should let the people of New Zealand," however similar they are to us, "decide fundamental questions about our law. Why do we submit to the decisions of much more distant and alien founders" (24)? On behalf of originalism, differing answers have been given, but none of them support the theory. One defends it because "the Constitution is law," but this "does not determine how it should be interpreted"; another says "that we are engaged in a multigenerational project" begun by the founders, but we still "have to determine the nature of" this project; yet another says "that we must show 'fidelity' to the founding generations," but this simply leads us to ask "what fidelity requires" (24–25). The answers, in other words, all beg what Strauss elsewhere calls "Jefferson's question" (44).

Originalism, Strauss allows, sometimes takes a moderate form, on which the authoritative understandings do not include those with which drafters and ratifiers did or would have applied more general stipulations of the Constitution but, rather, are confined to the more general principles originally affirmed. "The key point about this moderate originalism is that it changes the level of generality at which the original understandings are described" (26). But this move, Strauss argues, allows citizens or judges "to justify any result we want to reach" because the general principle in question can be formulated at any convenient level of generality. Given the Eighth Amendment's prohibition of "cruel and unusual punishment," for instance, moderate originalism leaves "judges . . . free to declare any punishment unconstitutional, as long as they conclude that it is cruel" (27). If the Fourteenth Amendment is properly understood to assert a general principle, is it a prescription for racial equality or equal treatment of any minority contemporary judges or other interpreters consider oppressed? Changing the level of generality to which one appeals deprives originalism of the advantage it purports to have, namely, protecting the Constitution against arbitrary interpretation (see 27–29).

"For all its flaws," however, the theory persists, and one major reason is the want of an "established competitor" (31).[1] Absent an alternative, originalism is, for many, the only way to prevent capricious change in the

Constitution's meaning. As Strauss summarizes the indictment, permitting the Constitution to change "from time to time" means that "someone is changing it . . . according to his or her own ideas about what the Constitution should look like" (2). If originalism is indefensible, a constitution that is "invincibly stable and impervious to human manipulation" may seem impossible. "How can we escape this predicament" (2)?

"The living Constitution" is Strauss's answer. On this account, the Constitution includes a body of constitutional common law, the latter being what Strauss also calls "the small-c constitution," and this "along with the written Constitution in the archives . . . is our living Constitution" (35).[2] Toward explaining the "common law constitution" (43), he distinguishes "two competing accounts of how something gets to be law." On "the command theory," of which originalism is a version, "the law is, in the final analysis, an authoritative command from someone," so that one determines "what the law is" by asking what the sovereign said or did (36–37). On "the common law view," in contrast, the law is similar to custom in that both "can develop over time" and "can be the evolutionary product of many people, in many generations" (37). Because in part a body of common law, the US Constitution "evolves, changes over time, and adapts to new circumstances, without being formally amended" (1). At the same time, this adaptation is "impervious to human manipulation" (2) because common law changes "through the development of a body of precedents" and gains its "authority" from its "evolutionary origins and its general acceptability to successive generations" (37–38). There are indeed times when precedents do not settle a current issue, so that contemporary judgments "about fairness or good policy come into play"; when this occurs, however, "the precedents will usually limit the possible outcomes a judge can reach" (39). Judgments about fairness or good policy also become relevant on other occasions, namely, when judges rightly overrule precedent—but they do so only "in a limited way" because common law includes "complex" restraints (40) on such decisions, at least in part because, if I understand correctly, there are precedents with respect to the practice of overruling precedent.

In fact, Strauss argues, a common law constitution is transparent in the history of Supreme Court rulings. If one examines almost any opinion, "the text of the Constitution will play, at most, a ceremonial role. Most of the work will be done by the Court's analysis of its previous decisions" (33). This should not be surprising because originalism is, in fact, "an invitation" to judges and other interpreters "to be disingenuous" (45). As applied to controversial provisions of the text, originalism is "shot through with indeterminacy," in the face of which "it will be difficult for any judge to sideline his strongly held views about the issue" (45). Given the evolution of circumstances in which constitutional stipulations are to be specified and the recognition, once appeal to original understandings is no longer appropriate, that significant words in certain constitutional stipulations (e.g., "Congress shall make no law . . . abridging freedom of speech") are "not self-defining" (57), the emergence of a body of constitutional common law was all but inevitable.

Strauss explains in detail how this development led to principles, now generally accepted, that are required for reasonable application of the free speech clause (the priority of protecting political dissent, the distinction between "high-value" and "low-value" speech, and the distinction between different kinds of regulations)—principles hardly contained in the terse phrase of the First Amendment. Nor does appeal to original understandings justify these principles. Eighteenth-century understandings disagreed on what speech was constitutionally protected, but significant opinion at the time held that "seditious libel" (certain kinds of political dissent) could be suppressed—and, when we consider nonpolitical speech, it is likely that free expression was not understood to include blasphemy or, in ways now taken to be constitutional, defamation (see chapter 3). Strauss then argues for *Brown v. Board of Education* (1954) as a classic instance of overruling precedent, in this case the precedential status of "separate but equal" set by *Plessy v. Ferguson* (1896). A prior series of decisions, all formulated consistent with the *Plessy* precedent, increasingly gave persuasive reason to see "separate but equal" as impossible, whereby the *Brown* decision established a reversal recommended not only by fairness or good policy but also by the evolution of precedent itself (see chapter 4).

To be sure, one might confront even constitutional common law with Jefferson's question: why should the current generation submit to or, at least, be limited by past precedents, so that today's decisions are responsible to an evolution that precedes the present? Here, however, Strauss has an answer—namely, constitutional common law, as common law generally, "is governed by a set of attitudes: attitudes of humility and cautious empiricism" (40). The humility is "about the power of individual human reason" and is, therefore, a reliance on "the collective wisdom of other people" over a longer period of time (41). The empiricism expresses "a sense of the complexity of the problems faced by our society" (139) and a reliance on what has previously been found to work in practice (see 41)—and thus a "distrust of abstractions" (41) that counsel otherwise. Together, these attitudes "make up a kind of ideology," which Strauss calls "Burkean" because he takes Edmund Burke to be "its most famous exponent" (40, 42, 41). Given present acceptance of these attitudes, the common law approach is both "more workable" and "more justifiable" than originalism. Moreover, this approach explains what has actually happened in our constitutional law over the past two centuries, confirming that we have accepted and can be presumed now to accept the ideology (43–44).

As noted earlier, however, the living Constitution is not exhausted by the constitutional common law. The former includes the written Constitution—allegiance to which, along with "a certain kind of respect for the founding and for crucial episodes in our history, seem, to many people, central to what it is to be an American" (101). But the function of this document "does not have to depend on veneration of our ancestors"; to the contrary, "the written Constitution is valuable because it provides a common ground . . . for us to settle disputes that might otherwise be intractable and destructive" (101). In part, this common ground consists in specific prescriptions with respect to political institutions—for instance, the length of terms in various political offices (president, congressional representative, senator, etc.) and certain qualifications for their occupants. While any such prescriptions might be questioned, "sometimes," Strauss argues, "it is more important that things be settled than that they be settled [exactly] right" (101-02), and in these cases, the written Constitution "give[s] us good enough answers to important questions, so that we do not have to keep reopening those issues all the time" (102). Even where its formulations are more general, as in the religion clauses of the First Amendment, "having the text . . . as a starting point at least narrows the range of disagreement" (104), and contemporary interpretations are unlikely to be persuasive unless they can be plausibly understood as consistent with "the most straightforward understanding of the text" (108).

That the document provides contemporary common ground is, as is the ideology behind our constitutional common law, "an essential element of our constitutional culture" (103)—and this fact about both provides, if I understand Strauss rightly, our best solution to Jefferson's problem. Still, the implication of so understanding the text's function is this: "usually . . . the words of the Constitution should be given their ordinary, current meaning—even in preference to the meaning the framers understood. . . . The current meaning of words will be obvious and a natural point of agreement. The original meaning might be obscure and controversial" (106). Although Strauss makes this point while attending to the text's specific prescriptions, there is every reason to conclude that he means the same with respect to more general provisions. If "a court can show that its interpretation can be reconciled with some plausible ordinary meaning of the text . . . the text can continue to serve the common ground of narrowing disagreement" (107). To all appearances, "plausible ordinary meaning" intends plausible to contemporary citizens. The common ground is contemporary ground, as Strauss's answer to Jefferson's question seems to require, and "the common ground justification" is consistent with "the reverence that many people feel for the Constitution but that does not make that reverence an admission ticket to full U.S. citizenship" because this justification is also consistent with citizens "who feel . . . no such attachment" and "venerate other ethnic or religious traditions or no traditions at all" (102).

"The living Constitution," meaning a previous text and the evolution of constitutional common law, "is the primary—I will go so far as to say the all-but-exclusive—way in which the Constitution, in practice, changes. The formal amendments are a sidelight" (116). In saying this, Strauss leaves aside the first twelve amendments. Written so soon after the 1787 document, they are better seen as additions to the original text (see 117). Those twelve aside, then, an amendment is likely to be ineffective absent a change not derived from it, including general acceptance of the change—as was the case, Strauss argues, with the Fourteenth and Fifteenth Amendments subsequent to the Civil War (ratified in 1868 and 1870, they were widely nullified until the twentieth century and, especially, until the civil rights revolution of the 1960s [see 128–31]). Alternatively, amendments adopted "often do no more than ratify changes that have already taken place in the living Constitution without the help of an amendment" (116)—as, for instance, the Seventeenth Amendment prescribing direct election of senators (which formalized a practice many states had, in effect, reached without technically violating the original text [see 132–35]) and even the Thirteenth Amendment prohibiting slavery (which formalized an achievement of the Civil War [see 127]).

Moreover, constitutional change can occur without the benefit of written amendment, as in "the enormous growth in the permissible range of federal legislation" (120) and "the growth of a federal bureaucracy" and regulatory agencies (121–22)—or again, the prohibition of "discrimination on the basis of sex," notwithstanding the failure of the Equal Rights Amendment (126). On the whole, the formal amendments are not responsible for constitutional change on high-stakes and contested issues but, rather, "serve . . . the common ground function of settling matters that are not particularly controversial but that have to be settled clearly" (e.g., the Twenty-fifth Amendment specifying procedures in case of presidential disability) or "serve the distinct function of suppressing outliers," turning "almost-unanimity into unanimity" (117, 118). "The living Constitution is the real show" (116).

JEFFERSON'S QUESTION: HERMENEUTICAL AND NORMATIVE

The Living Constitution is a notable achievement. Eminently clear and accessible, it presents in relatively short compass a detailed and challenging argument. As far as I can judge, the critique of originalism is convincing, and Strauss's case for restrained or evolutionary constitutional change, contrary to manipulative interpretation, is compelling. To be sure, a detailed argument permits disagreement with respect to details, but I am not sufficiently competent in constitutional law to enter those discussions. My intent here is to add a general amendment to Strauss's account. Summarily stated, his explication of the living Constitution is, as I will seek to clarify, incomplete absent an abiding character that marks our political tradition in distinction from others—and I will approach this accounting through focus on what Strauss calls Jefferson's problem. Strauss's formulation of the question can be paraphrased: why should we in the present submit to past understandings in defining the fundamental law of our political life?

On my reasoning, this question has force because each generation makes its own political decisions. Accordingly, present citizens have the right to ask whether and, if so, in what respects they should submit to decisions inherited from others. So stated, however, Jefferson's problem can be read in two different ways. On the one hand, we might ask how we today should understand our Constitution. In this sense, the question is hermeneutical:[3] how should we interpret this historically given set of fundamental laws, and in what respects, if any, should we submit to understandings in the past for our present interpretation? The failure of originalism, Strauss argues, is exposed by this hermeneutical question. Submitting present interpretation of constitutional provisions to the understandings of their drafters and/or ratifiers is indefensible because, among other reasons, originalism cannot offer a defense of its answer without begging the question. Hence, Strauss proposes an alternative: we today, given our political culture, should understand the Constitution as living, whereby this historically given set of laws is not exhausted by its written text, and at least some of its many provisions are open to evolutionary change generally accepted by successive generations. As hermeneutical, then, Jefferson's question asks in part for the general principle or principles of constitutional law interpretation and, thereby, for an account of the judicial task insofar as judges should sustain the Constitution.

Still, citizens differ from judges. In the end, the task of citizens is to pursue good politics. On the other hand, then, we might ask a normative question. Once we have somehow decided how we should understand the Constitution, the point of Jefferson's question becomes: is this Constitution morally authorized, and should we submit to this historically given set of fundamental laws in our decisions about the best political community? No doubt the US political tradition would not long endure unless a large majority of citizens affirm our Constitution as framing good politics or, in that sense, are patriotic. Indeed, many or most citizens may readily take for granted the moral authorization of our democratic political form. But noting these facts credits the distinction between hermeneutical and normative questions as readings of Jefferson. As normative, then, his question asks in part for the supreme principle or principles of moral decision and, thereby, for the ultimate terms of political evaluation.

As far as I can see, *The Living Constitution* is focused by the hermeneutical question, and thus Strauss does not explicitly address the normative one; his discussion offers a theory of our Constitution but does not explicitly offer a political theory. Nonetheless, he also does not, unless I have missed something, adequately distinguish these two readings of Jefferson—and in consequence, the living Constitution seems to be so explicated that, given proper transitions, it becomes patient of whatever good politics is thought to require. Given Strauss's presentation, then, we might be left with the following question: if a person agrees to the kind of evolutionary transition he describes and then asserts, "I agree that the Constitution we have is, in the sense Strauss articulates, a living Constitution, but we should, I think, have a different one," does she or he rely on an inapplicable distinction?

Consider how, as Strauss describes it, the common law develops. Constrained by precedent with respect to possible outcomes, present decisions sometimes require considerations of "fairness or good policy" (39). The same considerations are pertinent when, in accord with complex restraints, precedent can or should be overruled. As far as I can see, Strauss identifies nothing in our Constitution that intends to define or help define fairness or good policy, notions that, in themselves, are indefinite and, in fact, have expressed radically competing understandings, even in Western thought. Accordingly, one might see Strauss's proposal as having so answered the hermeneutical question that any answer citizens give to the normative question can itself belong within the living Constitution, at least so long as the change, if sought, occurs in an evolutionary way and is generally accepted by successive generations. Hence, persistence of the male or racial aristocracy with which the Union began would not have been in principle ruled out—nor, for that matter, can some constitutional aristocracy in the future—as a consequence of common law development. Thus, to repeat the question: what, if anything, so marks this Constitution or the US political tradition framed by it that one may then question whether it is good?

What this asks about is the changeless meaning or abiding character of the Constitution and thus the US political tradition. In the nature of the case, moreover, this character must be present from the outset. That which defines a political tradition does so throughout and thus cannot emerge sometime during the tradition. Given a changeless meaning of the Constitution, in other words, a proper answer to the hermeneutical question depends in part on looking to past meaning; something about the original understanding of our Constitution is inescapable in any proper interpretation of it—or is an "authoritative command" (36) issued to later participants in the tradition.

Perhaps some will find such an abiding character in Strauss's living Constitution because, on his account, our constitutional culture takes the written Constitution to constrain constitutional change. This reading is, I think, unconvincing. On Strauss's explication, the common ground provided by the document is of two kinds: On the one hand, the text includes highly specific provisions, such as those regarding the length of terms and certain qualifications for given political offices—stipulations that "give us good enough answers to important questions, so that we do not have to keep reopening those issues all the time" (102). On the other hand, common ground consists in the text's more general prescriptions, because "having the text . . . as a starting point at least narrows the range of disagreement" (104). But any changeless meaning for our political tradition that either kind might be thought to provide seems to become indeterminate when Strauss adds: "the words of the [written] Constitution should be given their ordinary, current meaning—even in preference to the meaning the framers understood" (106). The meaning of these words, then, appears patient of evolutionary change and finally depends on understandings that have, over generations, secured general acceptance.

Others may see the evolutionary and, over generations, generally accepted nature of development within the common law to be itself an abiding character in Strauss's living Constitution. In other words, the virtues of "humility and cautious empiricism" (40) define our political tradition. But the ideology Strauss calls Burkean is not mentioned in the 1787 draft and, as far as I know, was not prominent in eighteenth-century constitutional discussions. Indeed, the drafting and ratification of the Constitution itself exemplifies, it might be argued, not evolutionary but, rather, dramatic change—replacing, as it did, the Articles of Confederation without adhering to their provision for change. Moreover, it is difficult to see how that ideology could be present until the constitutional common law practice itself emerged, and the latter, by definition, could not be present at the outset.

Yet others may embrace what they take Strauss to imply and deny that our Constitution requires an abiding character. Precision here counsels mention that Strauss, on my reading, intends no such denial. To the contrary, *The Living Constitution* discusses the hermeneutical meaning of Jefferson's question and does not consider its normative sense, and attention to the distinction is what raises the question about our Constitution's abiding character, that is, whether it is good. Still, if Burkean ideology is an emergent character of constitutional interpretation, one might wonder whether Strauss is, by implication, left with a denial of any changeless meaning in our political tradition. Emergent characters are themselves subject to change within a tradition. The living Constitution will be constrained by requirements of the common law—evolutionary change generally accepted by successive generations—only as long as our constitutional culture embraces the virtues of humility and cautious empiricism. Hence, that Constitution has no abiding character.

Whether Strauss so implies or not, in any event, some may deny the need for any such character. What marks our political tradition throughout, they may say, is that it started when and where it did. The events of 1787–88 began political rule of a given territory and the people living therein—and any subsequent change in the living Constitution occurred in *that* particular political community, including changes it accepted in territorial extent and in people numbered among the ruled. In effect, then, the Constitution is so understood that it can become any constitution—any change being a change *within* the Constitution.[4] Against itself, however, this account asserts its own abiding character to US politics: it is so constituted as to be inclusive of whatever change is thought to be good. Accordingly, we may ask, is *that* Constitution good—or should we have another that does not leave everything open to change? In other words, the denial of a changeless constitutional meaning becomes, in effect, the assertion of precisely this absence as the changeless meaning by which our political tradition is different from others or possible others. Hence, the question, we can say, is not *whether* US politics has an abiding character but, rather, *what* the character is—and the distinction between hermeneutical and normative questions remains.[5]

THE TRADITION OF POPULAR SOVEREIGNTY

In substantial measure, the US Constitution is directed to articulating proper relations between the federal or national government and the several states thereby united—the formation of, in James Wilson's term, a *confederate republick* (Wilson, I, 181)—and obviously many issues of constitutional interpretation concern proper understandings of such provisions. In asking about our Constitution's changeless meaning, however, I will abstract from those issues and focus on our national political tradition. Moreover, I propose to seek an answer to that question by first asking another, namely, about the source from which the Constitution receives authority to define US politics: what authorizes the Constitution to provide this definition?[6]

In so stating this latter question, I assume that our Constitution is indeed authoritative for our political community. But this authority is not with respect to good politics. Because the hermeneutical and normative questions are distinct, nothing can authorize good politics except the supreme principle or principles of moral decision or the nature and ground of the good—or, attending specifically to politics, the ultimate terms of political evaluation. The final appeal in decisions about the best form of political community can never rightly be to decisions of the past about the best form of political community. What is presently in question, then, is an authoritative definition of the US political tradition or, as we may say, the Constitution's authority to define US politics. As I will seek to show, this question is useful because its answer will provide clarity about just what abiding character the Constitution defines and thus in what respects its provisions are subject to change.[7]

The term "authority" is used in many contexts and has differing meanings. On my intention, asking in the relevant sense about our Constitution's authority seeks the source of its legitimation—of its authority *de jure* and not merely *de facto*. For present purposes, this distinction may be clarified as follows: *de facto* authority is present whenever a person attributes to some other or something the right to prescribe in certain respects the first person's actions or beliefs. In contrast, *de jure* authority is present when the right so to prescribe is legitimate and thus is present whether or not those subject to it recognize the authority in question (see Benn, DeGeorge).[8] Legitimate authority, then, depends on some source by which it is authorized or conferred and to which the authority is properly held accountable. In a US courtroom, for instance, the judge has legitimate authority to interpret the laws pertinent to the trial because her or his authority is conferred by the rules of the US judicial system, to which the judge is properly held accountable. Were its authority not *de jure*, the Constitution's changeless meaning could not answer the hermeneutical question: how *should* we today understand the abiding character of our political tradition, or to be repetitious, how should we today understand US politics? Given that it answers this question, the Constitution's right to do so is present whether or not any given US citizen recognizes its authority. As authoritative in this respect, the Constitution defines our political tradition, and asking further about the abiding character of that tradition will be asking about our politics in the normative sense.

Some will, I expect, find the source we here seek in the Constitution's ratification by the people. In Article VII, the 1787 text specified that "Ratification of the Conventions of nine States, shall be sufficient for Establishment of this Constitution between the States so ratifying the Same," and Article V of that text specified the process by which amendments could be ratified. The Constitution in its entirety, we may be told, derives its authority from such popular approval. After offering a different view, I will return to this proposal. Here, however, we may note that it implies originalism. What the people ratified, in 1787–88 and whenever subsequent amendments were approved, was the meaning of those texts as then understood. On this proposal, then, there can be no distinction between the Constitution's changeless meaning, defining our political tradition, and other original understandings subject to change.

If originalism cannot, as Strauss argues, answer the hermeneutical question, we cannot take ratification to be the source authorizing the Constitution's abiding character, and another reason for this conclusion is the following: were that view correct, the Constitution could not provide how we today should understand US politics because, absent something else, popular approval confers only *de facto* authority over those who so approve. In any event, I have posited that Strauss's critique of originalism is convincing. The issue pursued in our present discussion is not whether that constitutional theory can be redeemed but, rather, whether the living Constitution as explicated by Strauss is an adequate alternative. This does not deny the need, at least of the written Constitution, for ratification. Discrediting originalism implies only that something other than ratification authorizes the abiding character of US politics because such popular approval as the authorizing source is inseparable from the discredited theory. But whether ratification of the written Constitution is nonetheless required by its abiding character depends on what that other source authorizes.

In further pursuit of the Constitution's authority, it will be useful to see that an authorizing source may itself be an authority legitimized by a yet prior source. For instance, rules of our federal judicial system authorize the trial judge's authority in the courtroom because they (or at least some of them) are authorized to do so by the legislature, which is itself legitimized by the Constitution. But authority to define US politics cannot depend on an infinite regress of prior authorities because a given human tradition must have a beginning. If the Constitution has such authority, its legitimation must, at some point, depend on an authorizing source that is not itself an authority, and this may be called the primal source of US politics. To the best of my understanding, the founders of our republic were themselves eminently clear about this primal source, namely, what was often called the promise (or the promises, or the principles) of the Revolution (see Maier 2010, 2, 4, 6). This promise, as commonly experienced by those who first expressed it for the former colonies acting together, defines the US political tradition. If that is so, the primary authority for this definition is not the Constitution but, rather, the Declaration of Independence. The Revolution's promise as commonly experienced by those who first expressed it for the former colonies acting together occurred in the Continental Congress, and the Declaration expressed that promise, in support of which the signers pledged to each other their lives, their fortunes, and their sacred honor.

Appealing to the Declaration in this way does not mean what some have maintained, namely, that our eighteenth-century Constitution includes both the document of 1776 and the document of 1787. To the contrary, the hermeneutical issue here concerns the latter, along with whatever subsequent to it rightly belongs to a living Constitution, and concerns, specifically, the authority of that Constitution to define our politics. The point is, then, that such authority is derived from or conferred by a prior authority, namely, the Declaration of Independence. Thus, the Constitution, in defining US politics, is properly held accountable to the Declaration, because that expression of the Continental Congress is the primary authority authorized by the promise of the Revolution. Further, attention to this prior authority is important in the present discussion because, I have proposed, it will aid in clarifying the changeless meaning or abiding character of our living Constitution, in distinction from the respects in which it is subject to adaptation and change.

Most of the Declaration submits "to a candid world" the "history of repeated injuries and usurpations" by "the present King of Great Britain" and the history of colonial attempts to claim justice from "our British brethren." In addition, the opening paragraph announces why this submission is made, and the final paragraph explicitly declares independence. The Revolution's promise is given principal expression in the document's second paragraph: "all men are created equal and endowed by their creator with certain unalienable rights," among which are "life, liberty, and the pursuit of happiness" and to secure which "governments are instituted among men," so that governments receive their just powers from "the consent of the governed" and for their "safety and happiness." In a word, the promise of the Revolution was a republican form of government. I will here take for granted that James Madison in *The Federalist*, No. 39, speaks for contemporaries in the eighteenth-century nation generally in writing: "we may define a republic to be, or at least may bestow that name on, a government which derives all its powers directly or indirectly from the great body of the people" (Hamilton, Madison, and Jay, 182). Republican government, in other words, implies and is implied by popular sovereignty.

We may also state this conclusion by formulating the overriding political question to which the Revolution's principles were an answer. *De jure* authority is never unlimited authority. The right to prescribe belief and action is relative to some domain (see DeGeorge, chapter 2)—as, for instance, the trial judge's authority is relative to interpreting the law with respect to the courtroom's proceedings. At least typically, the relevant domain can be identified by the question the authority rightly answers—as, for instance, the domain of a trial judge's authority is identified by (something like) the question: what laws are pertinent and in what way are they pertinent to the proceedings in this trial? Hence, we can ask: what is the domain in which the Revolution's promise is authoritative for US politics—or what is the question to which that promise is an authoritative answer? As far as I can see, the question is about sovereignty—and the answer, expressed in the Declaration and the testimony of founding Americans generally, marks

US politics by its denial that ruling power should be possessed by one or the few through inheritance or the self-perpetuation of a select assembly or "some quality independent of the choice of the people" (Wilson, I, 278); that is, the answer denies government without consent of the governed. This is why republican government was almost always explicated in contrast to monarchy and aristocracy. Against sovereignty established in either of these latter ways, as in England's King (or Queen)-in-Parliament, the Revolution's promise was government that occurs through determination by the people.

To be sure, eighteenth-century US citizens typically took for granted some restriction on political participation—at least to free males, often to free white males, and typically to free males or white males who met certain property requirements—and I will discuss this later. Such limitations notwithstanding, however, the sovereignty of the people in contrast to rule stipulated without consent of the governed was paramount for revolutionary citizens. Indeed, this commitment, says Samuel Beer, made the conflict with England intractable (see Beer, chapter 4). Accordingly, the supposed difference, advanced by some, between republican and democratic governments is found in then current understandings of the nation only insofar as "democracy" designates what is sometimes called "direct democracy," in distinction from representative democracy. Wilson called "the nature and kind of that government" proposed by the Constitutional Convention "purely democratical," even if that principle "is applied in different forms" (Wilson, I, 193). On Jefferson's account, ancient Greece saw no alternative beyond, on the one hand, democracy, so understood as to be "impracticable beyond the limits of a town," and on the other, either aristocracy or tyranny, so that "full experiment of a government democratical, but representative, was and is still reserved for us" (Jefferson 1999, 218; see Amar, 277–81).

If popular sovereignty within the new political community was the Revolution's promise as attested by the Declaration, then the Constitution derives authority to define US politics because or insofar as it articulates this promise. In other words, the Constitution is authoritative because or insofar as controlled throughout by the Preamble to its 1787 text, in which the people are said to be the final ruling power: "We the people . . . do ordain and establish this Constitution." As Madison also wrote in *The Federalist* No. 39: "The first question . . . is, whether the general form and aspect of the government be strictly republican? It is evident that no other form would be reconcilable with the . . . fundamental principles of the revolution . . . If the plan of the [Constitutional] Convention therefore be found to depart from the republican character, its advocates must abandon it as no longer defensible" (Hamilton et al., 181–82). Jefferson agreed: "a government is republican in proportion as every member composing it has his equal voice in the direction of its concerns . . . by representatives chosen by himself, . . . and let us bring to the test of this canon every branch of our constitution" (Jefferson 1999, 211; see also Wilson, I, 183).[9]

Authorized to articulate republican or democratic government, the Philadelphia Convention of 1787 could only formulate a Constitution whose very design required ratification by the people—and provide therein a manner in which subsequent amendments might also be ratified. But such approval, we can now say, cannot authorize republican government itself because acceptance by the people cannot account for what was, in fact, the commission given to the Convention. As the authorizing source, ratification would imply that any product of the Convention subsequently receiving popular approval would define the US political tradition, and this is just to repeat that ratification as the authorizing source is inseparable from originalism. Had the Convention of 1787 assigned sovereignty to, for instance, a hereditary monarchy or a monarch-in-parliament, the people might have been asked to accept this outcome because, say, a transition from government in accord with the Articles of Confederation could not be effected without majority agreement from the political community (or the white, tax-paying males therein). But this need for popular approval would be external to the constitutional conception they articulated. There would be no imperative to design a form of government that internally required ratification.

In contrast, those who gathered in Philadelphia in 1787 were obligated to formulate a Constitution to which Article VII, stipulating initial republican consent, and Article V, stipulating the republican process of change, were essential. "If the plan of the [Constitutional] Convention therefore be found to depart from the republican character, its advocates must abandon it as no longer defensible" (Hamilton et al., 182). Final ruling power could be assigned only to the people, so that no constitutional provision or change within the Constitution may cancel or replace their sovereignty. If the Constitution is indefensible unless "we the people" are sovereign, the provisions purporting to articulate this form of government internally required and require popular approval, precisely because that approval was *not* the authorizing source of popular sovereignty. Ratification in 1787–88 by state conventions elected, given eighteenth-century standards, under especially populist rules was dramatically novel. James Wilson called the event "the most dignified one that has yet appeared on our globe" (Wilson, I, 285)—although the process of ratification in his home state of Pennsylvania was apparently less than a model of popular deliberation (see Maier 2010, 97–124). Absent approval by the people—in accord with Article VII or Article V or through informal general acceptance characteristic of common law—neither the 1787 document nor any subsequent changes could constitute a political community authorized by the Revolution. But *whether* republican government is what the Constitution should design was never a question for the Constitutional Convention or for subsequent changes within the Constitution to consider. The imperative to do so was prior to the 1787 assembly in Philadelphia.

To be sure, Wilson speaks of the people not only as "the supreme, absolute, and uncontrollable power" but also as "the supreme, absolute, and uncontrollable authority" (Wilson, I, 191, 213), thereby apparently designating the people as the primary authority and authorizing source of the Constitution. As Wilson also said, however, we thereby mean that such power or authority "*remains* with the people" (Wilson, I, 213). All other political power or authority is delegated by them and so delegated that the people retain the power or authority to recall what has been given. In other words, their sovereignty cannot be canceled. But, then, ratification of the Constitution by the people of 1787–88 cannot be the authorizing source of this permanence and the permanent need for ratification of all constitutional changes. If popular approval conferred whatever authority the Constitution has, sovereignty in the nation's political tradition could have no permanent locus; some succeeding generation could effect a change by assigning sovereignty elsewhere (to, say, a self-perpetuating select assembly)—that is, the US political tradition would become patient of whatever the current people take good politics to require.

On this accounting, then, we can call "the people" the primal source of authority only if doing so designates, not the people who ratified the Constitution but, rather, the people who, in distinction from loyalists, engaged in or supported the Revolution and thereby so communicated its promise to the Continental Congress as to make possible the Declaration.[10] Hence, authorization of a republican government as what always remains must be found in that promise as experienced by those in the 1776 Congress who declared independence. And this recognition, as I will discuss further later, is significant because it opens an alternative to both originalism and Strauss's apparent proposal, namely, a conception on which the living Constitution nonetheless includes a changeless meaning—its affirmation of popular sovereignty in the United States. With Wilson, perhaps, we can also call "we the people" the primary authority in US politics—but this rightly means their authority *within* the form of sovereignty authorized by the Revolution's promise, the authority that delegates and may recall all other political authority. They are not, in other words, the primary authority for democracy itself but, rather, are authorized through the Declaration of Independence to determine governmental institutions and activities within the abiding condition that no such determination can rightly cancel their sovereignty.

In this sense of the people's authority, then, we can speak of ratification—in accord with Article VII or Article V or through informal general acceptance characteristic of the common law—as a conferral of constitutional authority. The Constitution not only asserts popular sovereignty but also provides a detailed institutional design for the political community, a design purporting to be republican and whose details might have been, in some respects, different. Changes in the Constitution, by formal amendment or otherwise, alter this design. Precisely because this republican government was to be "democratical, but representative" (Jefferson 1999, 218), its constitutional details, as Madison most famously insisted, were bound so to stipulate the delegation of power as maximally to protect against its despotic corruption. The institutional design proposed in the 1787 Constitution was in large measure concerned to provide this protection, and a perceived insufficiency in this respect was the principal point of those in the several states who opposed ratification, even while the specific criticisms varied (see Maier, 2010). Given the Revolution's promise as conferral of *de jure* authority to the Constitution of popular sovereignty, ratification, we might say, confers not mere *de facto* but, rather, *de jure* authority to the constitutional details.

For this reason, as mentioned earlier, the formal process of constitutional amendment, specified in Article V, and possible change in the constitution occurring, as Strauss describes, through the general acceptance characteristic of the common law become essential to the Constitution. The *de jure* authority for constitutional details conferred by the people requires their continuing ratification—as Jefferson's question, in its hermeneutical sense, implies. At the same time, an institutional design is requisite if politics is to occur at all. Accordingly, ratification of the details may be taken to confer continuing authority as long as the people do not exercise their ever-present authority to change the design. Even then, however, the authority conferred by ratification on institutional details is subject to qualification because they should never violate popular sovereignty.[11] This issue, I think, demands an extended discussion, and I will here attempt only to suggest its complexity.

All ratified constitutional provisions consistent with popular sovereignty are authoritative for political participation; that is, they define the ethics of political participation. But a given constitutional provision or set of provisions may fail in some greater or lesser measure to institutionalize democracy. In one sense, then, such a provision or set of provisions is insofar not authoritative. It lacks authority because inconsistent, ratification notwithstanding, with why ratification must occur—namely, the prior authorization of popular sovereignty. Still, precisely this prior authorization gives the political decision about whether a provision or set of provisions is democratic to "we the people"; ratification is a "whole people exercising its first and greatest power—performing an act of sovereignty original and unlimited" (Wilson, I, 286). In another sense, then, ratification may be a source of authority even for provisions that are in some measure nondemocratic, namely, in this respect: citizens who contest such provisions are nonetheless bound to do so legally, so that nondemocratic features are obeyed as law until the Constitution is revised. Summarily stated, this possibility occurs if US politics as a whole remains sufficiently democratic; that is, the greater probability of achieving a more completely democratic constitution through extra-constitutional action is absent. In that case, citizens who seek to purge an offending provision should not violate its legal prescription until "we the people" are persuaded to alter the Constitution through constitutionally appropriate procedures (either those stipulated by Article V or those of the constitutional common law).[12] As it happens, most nondemocratic provisions of the 1787 constitution that were subsequently changed (e.g., the exclusion of women from the franchise) had been treated as authoritative in this sense for the political community—even by those who sought to change them.[13]

For all that, however, we should not rule out constitutional provisions or possible provisions that may be so destructive of democracy as to occasion exercise of a patriotic right to seek constitutional change by way of extra-constitutional action. To be sure, the only basis for such action consistent with the Constitution's authority is pursuit of more complete democracy—and however destructive certain ratified prescriptions may be, the opportunity to achieve this end must be sufficient to warrant the civil disruption involved. Nonetheless, such circumstances are possible. In the 1850s, for instance, extra-constitutional action to end the constitutionally recognized practice of slavery (through, say, violation of the Constitution's fugitive slave provision or through slave rebellions or the abetting thereof) was, perhaps, permitted for the sake of democratic government. This might well have been even more the case if the proposed constitutional amendment of 1860, which prohibited a subsequent constitutional amendment giving Congress the power to abolish or interfere with slavery in the states (see Foner, 148–59), had been ratified and the Civil War thereby avoided or postponed.[14] But these several comments on how ratification relates to constitutional authority merely anticipate the more extended treatment needed. However that discussion turns out, the point I wish to underscore concerns the source of authority for stipulating, as the Constitution's Preamble does, popular sovereignty itself, in distinction from assigning sovereignty elsewhere.

Some may object that republican government—or, in the words Abraham Lincoln later impressed on our national memory, government "of the people, by the people, for the people"[15]—does not exhaust what the Declaration attests as the promise of the Revolution. In addition, this primary authority, as I have called it, takes republican or democratic government to be itself sanctioned by "the laws of nature and of nature's God," whereby the governed are the final ruling power because they are "created equal" and "endowed by their creator" with certain natural rights.[16] In contrast, the claim to divine sanction is absent from the Constitution. Moreover, any explicit constitutional claim of this kind is likely denied by the stipulation in Article VI that "no religious Test shall ever be required as a Qualification to any Office or public Trust under the United States," that is, by the disestablishment of religion, which, as the First Amendment made explicit, was understood to mean religious freedom. Thus, this objection concludes, the Constitution's derived authority to define the US political tradition is incompletely represented because the Constitution fails explicitly to affirm dependence on the divine creator.

In response to this objection, we should first recognize how a constitutional provision affirming theism would be inconsistent with the constitutional articulation of popular sovereignty. A divine reality on which natural rights depend is, to all appearances, a reality that grounds or defines the most fundamental principle or encompassing purpose in terms of which all human decisions ought to be taken. But the people cannot be sovereign unless each member thereof is sovereign over her of his evaluation of every political claim; that is, government may never stipulate how any member of "we the people" should evaluate any actual or proposed activity of the state. Accordingly, each citizen has the right to affirm any understanding of the most fundamental principle and thus the ultimate terms of political evaluation she or he finds convincing—and constitutional provision of our dependence on nature's God would contradict popular sovereignty by stipulating the reality that grounds or defines those terms. For this reason, on my accounting, the same Jefferson who authored the Declaration of Independence correctly concluded his Bill for Establishing Religious Freedom in Virginia, written in 1777, by calling its provision a right that government may never properly violate—in his words: "the rights hereby asserted are of the natural rights of mankind" (Jefferson 1999, 391–92). Indeed, generalizing from the Declaration's theism, I am inclined to interpret "religious" in the constitutional principle of "religious freedom" to mean any explicit belief about the ultimate terms of political evaluation and their ground in reality—so that the principle both implies and is implied by a democratic constitution.

Whatever the merit of this last suggestion, we are left with the question: how shall we understand the Constitution's authority in relation to the Declaration's reference to God? Because the attestation of republican government and the theistic assertion cannot both be included in the Constitution, its authority as derived from the Declaration and, through it, the Revolution's promise must consist in the provision of popular sovereignty alone. This is the proper conclusion because it does not deny democracy's theistic grounding, while stipulation of that grounding within the Constitution would inescapably contradict government by the people. On this reading, in other words, the grounding in "nature's God" expresses what the Declaration's signers took to be *implicit* in popular sovereignty: "we the people" can be morally affirmed as the final ruling power only because all are equally endowed by their creator with certain natural rights. But what *explicitly* defines patriotic US politics is nothing other than profession of republican government in the United States. Accordingly, a US citizen is not unpatriotic simply because her or his conviction about the ultimate terms of political evaluation does not ground them in a divine reality—although insofar that person cannot rightly claim to agree with participants in the Continental Congress of 1776. Further, so understanding the Declaration's primary authority underscores the point asserted earlier, namely, relating the two in this way does not make the Declaration a part of our Constitution.

If this discussion properly clarifies the Declaration's reference to nature's God, the objection might still note the Constitution's failure to say expressly, as the Declaration does, that government by consent of the governed has its basis in the natural law. But this, too, I believe, should be understood as something signers of the Declaration took to be implicit in popular sovereignty. As noted previously, the constitution of government by the people explicitly provides the right of each citizen to believe any understanding of the ultimate terms of political evaluation she or he finds convincing. It is, then, no business of this constitution to stipulate whether or not those terms are given in or dependent on the natural law. Accordingly, the preamble to the Constitution explicitly makes no such assertion (however much the entire eighteenth-century nation may have assumed the implication) and, instead, is entirely focused on consent of the governed: "We the people of the United States, in order to form a more perfect union . . . do ordain and establish this Constitution."

Still, we citizens today who seek to understand and assess the Constitution's authoritative definition of popular sovereignty have reason to examine its implications—and thereby critically to assess whether these include those asserted by signers of the Declaration. If they took republican government to imply the natural law, formulating the point in that way alludes to a long tradition of Western thought and can at least be misleading, depending on what expressions of that tradition are taken to be assumed. This recognition allows a return to the previous discussion of authority and, specifically, to the relation between a primary authority and its primal source—in this case, the authorization of the Declaration by the promise of the Revolution. As reviewed earlier, the latter means the Revolution's promise as commonly experienced by those who first expressed it for the former colonies acting together. Accordingly, we have no access to the Revolution's promise in the relevant sense except as expressed in the Declaration, so that the two are correlative concepts. Nonetheless, the two are not identical; the Declaration gives expression to something by which it is authorized and, in that sense, is properly held accountable to its own source.

I take this to mean that terms with which the Declaration expresses the Revolution's promise are not themselves essential to that promise—and therefore subsequent interpreters seeking to understand what the Continental Congress declared are not bound to use the same terms. An interpretation of the Declaration's signers is indeed bound to express what they took to be implied by the Revolution's promise and expressed in terms of natural law. Because what is said and what is meant are not the same thing, however, subsequent interpreters are free—indeed, required—to hold the Declaration accountable to its own source by expressing those implications in the most appropriate contemporary terms. For this reason, as I will discuss presently, we may formulate what the Declaration calls natural law as the universal principle or encompassing purpose of all human decision. Moreover, everything said here about explicating the Declaration's assertion of natural law should also be said, mutatis mutandis, of the signers' theistic affirmation.

ADVANCING THE TRADITION

If its commitment to popular sovereignty in the United States is the Constitution's changeless meaning and is, therefore, present from the outset of our political tradition, this accounting must somehow come to terms with the limits originally placed on who belongs to "we the people." In this respect, the 1787 document did not challenge stipulations provided by the several states. At its most inclusive, political participation was confined to tax-paying males. As fathers and husbands and brothers, they supposed themselves to represent the political interests of women. With few exceptions, these males were also white. There was then little or no pretense also to represent the interests of free black men and women—much less the interests of slaves or of Native Americans. Moreover, most states further restricted voting rights by setting property standards (although differing measures of property were often relevant to differing kinds of elections), thereby also excluding the poor.

Troubled by these original conditions, some may recur to the Declaration of Independence, wherein they find a more inclusive conception of the people said to be created equal than is found in the 1787 document, especially given the latter's commitment to slavery. Because the Declaration is the primary authority for US politics, this comparison may allow something like Abraham Lincoln's account, namely, that concessions to slavery at the Constitutional Convention were, for many participants therein, a compromise for the sake of Union, accepted with the expectation of or hope for slavery's eventual extinction (see Lincoln, 352–65 and 517–53; Jaffa 2000). Reading the Constitution in this way can, I expect, be sustained. Still, there is no escaping that some who signed the Declaration endorsed slavery, and a wider company expected African Americans to be denied the franchise. In addition, all or virtually all at the Congress of 1775–76 assumed the exclusion of both women and the poor (those who could not pay taxes) from political participation. Similar limitations on the relevant public were largely taken for granted throughout the colonies, especially among the white, tax-paying males. Accordingly, the question of popular sovereignty as the changeless meaning of our political tradition persists.

The country's redress of these and other denials has been fitful, delayed, often bloody, and in the 1860s, marked by horrific carnage—and cause remains, in my judgment, to doubt whether the nation's definition of "we the people" is yet adequate. At the same time, there is little question that constitutional changes stipulating who may act as political participants have occurred during the nation's history—and, moreover, changes along an obvious trajectory. During more than two centuries since 1787, formal amendments to the Constitution have, with relatively few exceptions, either sought to make governmental officials more responsive to the people or erased previous exclusions from membership therein—and, as Akhil Reed Amar observes, "no amendment has ever cut back on prior voting rights or rights of equal inclusion" (Amar, 19). What he there says of formal amendments might also be said of (at least most) relevant informal changes effected solely through the constitutional common law.[17] Just because the general direction of this evolution is apparent, then, one has the more reason to ask how popular sovereignty can be the abiding character of our political tradition.

Nonetheless, we can, I believe, call this trajectory a process through which that abiding character is worked out or advanced—because we today can see in the concept of popular sovereignty a meaning with which exclusions present in the eighteenth century and subsequently are inconsistent. This is not to say that earlier understandings saw any such inconsistency. To the contrary, the exclusions were once largely taken for granted. Liberty was widely thought to require the independence that only propertied, white males were widely thought to enjoy—and political participation was widely thought to require such liberty (see McPherson, 48–50). Still, the concept whose meaning is changeless is that of republican government on its original understanding, which denies that ruling power is properly possessed by one or the few through inheritance or through something else other than consent of the governed. As mentioned earlier, the denial of both monarchy and aristocracy, inherent in what "republican" meant to the founding generation, implies that government cannot stipulate to any among the governed the terms of political evaluation; each member of the people must be sovereign over her or his evaluation of every political claim. If this is so, the people can act in common or can be the final political power only if they can be together as equals in a full and free discourse about governing activities. Disagreement about the ultimate terms of political evaluation can be civilized or has a recourse other than force only if differences about the truth are, as Jefferson said, permitted their "natural weapons, free argument and debate" (Jefferson 1999, 391). In a word, popular sovereignty implies politics by the way of reason.

But, now, once the way of reason is, at least by implication, affirmed, there can be no consistent political process that excludes from equal participation any among the governed to whom this exclusion can be applied as a prescription—that is, who can consent to or dissent from their exclusion. Prescriptions claim to command adherence because the reason of those to whom they apply so requires, which means that individuals to whom they apply can also contest them as contrary to what reason requires. The issue is not whether excluded individuals do in fact accept or contest their exclusion but, rather, whether their exclusion can be applied to them as a prescription. Given the latter issue, the governing process that excludes them in fact invalidates by stipulation their possible contestation. But the way of reason recognizes no grounds for the denial of validity except the possibility of sound argument to the contrary. The sole criterion of validity is possible redemption in discourse, so that the government is prohibited from invalidating by stipulation.

In other words, exclusion from republican participation of any among the governed who can contest their exclusion claims to be defensible by reasons that command the assent of all who can contest this provision—and thereby implicitly claims, against itself, to include in the political discourse those who are, by stipulation, excluded. Because it entails the way of reason, popular sovereignty drives toward inclusiveness.[18] Hence, we today can see in the eighteenth-century concept an abiding character with which restrictions on "we the people" then taken for granted were inconsistent—and thus a changeless meaning that was nonetheless to be worked out or perfected. Indeed, we today may call republican government on its original understanding an ideal, even if those or some of those who first embraced it did not think of it in this way—because popular sovereignty, by its own logic, was subject to more complete articulation.[19]

If this conclusion is sound, we have presented grounds of a differing kind than those Strauss mentions for a constitutional common law and, therefore, a living Constitution. He reviews the importance of radically changed circumstances. Because drafters and ratifiers of the written text could not anticipate the altered situation, their understandings of certain constitutional prescriptions may be irrelevant to the new context, and it falls to common law interpretation to translate the original meaning—as Strauss illustrates by way of the Second Amendment and the commerce clause. Also on his account, the common law is required because some constitutional stipulations are terse and cannot control in a reasonable way the variety of cases to which they are possibly pertinent without the formulation of distinctions and guidelines—as Strauss illustrates with respect to the protection of free speech. While its history may include, in some respects, both of these reasons for change, the constitutional understanding of popular sovereignty also exemplifies a different kind of development because its trajectory follows or works out the logic of republican government. In this sense, the evolution can be seen as perfecting the changeless meaning of the US political tradition.

To be sure, changes of this last kind are not effected simply by common law but, rather, often occur through or include formal constitutional amendment. But Strauss's discussion of *Brown v. Board of Education* (1954) is nonetheless a convincing case for how nontextual development is important, perhaps necessary, to achieving more complete popular sovereignty. Let us leave open whether *Plessy v. Ferguson* (1896) was consistent with original understandings of the Fourteenth Amendment. However that turns out, the Court's interpretation in that case was for decades credited by a substantial segment of US jurisprudence and of the US public (although not of the African American community). As Strauss documents, the course of Supreme Court decisions within that context increasingly revealed the impossibility of "separate but equal." More or less simultaneously, a larger public constituency took tentative steps toward conceding the atrocity of racism in our common life. Further, the Civil Rights Movement of the 1960s quickened the public's recognition. All three were important to the *Brown* decision, either to preparation for it or to its effect, and all three belong, on my understanding, to what Strauss means by constitutional common law evolution. If so, that evolution was important, perhaps necessary, to the change effected in our nation's understanding of "equal privileges and immunities" or "equal protection of the laws" as stipulated in the Fourteenth Amendment.

But if we have added a reason for calling the Constitution living, the abiding character of republican government is also a limitation on constitutional change. Any translation or adaptation effected through the common law should be consistent with the constitution of—indeed, should, wherever possible, advance the articulation of—popular sovereignty. Were the body politic to effect a change in our political framework through which sovereignty is no longer assigned to "we the people"—for instance, assigned instead to a hereditary monarchy—US politics as framed by its Constitution since 1787 would end. Even if this transition were to occur through a decision by "we the people," it would nonetheless replace what has been the US political tradition because the defining character of that tradition would be terminated. Accordingly, this changeless meaning of our Constitution limits what Strauss calls judgments about fairness or good policy in our constitutional common law, which become necessary when precedent does not determine contemporary decisions or when precedent is properly overruled. The development of this common law is not patient of whatever good politics is thought to be. To the contrary, judgments of fairness or good policy have as their most general principle the realization of popular sovereignty.[20]

At the same time, the Constitution's changeless meaning allows a distinction between how it should be understood and whether it is good. Notwithstanding a living Constitution, it remains a question for citizens, in distinction from judges or other interpreters of constitutional law, whether popular sovereignty is good politics. For some readers, perhaps, only an academic would propose this distinction or think it important because, in fact, US citizens rarely ask whether another assignment of sovereignty would be better. Even granting this perception, however, we have reason to underscore the difference between hermeneutical and normative questions about our Constitution. The normative question of *whether* democracy is good becomes, when the answer is assumed to be positive, the question of *why* democracy is good. A positive answer to the former, in other words, is not fully explicated without answering the latter—which is also a moral question that citizens alone, in distinction from judges or other constitutional interpreters, properly ask and answer. Moreover, why democracy is, if it is, good is a question all citizens in some way or other must answer, at least in this respect: its valid answer depends on the ultimate terms of political evaluation, about which each citizen must have some express or inchoate understanding in order to assess any actual or proposed law, statutory or constitutional, and thereby act as a member of "we the people." Given a democratic political community, each citizen is, as we have seen, constitutionally sovereign over her or his conviction about these ultimate terms, whereby activities of the state are determined through full and free discourse.

Thus, the difference between hermeneutical and normative questions is politically important because it differentiates asking about the given Constitution, adherence to which the government explicitly prescribes for all citizens, and asking about the terms for all political evaluation, beliefs about which are properly explicit only in the discourse among citizens. As this conclusion suggests, moreover, the singular character of a democratic constitution is its affirmation of precisely the difference between these two questions. Such a constitution is explicitly neutral to all political disagreement, even disagreement about whether this constitution is good or, if it is, why it is. To assert "we the people" as the final ruling power is, in other words, also to affirm that claims to political goodness for proposals or decisions can be validated only by the way of reason and, therefore, never by appeal to tradition or any other authority.

Pursuit of this recognition, I believe, will clarify how a democratic constitution is itself properly understood. If popular sovereignty entails that all questions of good politics are properly answered by the people together in discourse, democracy's fundamental law can properly include nothing more and nothing less than a) the provisions necessary for every political claim, including claims for these very provisions, to be the legitimate object of contestation and argumentative assessment among the governed, and b) the institutions of political decision making through which discourse among the people is maximally effective in determining how the political community is governed. The latter is required because political discourse is constituted in order that governing activities are thereby decided, as the term "political" implies. Hence, common adherence to a democratic constitution should be nothing other than the practice of political discourse about every political claim, including claims for constitutional provisions.

In this way, the constitution is, in effect, self-democratizing, and we should distinguish between adherence to it and profession of it. Any explicit conviction about the ultimate terms of political evaluation, even those taken by its believer to deny the goodness of democracy itself, is constitutionally protected. Such people are legitimate citizens; they can adhere to a properly democratic constitution because doing so is nothing more than participation in discourse about all political claims, including claims for democracy itself. In contrast, when one takes her or his conviction about the terms for all political evaluation, whatever it is, to prescribe popular sovereignty, one not only adheres to that constitution but also professes it. Such people are patriotic citizens.[21] I call the provisions of a properly democratic constitution, to which all citizens as political participants can adhere without professing, formative in character—and I thereby distinguish them from substantive prescriptions for the communal order, to which no citizen as a political participant can adhere without professing and which, therefore, are properly prescribed only as statutory law or policy.[22]

To be sure, an existing constitution may, in fact, include substantive provisions that are inconsistent with its properly formative character. Any such provision contradicts popular sovereignty because adherence to it requires something other than the practice of political discourse about every political claim. A constitutional provision limiting "we the people" to, say, males would be an example. The way of reason excludes none of the governed who can contest their exclusion, and as constitutional, the provision in question would stipulate as illegitimate its contestation by females; indeed, even contestation of their privileged status by males themselves would be excluded. In other words, adherence to a substantive constitutional provision is inconsistent with contestation of it because the constitution defines the practice of politics or the ethics of citizenship, so that adherence to a substantive provision can only mean professing it.[23] But if an existing constitution puts citizens in this position, their dilemma occurs because the supposedly democratic constitution is inconsistent with itself—affirming the people in discourse as the final ruling power, even while including a provision that contradicts that affirmation. In their contestation of a substantive constitutional stipulation, in other words, citizens are allowed to contradict themselves because the constitution defining their political community is self-contradictory—and this simply confirms that a properly democratic constitution is exclusively formative in character.

Be that as it may, constitutional affirmation of the way of reason implies at least one conviction given explicit statement in the Declaration. My reference here is not to the Declaration's theistic affirmation (although it, or some other theistic affirmation, may also be implied) but, rather, the asserted authorization of republican government by the natural law. In common with this assertion, the Constitution implies that good politics depend finally on a universal moral principle or encompassing moral purpose—and this implication simply repeats that popular sovereignty implies a distinction between hermeneutical and normative questions about our political tradition or historical location. Whether our Constitution's changeless meaning also marks a good form of politics requires noncontextual or universal terms for political evaluation.[24]

Nonetheless, the affirmation of such terms is, I stress, solely an *implication* of the US Constitution, however explicit it may be in the Declaration. The denial that moral decision depends on a universal principle or encompassing purpose is entirely legitimate within the democratic discourse, the constitution of which provides nothing other than the practice of political discourse about every political claim. Indeed, the denial of any universal principle or encompassing purpose for moral decision may, so far as the Constitution explicitly provides, be true—even if taking it to be true is inconsistent with what the Constitution implies.

Having considered the abiding character of US democracy as politics by the way of reason, we may note that Jefferson's problem easily leads to confusion between hermeneutical and normative questions because his words can be read to mean either one. "The earth belongs . . . to the living," Jefferson wrote, and thus "it may be proved that no society can make a perpetual constitution, or even a perpetual law. . . . Every constitution, then, and every law, naturally expires at the end of [a generation] . . . If it be enforced longer, it is an act of force and not of right" (Jefferson 1999, 596; see also 593–98). That every constitution expires suggests the normative question, namely, whether good politics requires the political tradition begun in 1787 or requires some other. Still, the hermeneutical question and thus, in response, a living Constitution is also suggested because *every* generation has the right to decide for itself, which might be taken to mean that popular sovereignty is the one thing that cannot rightly be canceled. But if Jefferson's words can be read either way, there should be no question that he nonetheless implied a distinction between the two questions—because his affirmation of natural law and thus a universal moral principle is transparent.

In the end, some may argue that Strauss's account itself intends popular sovereignty as the abiding character of our living Constitution. On his presentation, evolutionary change requires general acceptance by the people over successive generations, and this implies, we may be told, that democratic process is of the essence of our political tradition—so that emergence of a politics in which sovereignty is assigned elsewhere is inconsistent with his proposal. To the best of my reading, however, he does not explicitly show why a proposed nondemocratic framework for politics, were it generally accepted over time, could not then be effected *within* our Constitution, in distinction from being a transition to some other. Correspondingly, he does not explicitly discuss any criterion or criteria, including the principle of popular sovereignty, for judicial considerations of fairness or good policy. Still, if something like my amendment does capture Strauss's intention, I will be delighted simply to have this discussion attempt to underscore his meaning—in which case, the amendment is indeed a friendly one.

But if Strauss finds the difference between hermeneutical and normative questions finally at odds with his understanding, we may hazard an explanation for the apparent absence of a changeless meaning in his living Constitution. In that event, my hunch is this: Strauss's philosophical commitments are aligned with the later thought of John Rawls. Rawls asks how a "stable society of free and equal citizens" is possible when they "remain profoundly divided" by "reasonable comprehensive doctrines" (Rawls 2005, 4, 12), and his answer, which he calls "political liberalism," assumes a modern democratic situation. On that account, the principles of justice are derived from values fundamental to the political culture and institutions of a modern democracy. Accordingly, these principles are "freestanding," that is, independent of any universal moral law or "comprehensive doctrine," and the society is said to be stable if the freestanding character of justice enjoys an "overlapping consensus" among the reasonable comprehensive doctrines (Rawls 2005, 12, 134; see also Lectures I and IV). Precisely how Rawls understood this framing of his proposal is, perhaps, controversial. On my reading, however, his account of political liberalism prevents an independent normative question about democracy as a form of government. If one asks about the moral validity of democratic justice, his appeal to a modern democratic context implies a thoroughly contextualist answer.

That Strauss may take his philosophical bearings from a similar reading of Rawls is suggested when, in treating the written Constitution as contemporary common ground, Strauss says:

> We ought to have an explanation for why we pay attention to the Constitution that does not offend people who venerate the founders and who feel themselves deeply attached to American traditions, but that also includes people who feel no such veneration and no such attachment—people who simply want to live by the rules and do their duty as citizens, while they venerate other ethnic or religious traditions or no traditions at all. (102)

In that formula, one might see an allusion to Rawls's freestanding justice on which there is an overlapping consensus among reasonable comprehensive doctrines, none of which is essential to the definition of good politics.

To be sure, Rawls is clearly focused on modern *democratic* society and the United States as an example thereof; on his account, all citizens are "free and equal" within a "fair system of cooperation over time" (Rawls 2005, 14)—and, for him, the notion that US political culture might become nondemocratic is, I expect, impossible or irrelevant. But absent a difference between what a modern democracy is and whether it is good, one cannot so define a political tradition as to permit its distinction from whatever good politics is thought to require. Perhaps equating good politics with a given tradition seems to define good politics in terms of that tradition's abiding character. But the equation also implies the contrary, namely, the tradition's abiding character is defined in terms of good politics—or, in the phrase previously used here, is patient of whatever good politics is thought to require. In other words, a political tradition can have the kind of abiding character Rawls's account of democracy is said to have only if the question of that character and the question of good politics are distinguished. On Rawls's apparent equation, then, the US political culture can evolve in response to whatever changes the current political community effects—or what finally comes to the same thing, whatever happens to become the object of an overlapping consensus.[25] Hence, alignment with Rawls's proposal may explain why Strauss's living Constitution appears to have no abiding character. If so, and if my argument is sound, Strauss not only disagrees with those in the Continental Congress who signed the Declaration of Independence but also with the implication of our constitutional commitment to government by "we the people."

CHAPTER THREE

DEMOCRACY AND NATURE'S GOD

The Legacy of Abraham Lincoln

No words were more elemental to Abraham Lincoln politically than those issued by the Continental Congress in its Declaration of 1776. As he confessed at Independence Hall in 1861, during his extended journey from Springfield to Washington to become president: "all the political sentiments I entertain have been drawn, as far as I have been able to draw them, from the sentiments which originated and were given to the world from this hall." This self-description might have reference to either or both the 1776 document and the US Constitution drafted in that same hall in 1787. But Lincoln clarified directly which document he meant: "I have never had a feeling politically that did not spring from the sentiments embodied in the Declaration of Independence" (Lincoln, 577).

LINCOLN'S POLITICAL SENTIMENTS

The sentiments principally important to Lincoln were expressed in the Declaration's first two paragraphs, most especially: "that all men are created equal and endowed by their creator with certain inalienable rights, that among these are life, liberty, and the pursuit of happiness," and that governments, therefore, derive "their just powers from the consent of the governed." In 1857 and again at the Alton debate with Stephen A. Douglas in 1858, Lincoln thoroughly repudiated the explicit denial of these "self-evident" truths (see Dred Scott speech, June 26, 1857; Lincoln 360–61; Lincoln and Douglas, 312–13) advanced by, among others, John C. Calhoun, who called them "the most dangerous of all political errors" (cited in Jaffa

2000, 422). But Lincoln thought even more insidious a reading on which the plain sense of "all men are created equal" is implicitly denied by giving some circumscribed meaning to "all." Justice Roger B. Taney's Dred Scott decision, on which the phrase "did not . . . include negroes," did "obvious violence to the plain, unmistakable language of the Declaration" (Dred Scott speech, June 26, 1857, Lincoln, 360), as did Douglas, at the Lincoln-Douglas debate in Jonesboro in 1858, for whom "the signers of the Declaration had no reference to the negro whatever when they declared all men to be created equal. They desired to express by that phrase white men, men of European birth and European descent" (Lincoln and Douglas, 121). In Chicago, during the campaign of which the Lincoln-Douglas debates were a part, Lincoln replied:

> These arguments that are made, that the inferior race are to be treated with as much allowance as they are capable of enjoying; that as much is to be done for them as their condition will allow. What are these arguments? They are arguments that kings have made for enslaving the people in all ages . . . I should like to know if taking this old Declaration of Independence, which declares that all men are created equal upon principle, and making exceptions to it, where will it stop? If one man says it does not mean a negro, why may not another say it does not mean some other man? (speech in Chicago, July 10, 1858; Lincoln, 402-03).

Lincoln read the US Constitution through his understanding of the Declaration, as he confirmed in a fragment probably written subsequent to 1858:

> Without the *Constitution* and the *Union*, we could not have attained the result; but even these, are not the primary cause of our great prosperity. There is something back of these, entwining itself more closely about the human heart. That something is the principle of "Liberty to all" . . . The *expression* of that principle, in our Declaration of Independence, was most happy and fortunate. . . . The assertion of that *principle*, at *that* time . . . has proved an "apple of gold" to us. The *Union*, and the *Constitution*, are the *picture* of *silver*, subsequently framed around it. The picture was made, not to *conceal*, or *destroy* the apple; but to *adorn*, and *preserve* it. The *picture* was made *for* the apple—*not* the apple for the picture. (Lincoln, 513; the metaphor is from Proverbs 25:11)

Moreover, the Gettysburg Address began by dating the nation's birth, "conceived in liberty," at the event of that Declaration, "four score and seven years" previous to 1863 (Lincoln, 734). For Lincoln, accordingly, the Constitution's compromise with slavery is stated euphemistically (a "person held to service or labor") thereby to help express the founders reluctant concession to something already existing that could not be summarily removed, and thus the compromise did not erase their "hostility to the PRINCIPLE" but only stated their "toleration . . . BY NECESSITY" (speech in Peoria, October 16, 1854; Lincoln, 314). In other words, "they meant simply to declare the *right* [to equality], so that the *enforcement* of it might follow as fast as circumstances should permit" (Dred Scott speech, June 26, 1857; Lincoln, 361). They meant to put slavery, as Lincoln often said, "in the course of ultimate extinction" (speech in Chicago, July 10, 1858; Lincoln, 393).

Even if that reading captures the mind of Washington or Madison or Franklin or Wilson, some have argued, it was not the unanimous view of the Constitutional Convention. Lincoln "was wrong in claiming that those who viewed slavery as a positive good had no standing in the arguments of the founding generation, and he was wrong to imply that the founding documents did not take their views into account" (Burt, 275). Be that as it may, Lincoln never mistakenly claimed the Declaration as a "higher law" that sanctioned violation of the Constitution (see Burt, 651). Before the firing on Fort Sumter and notably in his 1858 debates with Douglas, he refused to evade the Constitution's fugitive slave prescription, and in the Cooper Union speech in 1860, his case for the right of Congress to regulate slavery in the territories turned entirely on what signers of the Constitution who subsequently served in the national legislature understood the relevant congressional powers to be. Having taken the oath "to preserve, protect, and defend" the Constitution, his presidential embrace of emancipation could be given political effect only in a proclamation justified as a necessary war measure, freeing slaves "in States and parts of States wherein the people thereof respectively, are this day in rebellion against the United States" (Lincoln, 690)—and for this reason, he zealously pursued, as the war approached its ending, the Constitution's Thirteenth Amendment.

For Lincoln, we can say, the Declaration of Independence did not inaugurate but, rather authorized the Constitution, whereby the former's assertion of equality and thus government by consent became the primary authority for a governmental design "ordained and established" by "we the people." Accordingly, the promise of political community in which the people are indefeasibly sovereign should, wherever and whenever relevant and the Constitution is itself unclear, control constitutional interpretations—and thereby the right to equality is enforced insofar as circumstances permit. So Lincoln also stated in Chicago during the 1858 campaign:

> In relation to the principle that all men are created equal, let it be as nearly reached as we can. If we cannot give freedom to

every creature, let us do nothing that will impose slavery upon any other creature. Let us then turn this government back into the channel in which the framers of the Constitution originally placed it. . . . Let us discard all this quibbling about this man and the other man—this race and that race and the other race being inferior . . . discarding our standard that we have left us. Let us discard all these things, and unite as one people throughout this land, until we shall once more stand up declaring that all men are created equal (speech in Chicago, July 10, 1858; Lincoln, 403-04).

In his continually instructive volume, *Lincoln's Tragic Pragmatism*, John Burt offers a similar understanding of how Lincoln viewed the Declaration—and does so through the "perhaps idiosyncratic" (Burt, 499) employ of H. L. A. Hart's distinction between concepts and conceptions in US law: A "law's concept" is "the deep . . . value it is intended to serve. A law's conception is its concrete working-out in the political and legal institutions of a particular time and place" (Burt, 719, n. 62). The difference, Burt continues, involves what he calls "implicitness" (Burt, 2; see 2–5) that is, the concept is only implicit in any given conception because the former is "always partly betrayed by articulation." Accordingly, the implicit concept "enables the kind of critique of the existing order of things that Lincoln engages in in his own critique of the Dred Scott decision" (Burt, 763 n. 47). Or, again: "The ruling values of the constitutional order, . . . their *concepts*, restlessly and endlessly become, because they are saturated with implicitness that no particular development of them, no *conception*, suffices to exhaust" (Burt, 3). Lincoln, then, "treated the Declaration . . . as a statement of the *concept* of American liberty, which could be brought to realization only through the *conceptions* of the Constitution" (Burt, 651).[1]

On Burt's argument, moreover, something like this distinction between concept and conception was present within Lincoln's own intentions. In what Burt calls a "surprising" conclusion to which his study of antebellum politics led, "Lincoln had chosen commitments whose entailments included racially equal citizenship . . . while he actively denied having made such a commitment" (Burt, x). Thereby, he shared a complexity also present in the Declaration's author:

> Jefferson, as Lincoln argued, both did and did not will the end of slavery. Lincoln both did and did not will racial equality. Both were in a position to deny embracing those intentions, and their denials may not have been entirely strategic. But both also, in the tangle of intuitions and doubts one finds in the penumbra where

human willing happens, did indeed will both things, and willed them more deeply than they willed their own denials. (Burt, 3)

In other words, the deeper intentions were "implicit commitments" (Burt, 3).

A contrary judgment was offered some decades ago by Richard Hofstadter, for whom Lincoln was an ambitious and opportunistic politician who opposed slavery because doing so served his principal concern with the cause of free labor, especially in the territories. "Never much troubled about the Negro, he had always been most deeply interested in the fate of free republicanism and its bearing upon the welfare of the common white man with whom he identified himself" (Hofstadter, 150). Having won the presidency, he fought the war "to defend not only Union but the sacred principles of popular rule and opportunity for the common man," and his thinking focused on "the free white worker: the Negro was secondary" (Hofstadter, 160, 167). Only when events left him no other course did he bow to "the tremendous forces of social revolution" that "storm[ed] about his head" (Hofstadter, 161).

Earlier in his life, Lincoln may have been, as Harry Jaffa says, "a hack politician" (Jaffa 1982, 185), someone principally concerned to advance his political party and his own success within it. That his critique of slavery, at least subsequent to repeal of the Missouri Compromise in the Kansas-Nebraska Act of 1854, was instrumental to his concern for free white labor is, however, not convincing. Lincoln's continual recurrence subsequently to the moral argument against slavery seems far too candid for that interpretation. Indeed, on Burt's account, Lincoln's implicit commitment led him "to reject [as the basis for nonextension of slavery] the purely political case for free soil . . . in favor of the moral case . . . because that moral case was the argument most suited to making a case for the moral equality of black and white, and thus the argument most suited to making the case for black citizenship later" (Burt, xiii).

This is not to impugn Lincoln's sincerity when "he actively denied having made such a commitment" (Burt, x), precisely because the commitment was implicit or inchoate. Lincoln, on Burt's reading, discovered his own intentions: "Over the course of the war, he came to understand that . . . [they] had a meaning and a purpose that even he himself had only partly understood, that emancipation had revealed itself to be in the space of implicit entailments of nonextension, in the shadows of his own willing. What is more, racial equality was also in that implicit space, even under denial" (Burt, 443). Such discovery is, for Burt, what Lincoln meant in his 1864 avowal: "I claim not to have controlled events, but confess plainly that events have controlled me" (cited in Burt, 443). Burt finds one clue to the implicit commitment in how Lincoln typically spoke of his own racism: "Lincoln was aware of his racism . . . [and] ashamed of it" (Burt, 225), and "most of Lincoln's racist remarks" were "defensive, intended to immunize him against . . . attack" as one who favored racial equality (Burt, 205).

To be sure, he endorsed, as did Jefferson before him, the settlement of blacks outside the United States. But "there was something halfhearted and unthought" about his "harebrained schemes" for colonization, "which suggests that Lincoln's commitment to them was shallow" (Burt 360). This formulation of the suggestion may be misleading. Lincoln's support of colonization began as early as 1852 in his eulogy for Henry Clay—Lincoln's self-confessed political sage, who was himself a member and died as President of the American Colonization Society (speech of July 6, 1852; see Lincoln, 275–77)—and continued well into Lincoln's presidency. Both his 1861 and 1862 annual messages to Congress included such schemes, and the latter proposed a constitutional amendment for financing this effect (see Lincoln, 629–30, 680). Notably, moreover, he claimed the merits of black emigration in an August 1862, meeting with African American leaders (see Donald, 367–68). Not until the Emancipation Proclamation, when he approved black participation in the Union Army, did he abandon colonization (see Donald, 430).

Still, Lincoln doubted, beginning no later than 1854, whether colonization was practicable, a concession he expressed more than once during the Lincoln-Douglas debates (see Donald, 167, 344). As Burt notes, moreover, Lincoln never spoke of or implied involuntary emigration (see Burt, 360), as did Jefferson and Lincoln's Postmaster General, Montgomery Blair (see Jefferson 1999, 474f.; Donald, 469). "Once the war began, [Lincoln] never treated colonization as a necessary precondition of emancipation" (Burt 360)—and the response of blacks to his proposals may have underscored the fantastic nature of such ideas. "For a man who prided himself on his rationality," comments one biographer, "his adherence to such an unworkable scheme was puzzling," although perhaps explicable by his general "lack of acquaintance among African Americans" (Donald, 167). So, his endorsement of colonization may have been "shallow" if we take this to mark, as Burt intends, Lincoln's implicit commitment. He persisted with this proposal "sometimes only for rhetorical purposes (so as not to have to give answers about what the shape of postwar society might be that it would have been fatal to give) but sometimes also as a way of not facing up to the meaning of the war," sometimes "to throw sand in the eyes of the voters" and sometimes "to deceive himself" (Burt, 446). When "colonization had been taken off the table" in January 1863, he began, "in a very tentative way, to rethink the question of political and social equality" (Burt, 413), that is, to make his implicit commitment in some measure explicit.

But Burt's more direct evidence of this underlying aim is, as mentioned earlier, that Lincoln's arguments continually implied "the moral equality of black and white" (Burt, xiii). "Despite repeated denials that he favored racial equality, Lincoln consistently chose the arguments that would lay the groundwork for racial equality later, and rejected arguments that would have supported preventing the spread of slavery into the territories but that would have ruled racial equality out" (Burt, 335). Wondering why "Lincoln persisted" in 1858 to condemn slavery as immoral when, by that time, "the people of Kansas, the one western territory where slavery might have imaginably had a chance of establishing itself, had decisively rejected it," Burt ends up "holding that Lincoln argued that way because of his allegiance to certain fundamental values among whose consequences was his ultimate commitment to seeking citizenship for black people" (Burt, x, xi). Accordingly, "Lincoln's views, despite his denials, really did point to racial equality, as Douglas said they did" (Burt, 176). Further, Burt is impressed by Lincoln's argument for the Emancipation Proclamation: "The key military necessity Lincoln built his case for emancipation upon was the need for manpower; slavery was ended ... to make possible the recruitment of black soldiers for the Union army." This was not itself a "direct promise of suffrage ... ; but one cannot ask people to die for the sanctity of the ballot while intending to withhold the ballot from them" (Burt, 407, 08)—a consequence Lincoln himself acknowledged in his last public address: "I would myself prefer that it [the elective franchise] were now conferred on the very intelligent [colored men], and on those who serve our cause as soldiers" (Lincoln, 799).

This reading of Lincoln's arguments is, Burt allows, "controversial" (Burt, 224). Still, even if one doubts any such implicit intention in Lincoln's willing, one should not deny that social and political equality was often implied by his formulations. I mean here to distinguish between what is implied by something someone says, on the one hand, and on the other, whether the person in question is in some way, even inchoately, conscious of or believes the implication. If Einstein's theory of relativity is true, for instance, any true statement made about relations among things in our universe implies that theory—but it does not follow that persons making such statements are in any relevant sense aware of or believe Einstein's proposal. Burt's analysis finds in Lincoln an implicit belief in full equality. Even if we doubt that conclusion, I here mean to say, we can still recognize that his statements often implied such equality. He could not recur so completely to the first paragraphs of Jefferson's Declaration without that implication.

As previously mentioned, that "all men are created equal ... [and] endowed by their creator with certain inalienable rights" means that governments derive "their just powers from the consent of the governed" (Jefferson 1999, 97); self-government is the proper consequence of equality. Nowhere does Lincoln embrace the point more clearly than in Peoria in 1854. Rebutting Douglas's argument for "popular sovereignty," Lincoln calls the doctrine of self-government "absolutely and eternally right" but relevant for Douglas only if "a negro is *not* . . . a man." If "the white man governs himself that is self-government; but when he governs himself, and also governs *another* man, that is *more* than self-government—that is despotism. If the negro is a *man*, why then my ancient faith tells me that 'all men are created equal'" (speech in Peoria, October 16, 1854; Lincoln, 303). In sum. "no man is good enough to govern another man, *without that other's consent*. I say this is the leading principle—the sheet anchor of American Republicanism." Having already alluded to the Declaration, Lincoln continues by citing its second paragraph, thereby to underscore "that according to our ancient faith, the just powers of governments are derived from the consent of the governed" (Lincoln, 304). To be sure, he then denies "contending for the establishment of political and social equality between the whites and blacks" and purports to be "combating what is set up as a MORAL argument for allowing" the extension of slavery (Lincoln, 304). But his denial would be consistent with his rebuttal of Douglas only if Lincoln also denied self-government as affirmed by the Declaration. Because the latter was Lincoln's own "ancient faith," his moral argument did indeed imply social and political equality.

THE DECLARATION'S LAWS OF NATURE

Whether or not the implication of Lincoln's argument was also an implicit willing, I am unclear to what, on Burt's reading, Lincoln's moral affirmation of the Declaration appealed. In Burt's "Introduction," he comments on his debt to John Rawls (see Burt, 10) and throughout the volume pauses to explain Rawlsian terms and distinctions used therein to help present a reading of the Lincoln-Douglas debates. While there is some attention to Rawls's earlier *A Theory of Justice*, especially to its terms "original position" and "veil of ignorance" (Rawls 1971, 18, 19), Burt refers more often to Rawls's later *Political Liberalism*, for instance, to its idea of an "overlapping consensus" (Rawls 2005, 134; see Burt, 11) and its distinction between the rational and the reasonable (see Rawls 2005, 48f.; Burt, 282f.). For Rawls in that later volume, liberal justice is not the application to politics of any universal principle or principles but, rather, is authorized by the specific public political culture of a modern democratic society. Hence, democratic principles are "freestanding" or independent of any "comprehensive doctrine" (Rawls 2005, 12)—and political decisions about society's basic structure, as he confirmed in a subsequent essay on public reason, should be defensible by reasons that do not imply any such doctrine but, rather, appeal solely to the specific public values of a modern democracy (see Rawls 2005, 435–90).

What is not clear to me, then, is whether Burt views Lincoln through the later Rawls's—or, in that sense, through a Rawlsian—account of democracy. Is Lincoln's appeal solely to the distinctive US political tradition or culture, or is there a more fundamental grounding by which he takes the Declaration to be itself morally valid?

Some of Burt's formulations seem to reflect a Rawlsian interpretation of Lincoln. Two illustrations may suffice. The "requirement of an overlapping consensus about public values does not mean that all parties must accept those values for the same reasons; evangelical Christians and secular Socialists may have different reasons for valuing freedom of speech or equal citizenship, but that difference does not matter as long as they both value them as strongly"—a statement suggesting that public values are freestanding—and this, Burt says, "was Lincoln's view, and Rawls's view as well" (Burt, 11). Or again: when Lincoln concludes his First Inaugural by evoking "the better angels of our nature," he "has in mind that half-conscious structure of habits and values against which our acts take their long-term meaning . . . The better angels of our nature tie us back . . . to the *nation*" (Burt, 642). This citation at least could mean that Lincoln's appeal is limited to the nation's common political culture rather than anything beyond, and that reading may be supported when Burt identifies these better angels with "a shared history" (Burt, 393).

On the other hand, other statements may count against a Rawlsian interpretation. Here, too, I will simply offer two illustrations: On my understanding, Rawls explicitly separates the rational "capacity to form, revise and . . . to pursue" a "conception of the good" (Rawls 2005, 19) from the reasonable because only so can reasonable political principles have the freestanding character on which comprehensive doctrines share an overlapping consensus—but Burt calls this distinction "rough-and-ready" (Burt, 282), and perhaps that characterization is apt for his appropriation: "rationality remains the prisoner of its own premises," while reasonableness "provides one . . . with an ability to critique one's own premises, to give reasons for believing that one's premises are deep, or neutral, or universal . . . Reasonable promises no special access to the absolute" (Burt, 282–83)—a formulation that may imply, as Rawls does not, that universal premises on which justice is said to depend can be verified or falsified by argument. Accordingly, a more inclusive meaning of "reasonable" than Rawls intends may be at work when Burt says: "it is fruitful to conceive of their argument [that of Lincoln and Douglas] as an argument about the nature of the reasonable" (Burt, 282). Or again:

> The legal realists . . . are right that laws are creatures of culture and history, and are marked as much with the social contradictions and forms of special pleading of their era as they are with

the majesty of justice. But the advocates of natural law are right that law is as much a critique of its society as an expression of it. . . . Embracing the distinction between concept and conception, this is to say, enables one to mark also the distinction between tragic pragmatism and relativism. (Burt, 499)

Although this latter passage could mean that some abiding aspect of the specific political tradition critiques more immediate social constructions, the citation might express instead a belief in some universal principle of moral judgment.

But however Burt's view of Lincoln should be understood, I rehearse its relation to Rawls's political liberalism as context for asserting that Lincoln was no Rawlsian. With the Declaration, Lincoln took the principle of equality to be universally human in the sense designated by "laws of nature" or "natural law" in a straightforward sense. Accordingly, he could without evasion cite this declared truth as "self-evident." Burt denies to this principle that character: "Something that is truly self-evident, in the sense of being immediately obvious to everyone, would not require that anyone announce that they hold it so. . . . That all men are created equal is not a self-evident truth in the way that a tautology is a self-evident truth" (Burt, 257). As it happens, "self-evident" was not Jefferson's original term. His draft spoke of "undeniable" truths. Both terms, says Morton White, refer to truths apprehended by rational intuition (see White, 72–78). But whatever one thinks such intuition might be, it seems clear that something can be undeniable or self-evident without being so transparent as to need no mention. If, for instance, a statement articulates some necessary condition of self-conscious existence as such, a truth about all possible subjects that depends on no specific characterization by which some are distinguished from others, it would be a truth any sufficiently reflective person may recognize as implied by her or his own consciousness—and thus a truth one cannot deny without the act of denial presupposing what is denied. Such a truth might well be called undeniable or self-evident or even discernable by rational intuition, even if not "immediately obvious to everyone."

In accord with this meaning, Lincoln would proclaim in Peoria: "Slavery is founded in the selfishness of man's nature—opposition to it, is his love of justice. These principles are an eternal antagonism . . . Repeal the Missouri compromise—repeal all compromises—repeal the declaration of independence—repeal all past history, you still cannot repeal human nature" (speech in Peoria, October 16, 1854; Lincoln, 309). No principle specific to a given political culture or tradition could survive all such repeals. "All honor to Jefferson," Lincoln wrote in 1859, "who, in the concrete pressure of a struggle for national independence by a single people, had the . . . capacity to introduce into a merely revolutionary document, an abstract truth, applicable to all men and all times" (Lincoln, 489). Moreover, no account of equality circumscribed by historical location could, as Lincoln's 1862 message to Congress announced, "light us down, in honor or dishonor, to the latest generation" because the Union defines "the last best hope of earth" (Lincoln, 688). For Lincoln, the US experiment in self-government was a light on humanity's universal moral possibilities, which is why the "great task remaining before us" after Gettysburg was "that government of the people, by the people, for the people, shall not perish from the earth" (Lincoln, 734).

In seeking to clarify Lincoln's meanings, Burt tells us, he turns not only to Rawls but also to Kant (see Burt, 10), although Burt's references to Kant are far fewer than those to Rawls. If these two philosophers exhaust the options, Lincoln's reading of the Declaration is surely Kantian rather than Rawlsian. On this issue, in other words, Harry Jaffa has Lincoln right—even while Jaffa's philosophical resources are not principally Kantian: "If self-government was a *right*, and not a mere *fact* characterizing the American scene (more or less), then it must be derived from some primary source of obligation. There must be something, Lincoln insisted, inhering in each man, *as a man*, which created an obligation in every other man . . . [something] other men were bound to respect" (Jaffa 1982, 348). Speaking of those who supported the South's "peculiar institution," Lincoln often said in differing ways what he stated in his First Inaugural this way: "One section of our country believes slavery is *right*, and ought to be extended, while the other believes it is *wrong*, and ought not to be extended. This is the only substantial dispute" (Lincoln, 586). He did not mean "right" and "wrong" simply in view of the nation's political tradition; he had in mind also the universal order that, for him, morally validates the Declaration of Independence. Our common human relation to that moral order is, I expect, the best candidate for Lincoln's "better angels of our nature."

Mention of Kant, moreover, opens a possible way to strengthen Burt's case that Lincoln's moral arguments against slavery not only implied social and political equality but also expressed an implicit or inchoate commitment to it. For Kant, the moral law must be a priori in practical reason, that is, self-evident because a necessary condition of self-conscious freedom as such—and since what is thereby implied in every exercise of practical reason is a *moral* law, no human can ever be ignorant of it. On his analysis, a moral prescription cannot be applicable to one's decision if one cannot act accordingly *because* one ought to do so; ignorance of the moral law would then mean that some occasion of decision with understanding would not be morally bound, and thus conditions without which self-conscious freedom cannot occur could not include a moral law. Accordingly, an a priori principle of human freedom defines an obligation of which all humans are aware, even if to some it is not explicitly obvious. It is, in other words, always understood and believed, at least implicitly, even when pragmatically contradicted by decisions against it. Let us accept this analysis. Let us further credit as a priori a moral principle that, when applied to US politics, more or less obviously prescribes social and political equality. If Lincoln's moral arguments against slavery also implied this application of a principle he, as all subjects, necessarily believed, social and political equality becomes the more plausible as something he implicitly willed. Absent that inescapable moral awareness, in other words, one might have cause to wonder why the implications of Lincoln's arguments should be seen as intentions of which he was inchoately aware.

To the best of my reasoning, the moral law is indeed a priori in human freedom and thus self-evident (although the principle is, on my thinking, more inclusive than Kant's categorical imperative), and this principle applied to US politics does more or less obviously prescribe something very like the Declaration's apparent meaning of equality among persons. In this context, and given Burt's evidence, I find his conclusions about Lincoln's inchoate intentions persuasive. But the transcendental context, to give the self-evident moral law another name, and the historical evidence available on Lincoln, beg for extended discussion, and I will not pursue these arguments here. Instead, I wish to make another point about what follows given that Lincoln was not a Rawlsian.

Lincoln's belief in the Declaration, such that rights therein affirmed are *human* rights, allows a distinction between what is meant when democratic equality is affirmed and whether democratic equality is morally good or right. For Lincoln, to be sure, American democracy as defined summarily by the Declaration was indeed good or right—but this is another way of saying that, for him, the Declaration was itself morally valid, that is, "derived from some primary source of obligation" (Jaffa 1982, 348). If, to the contrary, democratic equality neither has nor needs a moral ground other than the US experience or the historically specific US tradition, as the later Rawls apparently asserts, the moral question about the Declaration's affirmation makes no sense. At best, self-government then is, as Jaffa has it, "a mere *fact* characterizing the American scene"—or, as he also says, "any constitution is merely a document of positive law" (Jaffa 1982, 348).

This difference between what the Declaration means and whether it is morally good or right is important because, without it, government by consent of the governed or popular sovereignty cannot be complete. On a Rawlsian account, as far as I can see, self-government is "a mere fact characterizing the American scene" (Jaffa 1982, 348); that is, democracy with its legitimate plurality of "religious, philosophical, and moral doctrines" (Rawls 2005, 4) is posited or taken for granted. Accordingly, democracy is then immune to contestation and thus its validity cannot itself be the object of moral or political debate. The democratic constitution must, in other words, be imposed on the political community, such that dissent from its validity is illegitimate. "The question of democracy," we may note, is an ambiguous phrase, depending on whether the genitive is subjective or objective. As a subjective genitive, the phrase means democracy's question, which assumes the moral validity of democratic politics and concerns the principles of justice and their application that democratic citizens pursue. As an objective genitive, the phrase means the question about democracy, that is, whether democracy itself as a form of government is morally good or right. Given Rawls's account, we can now say, democracy's question cannot include a question about democracy; there can be no debate about democratic government because its backing is the historically specific democratic tradition.

In contrast, complete popular sovereignty means that each citizen is sovereign over her or his assessment of every political claim, including any claim for the democratic form of government itself.[2] Strictly all prescriptions for political order, including those for democracy itself, are open to contestation in discourse among the citizens together as equals. Only so, if I see the matter clearly, can the political constitution be, not an imposition on citizens but, rather, ordained and established by "we the people"—even if a decision for some nondemocratic form of discourse would deny (not the authority of the Declaration for the Constitution but, rather,) moral validity for the Declaration. To be sure, including within full and free political discourse the question about democracy is itself a democratic provision, and thereby any citizen who contests the morality of a democratic process is constitutionally bound to honor the democratic form of discourse and thus the rights of all who belong to "we the people"—at least until, through discourse, "we the people" decide for another form of sovereignty. I will call such constitutional rights, those a democratic constitution should stipulate for every citizen, formative in character—and adherence to the practice constituted by the formative rights of all is, I will say, adherence to the ethics of citizenship.

But stipulating such adherence does not explicitly proscribe asking whether democracy itself is good or right—and, in truth, this question cannot be answered in democracy's favor unless popular sovereignty can indeed be defended as morally good or right. In his classic volume, *We Hold these Truths: Catholic Reflections on the American Proposition* (1960), John Courtney Murray said of "the American Consensus," which is his account of the ethics of citizenship: "we hold certain truths, therefore we can argue about them" (Murray, 27). Whatever he meant or may have included in those truths, this cryptic statement can, I believe, be recrafted to capture the formative character of a properly democratic constitution: "we adhere to this constitution, therefore we can argue about it." The one commitment that does not take sides in any political disagreement is the commitment to argument about the contending claims; hence constituting government as a full and free political discourse is not inconsistent with argument about whether the government should be so constituted—and only if democracy is morally good or right can it be redeemed in that discourse.

I do not say that Lincoln's explicit understanding of equality distinguished the formative rights properly provided in a democratic constitution. Until late in his life, as already mentioned, he publicly denied endorsing equal political rights for blacks—although on Burt's account of the complexity in Lincoln's intentions, he earlier became, likely sometime during the 1850s, implicitly committed to full equality for all (at least for all men). Whether or not he somehow pursued black membership in "we the people," however, Lincoln's explicit understanding of equality apparently focused on the substantive good or happiness of all citizens, that is, on the right to substantive justice that statutory law should secure for all in a democratic community. Discussing in 1857 the standard given by the Declaration, he spoke of government "augmenting the happiness and value of life to all people of all colors everywhere" (Dred Scott speech, June 26, 1857; Lincoln, 361)—and Jaffa summarizes: "Lincoln's interpretation of human equality . . . is that every man had an equal right to be treated justly, that just treatment is a matter of intrinsic worth, that a man's rewards from society ought to be proportional to the value of his work" (Jaffa 1982, 320).

Still, if we allow, as Burt argues, that Lincoln's implicit willing included political equality for all, his substantive view of the Declaration's standard expressed his conviction that democracy as a form of government is good or right. Government by consent of the governed is the proper political constitution because justice as authorized by the moral law affirms the substantive equality of all citizens; equal membership in "we the people" is morally prescribed because participation in self-government belongs to the happiness of all at which politics properly aims. This offers one way to appropriate Lincoln's distinction between "government by the people" and "government for the people." The former means that final power properly resides with the entire community, whose members are together as equals in discourse about every political claim—and "for the people" prescribes that government, whose decisions are properly determined through that discourse, is properly aimed at the flourishing of all. Hence, Lincoln's commitment to the Declaration perhaps argues that his implicit willing included something like the difference between formative and substantive principles of justice.

Finding this distinction in the complexity of Lincoln's intentions may, moreover, help to clarify his response to his antagonists in the South. Even as he asserted that "one man's making a slave of another" is not "self-government" but, rather, "despotism" (speech in Peoria, October 16, 1854; Lincoln, 303-04), he sought, during the events before 1861, to engage in moral discussion those for whom slavery was a positive good. If his First Inaugural described "the only substantial dispute" in terms of how each party understood right and wrong, he also spoke this way *to* his "dissatisfied fellow countrymen" (Lincoln, 588). In 1860, he wrote to Alexander Stephens, Lincoln's former colleague in Congress and soon to be elected vice president of the confederacy: "You think slavery is *right* and ought to be extended; while we think it is *wrong* and ought to be restricted. That, I suppose, is the rub. It certainly is the only substantial difference between us" (Lincoln, 568). Because inconsistent with self-government, the "positive good" view of slavery was, for Lincoln, a political denial of democratic discourse. Nonetheless, he treated its advocates not as hostile aliens immune to discursive engagement but, rather, as participants in the democratic process.

As far as I can see, this treatment would be merely tendentious if Lincoln's appeal were restricted to values entirely specific to US history. On that basis, one might critique the Southern defense of slavery as inconsistent with the country's founding documents, but there could be no argumentative engagement with those for whom "all are created equal" was "wild and dangerous nonsense," as it was to Calhoun and other "pro-slavery ideologues" (Burt, 73)—including Stephens, for whom the founders' "assumption of the equality of the races" was "fundamentally wrong" (cited in Jaffa 2000, 217). Only because the moral law prescribing democratic equality is universal to humanity is there, at least in principle, common ground to which discourse about whether slavery is right or wrong may appeal.

Perhaps, moreover, although here I only speculate, Lincoln's affirmation of a full and free democratic discourse was among his motivations when the crisis at Fort Sumter faced him. The government, he promised in his First Inaugural would not initiate war: "In *your* hands, my dissatisfied fellow countrymen, and not in *mine*, is the momentous issue of civil war. . . . You can have no conflict, without being yourselves the aggressors" (Lincoln, 588). Whatever other considerations were relevant, including his other First Inaugural promise to "possess the property and places belonging to the government" (Lincoln, 583; see Donald, 294-95) and the need to ensure support in the North for an armed conflict, his eventual decision to provide the fort but only with nonmilitary necessities, so that no shots would occur unless first fired by confederate batteries in Charleston harbor, was at least consistent with his commitment to a discourse in which even the denial of democracy can be included.

THE ALMIGHTY'S PURPOSES

Whatever may be the case with Lincoln's implicit willing, his commitment to the Declaration will not be adequately represented without attention to his religious beliefs. On his explicit accounting, the moral law defining good or right human community is not merely the normative structure defining the human community in an otherwise indifferent or heedless universe; the moral order is, rather, providential. With Jefferson, the relevant laws are given in the nature of things, and they are laws of nature because laws of nature's God. When Lincoln cited the Declaration, as he often did, to express what he called his "ancient faith"—"my ancient faith teaches me that 'all men are created equal'" (speech in Peoria, October 16, 1854; Lincoln, 303)—the term "faith" was entirely apt, because he meant the providential moral order specified to politics. As one biographer comments, "Lincoln found the scriptural basis for the Declaration in the book of Genesis: if humankind was created in the image of God, then 'the justice of the Creator' had to be extended equally 'to *all* His creatures.'" (Carwardine, 40; internal citations are Lincoln's words). "Nothing stamped with the Divine image and likeness," Lincoln once said, "was sent into this world to be trodden on, and degraded, and imbruted by its fellows" (cited by Carwardine, 40)—and he thereby echoed Jefferson's words: "the mass of mankind has not been born with saddles on their backs, nor a favored few booted and spurred, ready to ride them legitimately, by the grace of God" (Jefferson 1999, 149).

There seems little doubt that Lincoln was a fatalist. Likely influenced by the Calvinism to which he was exposed as a child, he professed a kind of divine determinism, whereby God controlled all or virtually all from eternity. "I have found my life as Hamlet says," he apparently testified: "'There's a divinity that shapes our ends, Rough-hew them as we will.'" Lincoln's law partner, William Herndon, wrote after Lincoln's death that Mary Lincoln noted how many times her husband said: "What is to be will be and no cares of ours can arrest the decree." Urged to take measures against assassination as he left Springfield for Washington and his inauguration, he reportedly replied: "I will be cautious . . . but God's will be done. I am in his hands . . . and what he does I must bow to—God rules, and we should submit" (cited in Carwardine, 39). His "Meditation on the Divine Will," written during the war years, begins, "The will of God prevails"—leading Lincoln then to entertain, as he again supposed in his Second Inaugural, that God willed the war and willed its continued horror through "His appointed time" (Lincoln, 655, 793).

Still, his belief in divine control did not evoke passivity. To the contrary, Lincoln's sense of moral responsibility was acute. To affirm both detailed determination of events and a moral order appears to be—and, on my accounting, finally is—a contradiction. Lincoln transparently embraced the latter and thus may have sought to limit the former. Although Herndon reported Lincoln's often expressed belief that "all things were fixed, doomed in one way or the other" (cited in Carwardine, 39), Herndon also noted Lincoln's qualification: "the will to a very limited extent, in some fields of operation, was somewhat free," so that humans could "modify the environments" by which they were created (cited in Carwardine, 43). But Lincoln, I expect, more often reconciled the moral demand with God's determination of events by understanding human actions and, indeed, human decisions to be the worldly medium through which the divine effects its historical control. In 1846, he announced belief in the "Doctrine of Necessity," such that "the human mind is impelled to action or held in rest by some power, over which the mind itself has no control" (cited in Carwardine, 40). During the 1860s, he meditated that God's will is effected by "his great power on the minds" of agents (Meditation on the Divine Will; Lincoln, 655). Further, he likely came to see himself as God's vehicle: according to one close friend, Lincoln concluded "that he himself was an instrument foreordained to aid in the accomplishment" of both saving the Union and ending slavery (cited in Carwardine, 44). Accordingly, "Lincoln the limited fatalist," as one recent biographer has called him (Carwardine, 40), could affirm responsibility, insofar as God gives one to see God's will, to act for outcomes nonetheless controlled by God. It is worth noting, moreover, that some forms of Calvinism exhorted a rigorous morality even while they asserted without compromise the determinism of God's "special providence," and a similar active commitment characterized some communists who pursued by choice a culmination of history they also believed—with, as they understood him, Marx—is inevitable.

During the 1830s, in any event, Lincoln's abiding concern to follow reason and evidence with respect to theology was impressed by skeptical writings about Christianity, including those of Thomas Paine (see Donald, 49), and may have been drawn to the pursuit of rational theology. In New Salem, Lincoln apparently wrote an essay questioning the Bible as divine revelation, subsequently burned at the urging of friends who feared damage to his public career. On the testimony of many witnesses, however, his reflections were always those of a theist, who affirmed a providential creator (see Carwardine, 35, 36). What he could not believe were supposed truths supposedly available only through inspired Scripture—and this included the orthodox Christian claim for the uniqueness of Jesus. As far as we know, affirmation of anything approaching orthodox christology cannot be found in the evidence Lincoln left us, and the conclusion seems secure that he never became a Trinitarian. Some have argued for his conversion to Christianity during the 1850s, when he attended and, in fact, purchased a pew at the First Presbyterian Church in Springfield. But he did not join his wife as a member of that church, and his son Robert later denied any mention by Lincoln of a change from his more Unitarian convictions (see Carwardine, 38). Theism was one thing and christology another—and this may be one reason why, prior to his presidency, Lincoln rarely, if ever, spoke publicly about his religious beliefs. Evangelical Christianity was pervasive in the United States, a consequence in part of the Second Great Awakening earlier in the century, and this significant political constituency would likely be troubled by any refusal of its christology.

Perhaps Lincoln is, then, best characterized as a religious inquirer. But if so, the inquiry, possibly excepting some quite youthful reflections, was never *whether* God is but, rather, always *what* God is. His thoughts in answer to this question became, it seems, increasingly public during the course of his presidency. During the war's first year, he began publicly to invoke providence, and his "public calls for God's assistance" increased as the war proceeded (see Carwardine, 226). He attended church, like other presidents, and now more regularly, typically at Washington's New York Avenue Presbyterian Church. His private "Meditation on the Divine Will" (perhaps written in 1862 but more likely in 1864 [see Miller, 406]) foreshadowed his comments on God in his letter, intended for publication, of April 1864 to Albert G. Hodges—and both foreshadowed his especially public accounting of the war, God's purposes, and the nation's proper response in his Second Inaugural. To be sure, evangelical Protestants in the North emerged as an especially important part of Lincoln's political backing, and it might be argued that, once having become president, he now needed to express or imply agreement with their religious grounds for supporting the war. But charging his increasingly public theistic beliefs even primarily to strategic political motives becomes entirely incredible once the exceptional discernment of his religious mediations is appreciated.

According to some, the course of Lincoln's presidency also occasioned a change in his beliefs about how politics relates to God. Perhaps influenced by Phineas D. Gurley, the pastor at New York Avenue Presbyterian Church with whom Lincoln apparently had several conversations,[3] the Calvinism to which he was exposed early in life is said to have been resurrected in his thought, but God's providence now becomes the directives of a more personal actor, even while the divine will controlling events becomes more unpredictable and mysterious (see Carwardine, 224–28). Burt speaks approvingly of the emergent clarity in "Lincoln's . . . negative theology," expressed eminently in his Second Inaugural. "We do not know God's will," and every claim to know it is a betrayal of it, a disclosure of our fallenness, whose consequence is violent conflict with one another. Still, "it is . . . a crucial matter" Burt continues, "to do God's will, to be subject to a moral demand"

(Burt, 700)—to act for the right even though "urgently prevented from knowing whether what we seek to do really is the right or whether we are doing the right thing in the right way and for the right reasons" (Burt, 705).

Whether or not and, if so, in what ways Lincoln's understanding of God changed during the 1860s, we can, I believe, at least say this: as the war proceeded, it led him increasingly to ask about the providential purposes of a God whose moral order includes such slaughter and ruin. "By his mere great power on the minds of the now contestants, he could have either saved or destroyed the Union without a human contest. Yet the contest began. And, having begun, he could give the final victory to either side any day. Yet the contest proceeds." That "God wills this contest, and wills that it shall not end yet" (Mediation on the Divine Will; Lincoln, 655) must be so; that God's order is good is undeniable. Lincoln's abiding belief in God's eternal control of history required some reconciliation with God's "justice and goodness," and his resolution is this: the duration of this repeatedly awesome bloodshed, entirely beyond what either party expected or sought, can only be what God wills in order that both North and South "shall fairly pay for our complicity" (Hodges letter, April 1864; cited in Burt, 444) in the nation's offense and, thereby, wills in order to achieve the war's profound result.

But however unknowable Lincoln found God's governance to be, he did not doubt the Declaration: because nature's God created all equal, slavery was a "great wrong" (Hodges letter, April 1864; cited in Burt, 444). It was, he said plainly in the Second Inaugural, an offense in which both North and South were complicit—and, as all "somehow" knew (Lincoln, 792), caused the war. Hence, whatever merit there may be in calling Lincoln's theology negative, there was a limit to its negativity. God's moral response to slavery was not mysterious. Emancipation was "the way which, if followed, the world will forever applaud, and God must forever bless" (Annual Message, 1862; Lincoln, 688). And if we agree that black citizenship was not only implied by his moral commitments but also implicit "in the penumbra of his intentions" (Burt, 700), Lincoln "somehow" knew that anything less than social and political equality would be a violation of God's moral order. Given that account, we might find this implicit recognition expressed more or less explicitly in 1865 even when he defended the reconstructed Louisiana constitution others wished him to reject for failing to provide black citizenship. "Grant that he [the colored man] desires the elective franchise," Lincoln said, and he may well have meant *rightly* desires. "Concede that the new government of Louisiana is only to what it should be as the egg is to the fowl, we shall sooner have the fowl by hatching the egg than by smashing it" (Lincoln, 800).

THE HOUSE DIVIDED

As is well known, Lincoln began reading the Bible as a youth and could, throughout his life, cite or refer to it with ease. Among his biblical allusions, none other captures so well his ancient faith and its critique of slavery than the "house divided" metaphor he exploited on receiving the Republican nomination for the Senate in 1858. The lion's share of that speech develops the conspiracy he charges against Stephen Douglas, Presidents Pierce and Buchanan, and Chief Justice Taney and then the specter, along the trajectory carved by that conspiracy, of yet another Supreme Court decision declaring slavery constitutionally protected in all of the states. While aspects of the charge were not without some backing, Douglas's responses to it during the 1858 campaign were, in my judgment, effective, and many historians have doubted that anything like the conspiracy Lincoln proposed occurred (see, e.g., Donald, 208). But my interests here are elsewhere, namely, in how the biblical metaphor from which that speech takes its title can be used to express Lincoln's conviction about the universal moral order and its divine ground.

"A house divided against itself cannot stand," Lincoln cited, alluding to Mark 3:25 and Matthew 12:25. "I believe this government cannot endure, permanently half *slave* and half *free*. I do not expect the Union to be *dissolved*—I do not expect the house to *fall*—but I do expect it will cease to be divided. It will become *all* one thing, or *all* the other" (speech of June 16, 1858; Lincoln, 372). My resources are not competent to the proper exegesis of this metaphor as it appears in the biblical passages. On one reading, however, Lincoln might be said here to take license with the New Testament. Its use of the house divided image, this reading contends, does not portray social and political conflicts that threaten human communities or governments but, rather, involves the Gospels' focus on the condition of each human soul. The relevant division is not between nations or within nations but, rather, the war within a person's spirit when it is possessed by demons—and a brief word about what is at stake in this accounting of the Gospels' message will, I think, help to clarify Lincoln's ancient faith.

"Religion," as Alfred North Whitehead famously defined it, "is what the individual does with his own solitariness" (Whitehead 1926, 16). In comparison with all other known creatures, our defining power as humans is to live in some extended measure self-consciously, in the sense that what we become is not simply another natural result of prior forces or instincts but, rather, depends on our own conscious choice. On Whitehead's definition, we are distinctively human because each individual makes with every choice a fundamental and all-embracing decision about what gives ultimate meaning or significance to everything we are or could be. Our many choices about work and play, family and public life, always take their bearings from that inclusive decision in which we name the someone or something from which the very worth of life itself derives and which, therefore, commands all our heart and soul and mind and strength. The choice, we may say, is original to humans as such, and it is this original decision that is distinctively religious and incurably solitary.[4] And in this household of the human soul, the Gospels speak of a division against itself.

The schism occurs, this reading attests, because we humans so readily yield to pervasive temptations pressing decision for some or other false understanding of our ultimate meaning in competition with the true God who alone gives significance to our lives. Profit, privilege, position, or pleasure; family, class, country, institution, or inherited way of life—virtually anything else at all can become a demon whenever we choose it in conflict with the God who alone rightly evokes our worship.[5] The Gospels' metaphor describes a self in fundamental self-contradiction and reminds one of the other saying in Matthew: "No one can serve two masters . . . You cannot serve both God and mammon" (Matthew 6:24). But this latter saying can be misleading: if two masters create a problem, the conflict would seem resolved by dismissing one or the other—God or mammon, God or the demon, and neither Mark nor Matthew speaks of a divided soul or religious self-contradiction that allows any such escape.

On their witness, to the contrary, belief in God cannot be revoked, because only God can give life ultimate worth, and thus humans unavoidably affirm the divine presence in every moment of their lives by deciding to be or do something they claim to be worthwhile; we cannot escape this affirmation, even if the decision also affirms a false understanding of our ultimate meaning. With the latter, the self becomes a living contradiction because one raises up another alongside of God as if it, too, could provide what one simultaneously knows only God can provide. In this sense, admitting a demon is like adultery: the prior marriage defines one's true loyalty, and one is adulterous by acting as if someone else could occupy the place one has simultaneously vowed to one's betrothed—with the religious division being distinct because the vow to our divine source of worth is original to life with understanding. Within the soul, one's true loyalty is given by being a creature of God, and schism is the duplicity that occurs when a pretender is also avowed. This is the radical sense of division against oneself, because the problem is not simply two competing commitments but, rather, a soul at odds with its own integrity, having embraced an enemy to its own essential nature.

Lincoln did not doubt that history has ultimate meaning. Divine control implies ultimate importance. "Again and again, he reverted to the idea that behind all the struggles and losses of the war, a Divine purpose was at work" (Donald, 514)—and thus, as he wrote to Eliza Gurney in September 1864: "we must work earnestly in the best light He gives us, trusting that so working still conduces to the great ends He ordains. Surely He intends some great good to follow this mighty convulsion, which no mortal could make, and no mortal could stay" (Lincoln, 757). Indeed, even if God wills the war to continue "until all the wealth piled by the bond-man's two hundred and fifty years of unrequited toil shall be sunk, and until every drop of blood drawn with the lash, shall be paid with another drawn with the sword, so still it must be said 'the judgments of the Lord, are true and righteous altogether'" (Second Inaugural; Lincoln, 793).

In this context, moreover, he saw the national conflict as division in the radical sense. To first appearance, his "House Divided" speech might seem to pose the problem simply as being half slave and half free, two incompatible commitments, whereby the government could endure and the Union remain intact if she became all the one or all the other. "I do not expect the Union to be *dissolved*," he said, "but I do expect it will cease to be divided. It will become *all* one thing, or *all* the other" (Lincoln, 372). Whatever he intended with those sentences, however, a mere choice between the two can only be the mere appearance of how he understood the division. Lincoln was lucid that slavery betrayed the Republic itself, was an enemy that threatened the very essence of the Union. This is transparent given that, on his conviction, the Declaration authorized the United States Constitution and thus the democratic form of government established thereby. That "all men are created equal" and "endowed by their creator with certain unalienable rights," and therefore governments derive their "just powers from the consent of the governed," cannot be a principle to which this body politic is dedicated if slavery exists in one half of the states or all of the states or any of the states because slavery contradicts the essence of democracy.

To be sure, Lincoln might still be accused of misusing the metaphor because he departed from the innermost question of ultimate meaning each individual must ask and answer in her or his soul and spoke instead about conflict within our common life. But division in the soul has its effects in the world. Defining religion as "what an individual does with his own solitariness," Whitehead also wrote that "religion is world loyalty" (Whitehead 1926, 16, 60), meaning that decision for the ultimate source of worth is a pledge of allegiance to all of the world because the world in its entirety is included in the divine reality. By implication, then, those who raise up something else as if it, too, could be God pledge their ultimate loyalty also to something within the world and, thereby, debase the rest. Whoever chooses against the whole chooses for some part, and worship of something within the world implies division in the world as surely as it contradicts the self: worship of one's own race, to take one example, creates racism. Religious duplicity may have political consequences. Assuming the Gospels' house divided image is given the reading we have been pursuing, one can still say that Lincoln's use follows the metaphor's full meaning.

For some, Lincoln's focus on the Union has occasioned a critique of his concern with slavery; his intentions, the argument goes, were directed elsewhere. Hofstadter may assert or imply this in summarizing, as noted earlier, why Lincoln fought the war, namely, "to defend not only Union but the sacred principles of popular rule and opportunity for the common man," such that his thinking focused on "the free white worker: the Negro was secondary" (Hofstadter, 160, 167). Indeed, Lincoln became "The Great Emancipator," others believe, only because he was, as one author has it, "forced into glory" while in pursuit of these other purposes (see Bennett). "In Lincoln's view," as another historian says (I do not intend to align him with the critique here being reviewed), "the event that precipitated it [secession] was Lincoln's own election, which had been achieved by a constitutional majority according to constitutional procedures," and the South "now decided to leave the Union just because it had lost an election" (McPherson, 28)—and to this, Lincoln replied: "ballots are the rightful and peaceful successors of bullets; and . . . when ballots have fairly and constitutionally decided, there can be no successful appeal back to bullets; . . . There can be no successful appeal except to ballots themselves at succeeding elections" (Message to Congress, July 4, 1861; Lincoln, 608). On some readings, then, Lincoln was fixed on proving the futility of this appeal back to bullets and, thereby, showing that a Republic can ensure its own protection against fracturing dissension, lest popular government be forever buried with the failed American experiment. Slavery itself, therefore, was never the issue for him.

As already noted, Lincoln surely considered the Declaration and thus US democracy a light to all nations. Because of this, some may further indict him for aiding later and often pernicious beliefs in American "exceptionalism," although it should be noted that, for Lincoln, "the last best hope of earth" (Lincoln, 688) was not American power or privilege but, rather, the ideal of popular government. It is also true that he understood the war as a test of whether, as he said at Gettysburg, popular government "can long endure" (Lincoln, 734). Hence, the issue raised by rebellion, he reported in his first presidential message to Congress,

> embraces more than the fate of these United States. It presents to the whole family of man the question, whether a constitutional republic, or democracy—a Government of the people, by the same people—can or cannot maintain its territorial integrity against its own domestic foes. . . . It forces us to ask: "Is there, in all

republics, this inherent and fatal weakness?" "Must a Government, of necessity, be too *strong* for the liberties of its people, or too *weak* to maintain its own existence?" (Lincoln, 598)

Many in the North—notably George McClellan throughout the war, including his two terms as commander of the Army of the Potomac and, further, his 1864 run for president—understood fighting for the Union to mean restoring the Union as it was before secession and, thereby, with slavery constitutionally protected at least within the states where it existed. Lincoln himself, at least explicitly, initially shared this accounting of the war's purpose, as is suggested by his willingness, stated in the First Inaugural, to accept a proposed thirteenth constitutional amendment "to the effect that the federal government shall never interfere with the domestic institutions of the States, including that of persons held to service" (Lincoln, 587).

For all that, however, a separation of Lincoln's antagonism to slavery from his commitment to the Union is, I am persuaded, unconvincing. If Burt is correct about Lincoln's implicit intentions, his own initial construal of the war was subject to an implicit self-indictment because he somehow knew that social and political equality for all was finally demanded by the moral order he affirmed. In any event, Lincoln made clear, well before the war, that slavery could be tolerated where it existed, as the Constitution then required, only if "the public mind" understood it was wrong and "could rest in the belief that it is in the course of ultimate extinction" (speech in Chicago, July 10, 1858; Lincoln, 394; see also speech in Peoria, October 16, 1854; Lincoln, 283f.). That accounting required his insistence on excluding slavery from the territories. He was apparently persuaded early in his political career that slavery required expansion and would eventually cease, its constitutional toleration notwithstanding, if restricted to its then current locations (Donald, 134). Perhaps he never clarified why this result would occur. But his belief is at least consistent with holding that slavery within a democratic political community effects, in a radical sense, a house divided.

Further evidence on this point is Lincoln's recognition, at least as early as his Cooper Union speech in 1860, that advocates of slavery themselves were somehow aware of its contradiction to democracy. That perception of their consciousness is, at least, plausibly implied when he asks the question: "what will satisfy them [the southern people]" (Lincoln, 534)?—and he replies:

> This and this only: cease to call slavery *wrong*, and join them in calling it *right*. . . . We must place ourselves avowedly with them . . . suppressing all declarations that slavery is wrong, whether made in politics, in presses, in pulpits, or in private. . . .

> We must pull down our Free State constitutions. The whole atmosphere must be disinfected from all taint of opposition to slavery, before they will cease to believe that all their troubles proceed from us. (Lincoln, 535)

On their morality, in other words, democracy itself must be sacrificed wherever it so much as allows a challenge to enslavement. In Lincoln's so-called "lost speech" at the May 1856, Bloomington convention organizing the Illinois Republican party, he pledged himself, according to a report in the *Alton Weekly Courier*, "ready to fuse with anyone who would unite with him to oppose the slave power," explaining that "the Union *must be preserved in the purity of its principles as well as the integrity of its territorial parts*" (cited in Donald, 192).

Even more clearly to the point is his statement in 1859: we require

> a national policy in regard to the institution of slavery, that acknowledges and deals with that institution as being wrong. . . . I do not mean to say that this general government is charged with the duty of redressing or preventing all wrongs in the world; but I do think it is charged with the duty of preventing and redressing all wrongs which are wrongs to itself. (speech in Cincinnati, cited in Carwardine, 123)

And most evidential of all, Lincoln could only think slavery a wrong to the republic itself because, as mentioned previously, the primary authority for the Constitution, the Declaration, said so—and thus its authors "meant to set up a standard maxim for free society," so that "*enforcement* of it might follow as fast as circumstances should permit" (Dred Scott speech, June 26, 1857; Lincoln, 361).

During the years of war, then, he became explicitly mindful of the stakes God's moral order and thus his ancient faith presented to him. It was true, as many have said, that abolition required preserving the Union; accepting secession or an independent South could only mean the triumph of slavery as a "positive good" for the foreseeable future. But the greater truth was this: perfecting the Union required abolition, because slavery was an enemy within, violating the integrity of a democratic political community.[6] Once he saw clear to issue the Emancipation Proclamation, Lincoln would permit no turning back: "In giving freedom to the slave, we assure freedom to the free—honorable alike in what we give, and what we preserve" (Annual Message, December 1862; Lincoln, 688). Given the Declaration's authority, the Union could be saved, as he said at Peoria, only if "so saved . . . as to make, and to keep it, forever worthy of the saving" (speech in Peoria, October 16, 1854; Lincoln, 315).

LINCOLN'S LEGACY

On my accounting, Lincoln's extended explications of political division in the radical sense, delivered with singular command of the English language, warrant calling him our presidency's eminent public theologian. His ancient faith—that authorization of "government of the people, by the people, for the people" in 1776 is itself validated by a divine moral order—belongs to the deepest level of his enduring legacy. It is noteworthy, moreover, that Lincoln's relative silence about his religious beliefs prior to 1860 increasingly gave way to their public expression. Anticipated in the Hodges letter, this is most apparent in the Second Inaugural, in which he set the moral order within its divine backing. "The Almighty has his own purposes"—in relation to which, as noted previously, the North, too, is included among those "by whom the offense cometh" (Lincoln, 793). Lincoln surely had in mind not only common agreement in 1787–88 to the Constitution's approval of slavery, however euphemistically expressed, but also the ready consent to that agreement by northerners who had since benefited financially, the decades-long submission to slavery by all who neglected its inconsistency with republican government, and the racism so prevalent throughout the nation—and he did not exclude himself from those who were complicit.

He also included himself, along with virtually all others, in the common failure to see the war's meaning. "Neither party expected for the war, the magnitude, or the duration, which it has already attained. . . . Each looked for an easier triumph, and a result less fundamental and astounding." Even more damning, each side rushed to claim alignment with God's will and thus the absence of complicity in the nation's evil. "Both [parties] read the same Bible, and pray to the same God; and each invokes His aid against the other. . . . The prayers of both could not be answered; that of neither has been answered fully." That distance between God and humans required all to "judge not, that we be not judged" and, as Burt says, to proceed with recognition of one's own fault and with renunciation of moral privilege—and thus "with malice toward none; with charity for all" (Second Inaugural; Lincoln, 792–93).

"It was Lincoln's achievement," Reinhold Niebuhr wrote, "to embrace a spiritual paradox which lies at the center of the spirituality of all Western culture: affirmation of a meaningful history along with religious reservations about the partiality and bias which human actors and agents betray in their definition of that meaning"—and Burt cites this sentence with approval (Niebuhr 1965b, 173; see Burt, 680). Niebuhr's frequent use of paradoxical statement to express features of history and human life is, on my reading, typically incisive—never more so than when he reveals how ideologies become rationalizations for the narrow interests of someone or some group, and the inclination to injustice corrupts conceptions and achievements in politics. Niebuhr was also characteristically instructive in naming Lincoln as the US president most perceptive and articulate in marking the difference between abiding faults of the human condition and the moral law, such that firmness of political purpose should be attended by, as Niebuhr says, a religious reservation.

Still, something about Niebuhr's formulation of Lincoln's achievement cannot be quite right. Were strictly every attempt to express the meaning of politics compromised by partiality and bias, it would not be possible for Lincoln or Niebuhr correctly to assert this fact without partiality and bias, whereby their assertion, too, would be in some unspecifiable way false. The understanding that purportedly relativizes all human understanding cannot itself consistently be relativized. What we can say, however, is something like the following: while any given claim to political truth or goodness may be valid, the person making the claim may be wrong, and, further, the more she or he seeks to articulate other political claims said to be warranted by or inseparable from the initial one, the more probably partiality and bias invade the possible validity of her or his claims; accordingly, no such claim can be valid unless it can be validated by reasons or argument, that is, redeemed in discourse. Moreover, a claim for this complex assertion can itself be redeemed by reasons that argue from the fragmentariness of and pervasive fault within human life. As far as I can see, democracy as politics by way of full and free discourse implies the assertion of our fallibility and failures—and that implication is sufficient to proscribe malice and prescribe charity toward those with whom one disagrees.

For Lincoln that democratic spirit should prevail as the people "finish the work we are in" (Second Inaugural; Lincoln, 793), and the work to which he referred was not merely winning the war but, rather, giving to the nation "a new birth of freedom" (Gettysburg Address; Lincoln, 734). His vigorous commitment to the Thirteenth Amendment to the Constitution (see Miller, 394–95) testifies to this meaning and, further, to his clarity on why abolition was essential in reclaiming the Declaration's authority. Were he to violate that conviction, he reportedly said, "I should be damned in time and eternity" (see Miller, 386). At least by implication, then, speaking of God became publicly important for Lincoln in part because the public mind would be served through awareness that political freedom depends on a divine order. The truth of this conviction is what, on my accounting, is fundamental to Lincoln's legacy.

There is, I think, considerable room to contest some aspects of Lincoln's theology. This is most evident, perhaps, with his apparent belief that God controls history in more or less complete detail, which implies that God willed slavery in the colonies and states, willed its constitutional recognition, and willed its abetment by both North and South until, through the war's magnitude, God determined to remove it. In addition, divine control perhaps also implied, for Lincoln, a completely eternal deity who, while clearly righteous altogether, was not easily said to be forgiving. At least, I am not aware of any mention by Lincoln of God's love. Notwithstanding possible revisions in Lincoln's theism, however, what remains essential is his conviction that his nation's Declaration of Independence and thus its commitment to democratic justice are grounded in a divine purpose by which the ultimate meaning of history is defined.

A belief that theism is the necessary backing for democracy is, to be sure, controversial and, indeed, is rarely articulated today in academic reflection. I will not seek here to assess that conviction, except to offer the following comments: were there no ultimate worth to our lives, then ultimately our lives would have no worth. Every moment would be, as Whitehead said, "a passing whiff of insignificance" (Whitehead 1941, 698)—and decision with understanding, which cannot escape a claim for its own importance, also cannot affirm the final nullity of the difference it makes. This does not deny that what we do is or can be important in the world, makes a difference to ourselves, our family and friends, our wider communities, nonhuman creatures, and the worldly environment generally. But the worldly difference we make in deciding one way rather than another is temporary; it will, at least eventually, be erased by the sands of time. If our worth is confined to the world, that limitation adds to our worldly or temporary significance a solely negative condition, namely, the absence of any permanent value.

Were this supposed absence true, we could believe that sometime in the future, soon or late, whatever value our activities have will be annulled. On my reasoning, that thought would make decision impossible. To assert that other considerations commend some decision because of the temporary difference effected is irrelevant, because any such difference is precisely what would be erased. As far as I can see, the wider context of evaluation is the inclusive one; which alternative is better all things considered is the proper choice. Hence, final nullity would be the inclusive evaluative belief about our present alternatives, so that decision would have no worth at all. We can repeat the point this way: life with understanding decides through or with practical thought, that is, with evaluation of the alternatives. The thought of final nullity adds absolutely nothing to this evaluation; it is strictly meaningless to practical thought, so that decision with understanding could not really think it. Some may counter that thinking the permanence of value also adds nothing to evaluation, but that reply is mistaken. To think the ultimate worth of what one does is simply to think the reason for deciding, however one decides—is to think what makes our lives as such worth living, and thus to think what is implied in all practical thought.

But, then, the permanence of worth requires a permanent reality to which everything we decide makes a difference. The temporary character of any and all significance in the world itself argues for a divine reality to which the enactment of our deeds in all of their detail and whatever difference they make to our worldly context make an everlasting difference.

This argument, I recognize, begs for extended clarification, including explication and defense of the implied divine purpose and thus the moral order to which humans and history are bound. That is the assessment I will not here pursue (see Gamwell 2011)—and, in lieu of it, will only again assert my basic agreement with Lincoln's conviction: popular government depends on nature's God. But I do wish briefly to discuss the widely articulated view that our politics is properly secularistic or independent of a divine purpose because US democracy constitutionally so requires. Absent a nontheistic backing for morals and politics, we are told, our Constitution, especially its First Amendment, could not consistently stipulate religious disestablishment. Given religious freedom, the Constitution legitimizes any religious conviction any citizen finds convincing. Accordingly, the argument goes, the grounds for political decision must be constitutionally separated from any such conviction, and theism must be excluded from the reasons, explicit or implicit, by which understandings of justice, both in general and as specified in governmental decisions, are validated.

I see every reason to agree that a democratic government must proscribe governmental teaching of any religious understanding. Moreover, "religious" here should be taken in an extended sense to include what are often called nonreligious or secularistic views—because the democratic imperative is to prohibit governmental teaching of terms in which all political evaluation should occur. That prohibition, which recommends the extended meaning of "religious freedom," protects the right of each citizen to decide for herself or himself the ultimate terms of political evaluation, and only if all such decisions are legitimate can "we the people" be sovereign. To deny that justice implies theism, therefore, is itself one account of those ultimate terms, and whether it is true can only belong to the full and free discourse. A democracy's constitution, in other words, not only allows but also invites into the public discussion and debate the belief that justice depends on a divine purpose—the belief that all political goodness or rightness, including a proper constitution itself, implies nature's God. As far as I can see, the supposed constitutional separation of democracy from theism results from failure to distinguish what a democratic constitution explicitly provides and what it implies. Indeed, the entire point of its formative provisions, to recall terms I introduced earlier, is that "we the people" should discuss and debate and apply to contemporary political choices the substantive meaning of justice the democratic constitution, if democracy is morally valid, implies.

Moreover, the failure results, again as far as I can see, from the sometimes tacit assumption that religious disagreements cannot be the objects of discourse; that is, no such conviction can be validated by reasons. To the best of my knowledge, Lincoln never abandoned his early suspicion of views based solely on special revelation and his insistence in religious inquiry as everywhere else on reasons and evidence, and that demand is thoroughly sympathetic to this account of democratic discourse. Although he did not, again as far as I know, speak about democracy and religious freedom, I see no reason to suppose any disagreement with Jefferson's eloquence in the Bill for Establishing Religious Freedom in Virginia: "Truth is great and will prevail if left to herself . . . she is the proper and sufficient antagonist to error and has nothing to fear from the conflict unless . . . disarmed of her natural weapons, free argument and debate" (Jefferson 1999, 391). If Lincoln's conviction about the divine backing for our democracy is true, moreover, we should have no hesitation in calling it the embracing mark of his singular legacy.

CHAPTER FOUR

ON RELIGION IN THE PUBLIC SPHERE

A Conversation with Jürgen Habermas

During the past half century, Jürgen Habermas's contribution to Western thought has rightly drawn uncommonly widespread attention. His massive proposal—largely ordered as a reading of modernity's emergence, secular definition, and importance—unites singular learning and distinction in philosophy, social theory, and contemporary political criticism alike, such that current study of the human condition is impoverished when it fails critically to consider his achievement. At its core, that achievement prominently includes his *The Theory of Communicative Action* (Habermas 1984; 1987), whose title signals his formulation of an intersubjective understanding of rationality. This is a reformed Kantian project. It is Kantian because the understanding is universal and "postmetaphysical" (see Habermas 1992); Habermas finds in or through Kant, as do many others, a conclusive discrediting of the Western metaphysical tradition whose aim is knowledge of reality as such. The Kantian character is reformed because, on Habermas's reading, Kant mistakenly sought to explicate rationality in terms of a solitary subject. An adequate conception of rationality is, with Kant, properly postmetaphysical, but it can be achieved, contrary to Kant, only through analysis of the communicative practice in which a subject acts for purposes through seeking with another or others mutual acceptance of relevant validity claims.

On this analysis, communicative action is first-order human practice or life practice and includes, explicitly or implicitly, several claims to validity, of which the most pertinent to the present discussion are claims for some understanding of what is the case and some understanding of what ought to be the case—or, as Habermas also says, truth claims and rightness claims.[1]

Because they are *claims* to validity, they can be contested, and because they are claims to *validity*, the subject thereby pledges, at least implicitly, that if the claim is contested, reasons can be given by which it can be redeemed. When contestation occurs, relevant subjects may then suspend the purposes of life practice and engage in the second-order communicative practice of argumentation or discourse, the purpose of which is solely to problematize contested claims and critically to validate or invalidate them.[2]

This reformed Kantian proposal can also be expressed as a thesis about modernity, namely, that emergence of the modern lifeworld has released the exercise of reason from restraints on its critical form or on discourse—an emancipation inseparable from modernity's postmetaphysical commitment. In contrast, medieval civilization was distinguished by "religious and metaphysical worldviews," on which a "fundamental order," wherein "ontic, [and] normative . . . aspects of validity" are fused, lies "behind the visible world of this life" (Habermas 1987, 189). This inseparability of metaphysical fact and value left understandings of the fundamental order "immunized" against criticism (Habermas 1987, 189), and thus the critical exercise of reason could not be complete.

Habermas, I expect, credits Kant with providing a rigorous explication of why values cannot be derived from facts, that is, a convincing argument for why, as subsequent thinkers have formulated the point, naturalism in ethical theory is a fallacy. Accordingly, the modern lifeworld is postmetaphysical because "decentered" (Habermas 1984, 70), which means in the present context that statements about what is the case are separated from statements about norms for human interaction—or, as Habermas says, the objective world, about which truth claims are made or implied, is separated from the social world, about which rightness claims are made or implied (see Habermas 1984, 66–74). The independence of each kind of claim from the other emancipates both from limits on criticism and thus allows all claims of each kind to be validated or invalidated, when contested, by argumentative assessment or discourse. This is secularity in its best sense.

Thereby, to repeat the point, Habermas insofar agrees with Kant's separation of theoretical and practical reason: only their independence, each from the other, opens science, on the one hand, and morality and law, on the other, to complete rationalization. But if the modern lifeworld has occasioned this advance, the possibility of rationalizing the moral order has not been exploited. Dominated by noncommunicative understandings of reason, modern thought in the main has understood understanding to be a subject's relation to objects, in distinction from relation to another or other subjects, and has proceeded as if only empirical or scientific validity claims can be rationally contested and redeemed. Practical reason is then exhausted by the instrumental or strategic calculation of means to nonrational ends. This view is secularism in its reductive sense. Habermas calls it the "one-sided" or "selective" rationalization of modern society (Habermas 1984, 74, 240) and takes Max Weber's achievement to be a lucid description of modern rationalization in this one-sided sense, even while Habermas criticizes Weber's own failure to appreciate the alternative modernity has made possible (see Habermas 1984, 143–273).

In practical reason, that possibility includes a nonteleological moral theory. It must be nonteleological because Habermas again agrees with Kant in this: the notion of a telos or final cause or inclusive purpose that defines the most general moral principle for human purposes as such is inseparable from metaphysics in the sense Kant discredited. A good directing all human purposes in their entirety could only be defined by the character of reality as such, that is, given as a purpose in the ultimate nature of things—and precisely because medieval worldviews were typically metaphysical in this sense, medieval ethics typically took the form of a comprehensive teleology. The failure of metaphysical teleology does not, however, preclude moral universality. Kant's affirmation of a moral law separated from reality as such is, for Habermas, redeemed in the sense that moral claims are universal validity claims—which means, if I understand rightly, that discourse about such claims is bound by a universal or "universalization" principle (see, e.g., Habermas 1990, 57–65). As nonteleological, this principle assumes diverse persons with values or ends defining purposes, and discourse in accord with it then warrants norms that relate those individual pursuits to each other morally. "Practical discourses depend on content brought to them from outside," and the "universalization principle acts like a knife that makes razor-sharp cuts between evaluative statements and strictly normative ones, between the good and the just" (Habermas 1990, 103, 104)—or, as Habermas can also say, between ethical values and moral norms (see Habermas 1993, chapter 1; 1996, 95–99). He typically calls his moral theory "deontological," a term equivalent in his usage to "nonteleological" in mine.

THE INSTITUTIONAL PROVISO

The rationalization potential of a modern lifeworld provides the setting for democratic politics. "The public sphere as a space of reasoned communicative exchanges is," Habermas writes, "the issue that has concerned me all my life" (Habermas 2008, 12).* Properly speaking, democracy is or includes, if I understand rightly, discourse as exemplified in politics (see

---

*Subsequent citations from Habermas 2008 will be by page number or numbers alone. References to others of Habermas's works will be henceforth by year of publication and page number or numbers.

1996, 107f.), and thus "democratizing political power" means "secularizing government" (120)—although saying this is no endorsement of secularism in the reductive sense. More recently, then, Habermas has turned his attention to how religious traditions and communities contribute within a modern society and, specifically, how religious convictions or religious adherents properly relate, given the constitutional stipulation of religious freedom, to the democratic process. In this context, he is especially concerned to take up the achievement of John Rawls—the only other Western moral and political theorist of the past half-century who competes with Habermas for being the most widely read and debated. In addition to Rawls's prominence as a political philosopher, Habermas comments, "Rawls . . . deserves the immense credit of having addressed the political role of religion at an early date" (147). "Religion in the Public Sphere: Cognitive Presuppositions of the 'Public Use of Reason' by Religious and Secular Citizens," originally an independent essay that is now revised and included in *Between Naturalism and Religion* (2008), articulates an account of democracy and religion that may be considered a friendly alternative to Rawls, provoked in response to what, for Habermas, is a "compelling" objection (128) to Rawls's proposal.

The two thinkers disagree about democratic theory. Its character depends, for Habermas, on a reformed Kantian and thus postmetaphysical analysis of modernity and, specifically, on practical reason explicated in terms of the discourse principle—where the latter constitutes the moral point of view, on the one hand, and the democratic process of legitimation, on the other.[3] "I understand political liberalism (which I defend in the specific form of Kantian republicanism) as a nonreligious, postmetaphysical justification of the normative foundations of constitutional democracy" (102). On Rawls's account, Habermas's understanding is one among many comprehensive doctrines, from which Rawls's own political liberalism intends to be independent. For Rawls, the stipulation of religious freedom can only mean the separation of public reason from a plurality of "religious, philosophical, and moral doctrines" (Rawls 2005, 4)—so that political liberalism articulates solely the domain of the political in a modern democratic society. "I [Rawls] think of political liberalism as a doctrine that falls under the category of the political. It works entirely within that domain and does not rely on anything outside it" (Rawls 2005, 374). For this reason, principles of justice for what Rawls calls "the basic structure" (Rawls 2005, 257f.) depend solely on the public political culture of that society. In contrast, "Habermas's position . . . is a comprehensive doctrine that covers many things far beyond political philosophy" (Rawls 2005, 376).

But engaging this difference is not the purpose of Habermas's essay. To the contrary, he intends to posit their common affirmation of constitutional liberalism in order subsequently to consider the proper place of religious adherence among the citizens. As for Rawls, so for Habermas, "the form of state power that remains neutral toward different worldviews ultimately derives its legitimation from the profane sources of seventeenth- and eighteenth-century philosophy" (102), in the sense that modern democracy means reliance "exclusively on public arguments that claim to be *equally accessible* to *all* persons"—and thus constitutional liberalism means "a secular state that no longer depends on religious legitimation" (120). So understood, this secular state "makes the separation between church and state possible at the institutional level" (120). Accordingly, "citizens should respect one another as free and equal members of their political community" and "should seek a rationally motivated agreement when it comes to contentious political issues" (121)—and "only those political decisions can count as legitimate that can be impartially justified in the light of generally accessible reasons" and thus "justified equally toward religious and nonreligious citizens and citizens of different confessions" (122). It is, then, Rawls's account of public reason that provides the focus for Habermas's discussion of religious citizens, and the question Habermas will address is this: "How does the constitutional separation of church and state influence the role that religious traditions, communities, and organizations are permitted to play in civil society and the political public sphere, that is, in the political opinion- and will-formation of the citizens?" (119).

Rawls answers this question by formulating his famous proviso: "reasonable comprehensive doctrines, religious or nonreligious, may be introduced in public political discussion at any time, provided that in due course proper political reasons—and not reasons given solely by comprehensive doctrines—are presented that are sufficient to support whatever the comprehensive doctrines introduced are said to support" (Rawls 2005, 462; cited in Habermas 2008, 122–23). On Habermas's reading, however, this proviso so interprets religious freedom that religious adherents and communities must accept "not only the neutrality of public institutions, and hence the separation of church and state, but also the restrictive definition of the public use of reason" (123). Although hospitable to political advocacy that relies on religious reasons, Rawls's "overly narrow, secularist definition" (123) is restrictive because it expects "*all* citizens" also "to justify their political positions independently of their religious convictions or worldviews" (128)—and with this prescription, the state "encumber[s] its citizens . . . with duties that are incompatible with pursuing a devout life—it cannot expect something impossible of them" (126).

At least in part because "any 'ought' implies a 'can'" (127), Habermas credits what he sees as a "compelling" (128) objection to Rawls advanced by several critics: "A devout person conducts her daily existence *on the basis of* her faith," and the "totalizing trait of a form of faith that permeates the very pores of daily life resists . . . any nimble switchover of religiously rooted political convictions onto a *different* cognitive basis" (127). On the meaning relevant here, a religion includes some or other beliefs about ultimate reality and, in relation to it, a comprehensive way of life—and thus a self-understanding properly expressed in all activities of the religion's adherents. I will henceforth call this "religion" in the conventional sense. To demand that conventionally religious citizens also provide, even in due course, alternative or secular reasons for political advocacy is, Habermas says, to deny the comprehensive character of their self-understanding—because the political positions they take are inseparable from what is believed to be their relation to ultimate reality.

In order to credit the political advocacy of religious citizens without expecting something impossible of them, Habermas offers a differing account of "the role that religious traditions, communities, and organizations are permitted to play in civil society and the political public sphere" (119) of a liberal political community—namely, he replaces Rawls's proviso on political advocacy with an "institutional translation proviso" (130). The state's neutrality is preserved by imposing the "strict demand," namely, that political positions be justified "on a nonreligious footing" (121), only on "politicians operating within state institutions," that is, on "all those who hold a public office or are candidates for such" (128). These "institutional thresholds between the 'wild' political public sphere and the formal proceedings within political bodies also function as a filter that allows only secular contributions from the . . . informal flows of public communication to pass through" (131). Thereby, religious citizens are "allowed to express and justify their convictions in a religious language even when they cannot find secular 'translations' for them" (130). But "the truth contents of religious contributions can enter into the institutionalized practice of deliberation and decision-making only when the necessary translation already occurs in the pre-parliamentarian domain" (131).

This last qualification implies its own demand on religious citizens as they participate in the political public sphere. Each religious community must, from within its own religious viewpoint, relate its beliefs to a plurality of others within the public "universe of discourse" and must acknowledge the "internal logic of secular knowledge" (137)—and each of these "epistemic attitudes" (138) is implied by a third: the demand that religious citizens acknowledge "the priority that secular reasons also enjoy in the political arena" (137). In other words: "Religion must renounce . . . [its] claim to structure life in a comprehensive way that also includes the community" (261). Religious communities can do so successfully "only to the extent that they embed the equalitarian individualism of modern natural law and universalistic morality in a convincing way in the context of their comprehensive doctrines" and thus "do not jeopardize their own exclusive claim to truth" (137). Precisely because "every religion is originally a 'worldview' . . . [that] claims the authority to structure a form of life *in its entirety* . . . the major religions must reappropriate the normative foundations of the liberal state *on their own premises*" (261). In other words, only "the faith and practice of the religious community" can "decide whether a dogmatic processing of the cognitive challenges of modernity has been 'successful' or not." Insofar as it has, acceptance of democracy with religious freedom has become a "learning process" (138).[4] At least in some measure, Habermas holds, "Western culture has witnessed" already a relevant "transformation of religious consciousness since the Reformation and the Enlightenment" (136). Indeed, we can speak of a learning process through which "modern philosophical thought and a 'reformed' religious consciousness evolved simultaneously" in response to "*the same* cognitive challenges . . . nourished by secular sources of knowledge" (2013, 361, 351).

Although this demand on religions is a substantial burden (see 261), religious citizens are not only permitted but also encouraged to express their religious reasons for political claims. Democratic politics can benefit from religious traditions. "Secular citizens . . . can . . . learn something from religious contributions under certain circumstances, for example, when they recognize buried intuitions of their own in the normative truth contents of a religious utterance" (131). As one specific illustration, "human rights owe their equalitarian universalism (in addition to Stoic sources) to the secular translation of Jewish and Christian ideas of the equal worth of every person in the eyes of God" (2013, 361). Again, "the First Commandment," understood to empower the human transcendence of everything in the world, may also empower modern thought to sustain "the difference between facticity and validity" (Habermas et al., 82–83) and thus the universality in truth claims and moral claims. Indeed, postmetaphysical thinking properly recognizes that religious traditions "involve semantic potentials capable of exercising an inspirational force on society *as a whole* as soon as they divulge their profane truth contents" (142).

Accordingly, Habermas argues, the learning process without which political participation by religious citizens will not be democratic is complemented by an epistemic burden on secular citizens. They are expected to achieve a "self-critical assessment of the limits of secular reason" (139–40), that is, "to determine the relation between faith and knowledge in a *self-critical* manner" (264)—and thereby to effect a "self-reflexive overcoming of a rigid and exclusive secularist self-understanding of modernity" (138). If I understand rightly, Habermas here counsels overcoming the kind of reductive understanding of modern rationalization he has long criticized, the reduction on which validity and invalidity are exhausted by statements about empirical facts, and a scientific view of the world provides a sufficient self-understanding for modern life. Practical reason is then solely instrumental, and the consequences include the dominance of economic institutions and interactions and of bureaucratic politics throughout society. In keeping with such secularism, religions are seen as "archaic relics of premodern societies" without any "intrinsic justification" (138) and are destined to wither away.

In the sense that reductive secularism is denied, the learning process for secular citizens results in their "postsecular" consciousness, that is, "a shift in consciousness in largely secularized or 'unchurched' societies that . . . have come to terms with the continued existence of religious communities and with the influence of religious voices" (2013, 348). Secular reason can affirm the presence and importance of religion "while at the same time remaining agnostic" (143). Postmetaphysical thought "eschews the rationalist presumption that it can itself decide which aspects of religious doctrines are rational and which irrational" (143), at least in part because religions provoke modernity at its best to address in its own way vital human questions it has otherwise ignored. Thereby, modernity properly credits the place of religious doctrines in "the genealogy of reason" (140).[5] In any event, we may speak of "complementary learning processes" (144). Secular citizens in a postsecular society come to respect the "religious contributions" and, further, take responsibility to aid in translating their "potentially morally convincing intuitions and reasons into a generally acceptable language" (139).

On my reading, clarity on how, for Habermas, religion has continuing significance for modern democracy depends on his distinction between morality and ethics, such that postmetaphysical discourse about justice is nonteleological. No moral principle or principle of justice, in other words, can provide an existential self-understanding or conception of the good (see 1993, chapter 1), where this means an inclusive good or telos by which all of one's purposes in their entirety ought to be directed. "I start from the assumption that universalistic issues of justice can be distinguished from particularistic questions of the good. Whereas the former are geared to answers that can command universal agreement, the latter can be answered only relative to the values of the reference persons or reference groups in question" (2013, 379). In terms of this distinction, religions raise claims to truth for principles derived from "theologically or cosmologically justified paths to salvation" (Habermas et al., 79), that is, affirm comprehensive ways of life inseparable from conceptions of ultimate reality, and thus are properly treated by the constitutional state as a unique kind of ethical conviction.

For Habermas, then, the import of religion, just because it often has made or makes claims to comprehensive normative direction, may include affirmations that, when so translated as to be independent of their relation to ultimate reality, have moral significance—indeed, represent "buried intuitions" of secular thinking at its best. Moreover, ethical orientations generally are essential to democratic politics. The "equalitarian individualism of modern natural law and universalistic morality" (137) must assume individuals who have values and purposes, so that nonteleological moral and political principles may prescribe the right or just relations among these diverse aims—and thus democratic motivation depends on embedding such principles within the several ethical commitments democracy legitimizes.

> Moral insights effectively bind the will only when they are embedded in an ethical self-understanding that joins concern about one's own well-being with the interest in justice. Deontological theories after Kant may be very good at explaining how to ground and apply moral norms; but they are still unable to answer the question of why we should be moral *at all*. Political theories are likewise unable to answer the question of why citizens of a democratic polity when they disagree about the principles of their living together should orient themselves toward the common good—and not rather satisfy themselves with a strategically negotiated modus vivendi. Theories of justice that have been uncoupled from ethics can only *hope* that processes of socialization and political forms of life meet them halfway. (2003, 4)

In relation to this deficiency characterizing principles of justice, the "world-disclosive function" (2013, 374) of religions can be important (see 2013, 355–56).

In fact, the deficiency is twofold. On the one hand, democratic justice requires acceptance by its citizens of political outcomes with which they disagree—and in that sense a need for individuals to affirm more than a strategically negotiated modus vivendi. In this sense, religions, as ethical convictions generally, may contribute. Communities of faith may aid the mobilization of "modern reason against the defeatism lurking within it" because, absent the complicity of ethical and religious resources, "a modernization threatening to spin out of control tends to counteract rather than to complement" a morality "that despairs of the motivating power of its good reasons" (Habermas et al., 18). Habermas calls this the "motivational deficiency" (2013, 355, emphasis removed).

On the other hand, orientation to the common good includes commitment to collective action for justice and in that sense to political participation. Just because "postmetaphysical thinking is ethically modest in the sense that it is resistant to any generally binding concept of the good and exemplary life" (110), it cannot prescribe a commitment to what Habermas calls "civic solidarity" (275). Even if embedded in ethical convictions, "an ethics of justice . . . cannot make solidarity per se into a duty" (2013, 356). In relation to this "political deficiency" (2013, 356, emphasis removed), religions can be especially important. If their voices "eschew dogmatism and respect freedom of conscience," religions may preserve a "sensitivity to squandered lives, social pathologies, failed existences, and deformed and distorted social relations" that secular thought may lose (110). "The practice of religious communities," based on a "shared faith in the promise of 'redemptive' or 'liberating' justice," may elicit "action *in social solidarity*, which is required in times of crisis for the formation of social movements" (2013, 356, 355).

Perhaps Habermas has this special religious contribution in mind when he affirms a "semantic potential capable of exercising an inspirational force on society *as a whole* as soon as they [religions] divulge their profane truth contents" (142). In any event, the hope "that processes of socialization and political forms of life meet . . . [theories of justice] halfway" (2003, 4) may be taken as the hope for overcoming both deficiencies—and doing so entails, at least in part, the dependence of modern democracy on the learning processes Habermas has described. Those complementary developments among religious and secular citizens are essential to the democratic prospect and are, if I understand rightly, what the subtitle of Habermas's essay cited earlier—"Religion in the Public Sphere: Cognitive Presuppositions of the 'Public Use of Reason' by Religious and Secular Citizens"—anticipates.

HABERMAS'S PROPOSAL: A CRITIQUE

Beyond what is commonly the case with summary expositions, the foregoing abstracts from the considerable subtleties in Habermas's account, some of which I may have missed. Still, a more extended discussion would not, as far as I can see, change the meaning of "religion" implied in this review: a religion includes not only a belief or set of beliefs about ultimate reality and, in relation to it, a comprehensive way of life but also an appeal to authority as essential to knowing the truth of those beliefs. Thus, claims for religious beliefs are not open to discourse. If taken out of context, some of Habermas's formulations of constitutional liberalism may seem to be neutral to secular and religious grounds for politics—because the sole condition for democratic discourse is argument that claims "to be *equally accessible to all* persons" (120), that is, "the unrestricted quest for justification *that is equally open to all*" (2013, 352). But religious claims are thereby excluded because they are inseparable from an authoritarian appeal. "Religious claims to validity are tied to the thick experience of membership in a religious community and remain particularistic even in the case of proselytizing creeds that aspire to worldwide inclusion" (2013, 374). "I have no idea," Habermas concludes, "how one could convince the citizens of a secular state," marked as it is by multiple worldviews, of "the modern conception of toleration . . . without separating rational morality strictly from ethical and religious convictions" (Habermas et al., 79).

There is, in other words, a "kernel of an infallible truth left [in religion] which is immune against any objection whatsoever," so that "no theology can embrace the unconditional openness to critical self-revision" (2013, 383), and "the whole thrust of postmetaphysical thinking was to deconstruct the divine standpoint which has, by definition, the last word. Its place is taken by the impartiality of the practice of argumentation among participants" (2013, 365). Postmetaphysical thinking, therefore, "insists on the difference between the certainties of faith and publicly criticizable validity claims" (143). Only nonreligious or secular thinking in its best sense can rely "exclusively on public arguments" (120), and the important contributions of religiously based advocacy to the political process must be translated "into a generally accessible language" (143) before their "truth contents . . . can enter into the institutionalized practice of deliberation and decision-making" (131).

To all appearances, then, Habermas's current understanding of religion continues in all essentials what he earlier called the "religious and metaphysical" kind of worldview characteristic of medieval civilization, on which some account of a "world behind the world" or conception of ultimate reality provides a "fundamental order" that is "immunized" against criticism (1987, 189). Similarly, then, there is no change from his virtually constitutive belief in a Kantian discrediting of metaphysics as the rational attempt "to grasp reality as a whole" (278) or reality as such. "Today there is no alternative to the postmetaphysical mode of doing philosophy" (2013, 362).[6] Hence, postmetaphysical thought is nonreligious largely because religious thought is, by implication, typically metaphysical. A religious believer, at least absent the learning process for which Habermas calls, typically "travels with heavy metaphysical baggage" (263)—while, to the contrary, "postmetaphysical thinking refrains from making ontological pronouncements on the constitution of being as such" (140). Accordingly, Habermas asserts the "strict demarcation between faith and knowledge" (140; see also 2003, 101–15); that is, "the perspectives which are centered *either* in God *or* human beings cannot be converted *into one another*" (242), and "providing an apology for faith . . . is not a task for philosophy proper" (143). At least "in the European part of the West, the aggressive conflict between anthropocentric and theocentric understandings of self and world is yesterday's battle" (211), and "philosophy *circumscribes* the opaque core of religious experience when it reflects on the specific character of religious language" (143).

Given that religions are so understood, one might ask how postmetaphysical thinking can truly refuse "the rationalist presumption that . . . [such thinking] can itself decide which aspects of religious doctrines are rational and which irrational" (143) and, in that sense, remain agnostic about the certainties of faith. The "metaphysical baggage" religions carry, at least prior to the learning process for which Habermas calls, implies "metaphysical conceptions of the good" and, thereby, some all-inclusive or comprehensive teleology, such that "the good enjoys epistemic primacy over the right" (263). In what way, then, can modern reason credit even the possible rationality of metaphysical teleology without ceasing to be postmetaphysical? Unless I have misunderstood, there is at least a sense in which postmetaphysical rationality must take the certainties of faith to be irrational because, as Habermas says, the "core [of religious experience] remains . . . profoundly alien to discursive thought" (143). To all appearances, the assertion of a "fundamental order" in which ultimate fact and value are inseparable falls outside the emancipation of reason as effected by modernity's decentered lifeworld. As Habermas also says, secular reason "can accept as reasonable only what it can translate into its own, in principle universally accessible discourses" (Habermas et al., 16).

But if the possible rationality of "metaphysical baggage" remains to be clarified, the Kantian background Habermas critically appropriates offers another sense in which postmetaphysical thinking might be agnostic about nontranslatable religious beliefs. "The agnostic," he says, "only asserts that these semantic contents are *inaccessible* and refrains from making judgments concerning the truth claim that believers associate with them" (2013, 367). "Secular citizens, in their role as citizens, may neither deny that religious worldviews are in principle capable of truth nor question the right of their devout fellow-citizens to couch their contributions to public discussions in religious language" (113). On my understanding, Kant never denied that metaphysical beliefs in the sense he supposedly discredited might be true; he argued only that reason or understanding could neither establish nor refute them—and in that sense, they could not be known. Perhaps for Habermas, in a similar way, postmetaphysical thinking can only insist on the inaccessibility to discourse and thus to public reason of religion's metaphysical implications. Whether or not this accounting captures his point, however, it remains that no conception of a good enjoying epistemic primacy over the right can properly be implied by democratic decisions. Modern democratic decisions must treat the comprehensive norms of religious beliefs similar to ethical orientations, such that morality and justice are independent of them, and only secular reasons count within the formal political process or beyond the institutional threshold.

For this reason, there is cause to underscore an asymmetry between the "new epistemic attitudes" Habermas requires of religious and secular citizens respectively. He himself admits "that the burdens of tolerance are not equal for believers and nonbelievers" (262; see also 112)—even if he can also call the demands on secular thinkers "no less cognitively exacting" (139). In any case, secular citizens, although "expected to adopt a self-reflexive critical stance toward the limits of enlightenment" (112) and thus to abandon secularism in the reductive sense, are nonetheless privileged by constitutional liberalism. They alone advance arguments that pass beyond the institutional threshold and thereby belong within "the institutionalized practice of deliberation and decision-making" (131). Given that government is, in Habermas's sense, secularized, the reasons for political action-as-one are "independent of religious or metaphysical traditions" (104), and the contributions of distinctively religious advocacy to public discussion must be translated before passing through the institutional filter.[7]

As far as I can see, then, this postmetaphysical account of democracy with religious freedom is problematic—because the translation for which Habermas calls compels religions to renounce what he himself takes to be distinctively religious. Such beliefs, at least prior to the learning process he hopes their adherents will experience, include or imply "metaphysical conceptions of the good" (263); expecting religious citizens to acknowledge "the priority that secular reasons . . . enjoy in the political arena" (137) is calling them to deny that all human life is properly directed to a good defined by ultimate reality. Having metaphysical implications, a religious belief asserts that democracy itself can be authorized only by the good ultimate reality defines; if modern democracy means the secular constitution of the political process described by postmetaphysical thought, candor will conclude that beliefs implying a metaphysical good are, in truth, not legitimized therein.

With Habermas, to approach restating the point, let us endorse in "the 'wild' political public sphere" (131) advocacy based without qualification on religious and, by implication, metaphysical reasons, that is, without a proviso calling a religious citizen to offer in due course sufficient appeal to "proper political reasons" or reasons independent of her or his comprehensive doctrine. If that proviso is what Rawls prescribes, he expects "something impossible" (126). For the same reason, however, Habermas's own "institutional translation proviso" denies religious citizens participation beyond the threshold, that is, in "the formal proceedings within political bodies" (131), because therein these citizens would have "duties that are incompatible with pursuing a devout life" (126). Whether or not religious citizens do in fact participate in formal political institutions, then, it seems that no religious citizen could consistently accept sufficient reasons for political decisions independent of what, for her or him, is the ultimate good.

Accordingly, any religious citizen who could experience the learning process required by Habermas's institutional translation proviso could simultaneously accept a proviso on all advocacy. Given that experience, this citizen would acknowledge that her or his religious claim is, for political purposes, ethical rather than—or ethical as well as—moral in character, and thus the "universalistic morality" properly controlling political decisions might be embedded by other citizens within some or other different conception of the good. One could further acknowledge, therefore, that one's advocacy, insofar as it depends on one's distinctive religious orientation, requires translation "in due course," as Rawls has it, into a moral claim dependent on secular reasons—even if one requires aid in making the translation. But so formulating the point is designed only to underscore the more important question, namely, whether the learning process is itself consistent with any religious belief. The former requires a disavowal of any metaphysical implication, so that religious belief will then be consistent with the epistemic primacy of the right over the good and thus the priority of secular reasons.

Perhaps Habermas considers the learning process possible because, for him, claims for the truth of religious self-understandings are inseparable from an appeal to authority and thus not open to discourse. This fact itself, he may reason, is open to recognition by religious citizens, who may then acknowledge their own modernity and thus agree that a modern political community, with its plurality of religious and nonreligious worldviews, can only rely on "public arguments that claim to be *equally accessible* to *all* persons" (120)—that is, on secular arguments making no appeal to authority. This accounting may be implied when he calls "the religious consciousness that 'reformed' itself . . . and the postmetaphysical thinking that developed a 'critique of reason'" finally "*complementary* answers to the *same* cognitive challenges of the Enlightenment" (2013, 351).

Again, I am not clear whether this explication captures Habermas's mind, but if so, the reasoning simply assumes what he needs to show, namely, that religious adherents can affirm, in his sense, the secular character of democracy and thus can alter their religious adherence accordingly. In the end, that assumption is simply incredible because inconsistent with the recognition that a religious faith is "totalizing"—the "compelling" objection that led Habermas to seek a revision of Rawls. What he requires of religious adherents, in other words, are two inconsistent affirmations. On the one hand, "the faith and practice of the religious community" (138) derives all moral and political norms from ultimate reality, and on the other, each religious community or adherent must renounce the "claim to structure life in a comprehensive way that also includes the [political] community" (261).

One cannot consistently affirm the epistemic primacy of good over right and simultaneously accept the democratic priority of the right over the good.

The point is underscored when the change in religious consciousness on which democracy is said to depend requires, among other things, that each religion "embed the equalitarian individualism of modern natural law" in a way that does not "jeopardize" the religion's "exclusive claim to truth" (137). The claim to truth for a belief purporting to express a good defined by ultimate reality is indeed exclusive; that is, the belief entails that any contrary belief is insofar false. Hence, a given religion could successfully "embed the equalitarian individualism of modern natural law" (137) only by asserting its conviction about the good as necessary to the validation of modern natural law (as all political claims)—and thereby denying that principles of justice could be independent of any given comprehensive orientation. As far as I can see, that conclusion is inescapable given the meaning of "comprehensive" as characterizing religious belief. Accordingly, the change in religious consciousness on which, for Habermas, democracy depends could occur only if each religion renounced, at least with respect to principles of justice, its own religious claim. In other words, those committed by implication to metaphysical conceptions of the good cannot learn to be postmetaphysical without ceasing to be religious.

The assertion that religious claims to truth are authoritarian is, therefore, irrelevant. If religious self-understandings are correctly characterized in that way (and I will subsequently question whether they are), the apparent implication is not a possible acceptance of Habermas's secular democracy but, rather, the denial that good political decisions can be determined by public reason. If its supposed truth about ultimate reality and human purpose directed by it cannot be validated by reasoned discourse, a religious belief implies that good politics depends on the authority of that particular religion—and democracy by way of argument equally accessible to all persons is itself a denial of all such beliefs. Nor will it help to say, as Habermas does: "today there is no alternative to the postmetaphysical mode of doing philosophy" (2013, 362). Even if that is so, the postmetaphysical understanding of constitutional liberalism is inconsistent with a constitutional provision of religious freedom—because the former explicitly denies and the latter legitimizes freedom to affirm a comprehensive orientation.

HABERMAS AND RAWLS: THE BASIC PROBLEM

If the critique of Habermas I have presented is sound, his friendly alternative to Rawls fails to address the more basic problem in Rawls's political liberalism—and we may approach this point by noting, as implied in passing previously, why some might doubt whether Rawls's proviso is, in truth, finally different than the substitute Habermas offers. By reading the former as a demand on each citizen to provide "in due course" noncomprehensive reasons for whatever she or he advocates, this defense goes, Habermas fails to credit Rawls's refusal to specify any rules for "in due course." To the contrary, Rawls comments that "details about how to satisfy this proviso must be worked out in practice and cannot feasibly be governed by a clear family of rules given in advance" (Rawls 2005, 462)—and this may seem to leave open whether religious citizens themselves are bound in the end also to have nonreligious reasons for their political claims.[8]

But even if Rawls's account does not require Habermas's reading of it, the former nonetheless intends public reason or public political discussion, at least insofar as it determines the basic structure of society, to be independent of any given comprehensive doctrine—religious, philosophical, or moral. "To engage in public reason" is to argue from or for one of several "political conceptions . . . when debating fundamental political questions," where each such conception "can be worked out from fundamental ideas seen as implicit in the public political culture of a constitutional regime" or democratic political community (Rawls 2005, 453) and, therefore, remains entirely within the domain of the political. Each political conception is, in other words, properly "freestanding," neither explicitly nor implicitly dependent on any comprehensive doctrine. This remains the case even though, as Rawls further asserts, public justification for a political conception also requires that "all reasonable members of political society" succeed in "embedding it in their several reasonable comprehensive views" and, therefore, join in a "reasonable overlapping consensus" on the conception (Rawls 2005, 387).[9]

Rawls also speaks of political liberalism in his sense as "political and not metaphysical" (Rawls 2005, 10), and it is worth noting that he uses "metaphysical" in a different sense than does Habermas. For the latter, the term designates the object of traditional Western inquiry into, as Aristotle says, "being qua being" and thus into reality as such—so that "postmetaphysical" means thought that, with Kant, takes metaphysical knowledge in that traditional sense to be impossible or, as Habermas says, considers metaphysical understandings immune to criticism. For Rawls, however, "political and not metaphysical" means independent of any overall or inclusive theory of human life and thus a theory of all human practice. "A political conception of justice is not dependent on any particular comprehensive doctrine" (Rawls 2005, 387). In that sense, Rawls intends freestanding principles to be independent not only of traditional metaphysics but also of metaphysics in the sense Kant himself affirmed, namely, a comprehensive doctrine of human practice or purposes that denies any possible knowledge of reality as such.

As mentioned in the preface, my discussion here uses "metaphysical," unless otherwise noted, only in Habermas's sense. I will use "comprehensive" instead of "metaphysical" to designate the convictions from which Rawls intends principles of justice to stand free. In any event, the differing meanings of "metaphysical" betray the theoretical difference between these two thinkers that Habermas, as also previously mentioned, is not concerned to address in his essay on religion in the public sphere. In contrast, Rawls does note the issue. For him, to repeat this essay's earlier comment, Habermas is not politically liberal because his democratic theory, which applies to politics a discourse principle taken to be universal, depends on a comprehensive doctrine. That theory is a "metaphysical" view in Rawls's sense of the term and thus cannot legitimize a plurality of such doctrines. As far as I am aware, this criticism has not received an explicit response from Habermas. Although I here speculate, he may consider the indictment ill-conceived because, as discussed previously, he endorses a postmetaphysical distinction between morality and ethics—whereby the universal discourse principle yields nonteleological principles of justice that are independent of or impartial to all purposes inclusively directed and thus all conceptions of the good, which are specific to individuals and groups. If something like that does explicate the difference between them, Rawls may hold that universal principles said to be nonteleological always imply, against themselves, some conception of the good—so that principles of justice must be freestanding.

I am inclined to credit the stated implication of Habermas's nonteleology,[10] whether or not it expresses Rawls's intent. But it does not follow that freestanding principles of justice are consistent with a plurality of religious, philosophical, and moral doctrines. As I will discuss further in a moment, the problem for Rawls is analogous to the inconsistency Habermas introduces by separating moral and political principles from ethics and religion. An overlapping consensus among comprehensive doctrines on some freestanding principles (or, for that matter, on simply the freestanding character of justice) contradicts the meaning of every truly comprehensive doctrine or conception of the good—because "comprehensive" here means that, for adherents of a given doctrine, no valid moral or political prescription can be independent of the universal conditions they affirm. A refusal of freestanding principles is what the very logic of "comprehensive" here requires. It will not help to insist on each of many comprehensive doctrines embedding within its own view the freestanding principles or character of justice. A comprehensive belief about human life cannot consistently include the possible separation of justice from any given belief of that kind, such that justice could stand free from or would not depend on what is taken to be the truth about human life as such. I also recognize that Rawls's overlapping consensus is said to occur among *reasonable* comprehensive doctrines. As far as I can see, however, the term "reasonable" is, in the end, simply another way of asserting a freestanding object of consensus; that is, a doctrine is reasonable when it is able to accept some or other political conception of justice (see Rawls 2005, xvi). The meaning of "reasonable comprehensive doctrine" is, in other words, finally self-contradictory.[11]

The more I have reflected on and appreciated Rawls's achievement, the more I have wondered whether, against his apparent intentions, his political liberalism should be critically appropriated as a counsel for democratic citizens seeking to persuade other citizens that some political principle or policy is just. The context of modern democracy is taken for granted, such that its moral validity is not and, indeed, cannot be itself questioned in Rawls's project. This is the consequence of justifying principles by appeal to the ideas in the public political culture of a modern democratic society. The critical appropriation, then, might be formulated as follows: given the democratic legitimation of diverse comprehensive doctrines, and given how difficult discourse about the basic differences among those doctrines can be, Rawls advises citizens to seek political proposals and reasons for them that might persuade or be agreed to by other citizens in spite of their comprehensive differences. In that sense, political advocacy is counseled to seek freestanding proposals and reasons for them on which a sufficient overlapping consensus may be secured. Accordingly, citizens are advised to pursue, insofar as possible, what Cass Sunstein has called "incompletely theorized agreement" (see Sunstein, chapter 2). This reading, I have little doubt, misrepresents Rawls's intentions, but I also note how it gives a straightforward meaning to the phrase he has used to identify his account, namely, a "practical political" proposal (Rawls 1985, 225; 2005, 156).[12]

On that reading, in any event, Rawls's project is not, in the sense it is typically taken to be, a democratic theory. The counsel to seek freestanding proposals and reasons for them in order to effect political outcomes is not itself a coherent account of political unity with religious freedom—or political unity consistent with an open-ended plurality of comprehensive doctrines. To the contrary, defining democracy as dependent on incompletely theorized agreements is itself a theory of justice as freestanding and thus, as already argued, contradicts all comprehensive doctrines. Presented as such a theory, the counsel, even if often a wise one, would become in its own way a view of justice belonging to the same comprehensive order—because the denial that justice depends on any given comprehensive grounds is, against itself, a comprehensive denial, implying that justice is everywhere and always circumscribed by political context. For this reason, Rawls explicitly eschews either affirming or denying any comprehensive doctrine, practicing instead, as he says, "the precept of avoidance" (Rawls 2005, 29, n. 31). If his project is a democratic theory, however, avoidance is not possible; freestanding principles imply their own comprehensive belief, which simply repeats in another way that such principles contradict all (other) comprehensive doctrines in purporting to stand free.

This, then, is the inconsistency in Rawls's political liberalism that is repeated in Habermas, notwithstanding the friendly alternative he offers. Whether or not Rawls's proviso is so formulated as to burden all political advocacy, the more basic issue is Rawls's insistence on uniting a diversity of legitimate comprehensive doctrines by way of freestanding reasons for political decisions. Similarly, Habermas calls on religions inconsistently to affirm that sufficient reasons for political decisions can be independent of any metaphysical teleology. But a coherent account of democracy with religious freedom cannot be achieved by substituting for a proviso on advocacy an institutional proviso on decisions of the state, whatever other changes may also occur by virtue of philosophical differences between Rawls's political liberalism and Habermas's postmetaphysical liberalism. Behind any such proviso is the assumption that principles of justice can be independent of what at least some religions inescapably affirm. The point can be expressed this way: by implication, Habermas, with Rawls, calls for religious adherents, whatever the differences among their beliefs, to join an overlapping consensus, namely, a consensus on the institutional proviso. To be sure, Habermas does not explicitly speak of an overlapping consensus. Perhaps this is because, on his intention, these adherents have experienced or will experience a learning process through which they "renounce . . . [the] claim to structure life in a comprehensive way that also includes the community" (261) and thus understand their religion, in relation to political decisions, as similar to postmetaphysical ethical orientations. But if that learning process implies the denial of metaphysical claims and, therefore, denial of something essential to religious belief, Habermas's proposal asserts, by implication, an overlapping consensus at least among *religious* convictions on the political priority of secular reasons.[13]

In sum, then, Habermas's attempted clarification of modern politics with religious freedom is unsuccessful because it seeks to legitimize a diversity of religious beliefs by so constituting democracy that it denies every religious conception of the good. Thereby, he repeats Rawls's basic problem because Rawls, too, denies all comprehensive doctrines when he constitutes democracy by way of justice as freestanding. A constitutional denial of religious beliefs or, alternatively, comprehensive doctrines does not legitimize them—and thus cannot belong to a theory of democracy with religious freedom.

THE BETTER SOLUTION

In a 1998 interview, Rawls defended his proposal as the only way to make sense of modern democracy: "See, what I should do is turn around and say, what's the better solution, what's your solution to it. And I can't see any other solution" (cited in Stout, 71). Perhaps Habermas could make a similar appeal. To be sure, the critique of both presented here might seem to imply that democracy with religious freedom is impossible. But if that conclusion is difficult to embrace, each of these two thinkers has a right to ask for the better solution.

There is, I believe, another alternative: in contrast to Habermas and Rawls, democracy is not constituted by an overlapping consensus on freestanding principles or by an institutional threshold beyond which only secular reasons count—but, rather, constituted solely as politics by the way of full and free discourse,[14] inclusive of religious convictions. I propose, in other words, that these two philosophers formulate problematic theories of modern democracy because they assume that religious claims to truth cannot be validated or invalidated by argument or public reason. To all appearances, Habermas adopts this assumption more or less explicitly in his insistence on "a strict demarcation between faith and knowledge" (140). Although Rawls, as mentioned, purports to follow "the precept of avoidance" (Rawls 2005, 29, n. 31), making no statements about the truth or falsity of any given comprehensive doctrine, his decision to restrict the reasons for political decision to ideas and values in the political culture all reasonable citizens share implies that such doctrines cannot themselves be objects of public reason.[15] To the contrary, then, I also propose that democracy with religious freedom is a coherent form of political community if comprehensive doctrines are so many differing answers to a rational question.

Toward clarifying this account, I will understand "religious" as used in the political principle of religious freedom to designate in a broad or extended sense, namely, to mean any explicit conviction about the ultimate terms of political evaluation, including in that conviction, at least by implication, how those terms are authorized or grounded.[16] In that sense, "religious" designates, at least roughly, the class of convictions Rawls calls comprehensive doctrines. Indeed, he has, on my accounting, made clear what many others in the discussion of religious freedom have missed: a coherent understanding of this political principle must relate politics to this extended class of convictions. Within that broad class, then, are convictions properly called "religious" in a strict sense. In that sense, let us say, "religious" designates those cultural formations of concepts and symbols, including symbolic practices, in terms of which or through which a community of adherents seeks to mediate a conviction about the character of ultimate reality and, in relation to it, of human purpose as such, toward bringing all of their lives into accord with that conviction. On some accounts, the understanding of reality and human purpose marking any such religion also involves affirmation of a transcendent reality. With this addition, a religion in the strict sense is at least very close to the conventional view Rawls apparently intends in speaking of "religious" along with "philosophical and moral" doctrines—and, further, very close to what Habermas apparently intends when he asks about religion in the public sphere.

Still attending to religion in something like the conventional sense both thinkers apparently intend, let us allow that each religion is distinguished by its affirmation of some event or set of events as a decisive disclosure of ultimate reality and of realistic self-understanding in relation to it. This cultural system, then, is indeed authoritative for *what* self-understanding adherents of that religion take to be true. But whether the claim to truth thereby made for a religious "worldview," its conception of life in relation to the encompassing reality, is authoritarian is another question. That a religion takes some event or events as authoritative for what it *claims to be true* is fully consistent with a recognition of discourse as the only proper basis for determining whether its understanding of reality and human purpose *is true*. Accordingly, it is mere assertion to say that religions in a conventional sense are convictions whose claim to truth cannot be argumentatively assessed. Democracy, I propose, implies to the contrary, because it constitutes the body politic as a full and free discourse about all religious beliefs (in the extended sense) citizens find convincing, insofar as they are pertinent to political issues. Democracy with religious freedom I will say, constitutes politics by the way of reason.

In keeping with Habermas's own account of communicative acts, then, every religious claim to truth or claim for a comprehensive doctrine issues the pledge that it can, if contested, be redeemed by reasons convincing to anyone who understands the argument; that is, neither understanding the claim nor being convinced by the argument depends on having affirmed the religion or comprehensive doctrine in question. To make any such claim is to engage in a practice, whereby the act of participation has the pragmatic feature of pledging its readiness for argumentative validation. If, as the way of reason implies, differing religious beliefs or comprehensive doctrines are answers to a rational question, the constitution is indeed explicitly neutral to all such beliefs or doctrines. To establish a full and free political discourse imposes nothing on citizens they do not impose on themselves in making political claims. This is the case even if a religious belief purports to express truth established only by the authority of some special disclosure. Given that religions in fact answer a rational question, a claim for any religious answer based on such an authority issues, against what the religion says about itself, the pragmatic pledge that discourse can redeem the claim.

To be sure, one may contest whether the question religions answer is a rational one and thus maintain that, as Habermas says, a valid religious conviction is immune to discourse and thus validated only by authority. If that claim itself is valid, constituting politics by the way of reason is then an alien imposition on at least some (and finally all) explicit convictions about the ultimate terms of political evaluation, because the constitution then explicitly requires adherence to a political process or practice whose capacity to determine justice is rightly denied. Accordingly, religions are, in contradiction to religious freedom, delegitimized by a democratic constitution. In that event, as far as I can see, religious freedom is not a coherent political principle. Absent the possibility of union through full and free political discourse, fundamentally differing accounts of justice cannot be civilized. But my intent here is to propose, against the theories of Habermas and Rawls, a consistent account of democracy, and toward that end I will assume that religious freedom protects answers to a rational question. I thereby leave those for whom the assumption is false—so that this alternative, too, is incoherent—the invitation to argue for their view. On my reckoning, they cannot do so. The supposed nonrational or suprarational character of religious validation cannot itself be established by argument, so that its supposed truth must also claim to be suprarational. Accordingly, asserting that view can only beg the question of whether democracy with religious freedom makes sense.[17]

Constituted by the way of reason, we should recognize, democracy itself implies a comprehensive doctrine or religious conviction by which this form of political community purports to be authorized. Full and free political discourse is a practice whose claim to have a sufficient moral reason can be validated only by the ultimate terms of political evaluation, whatever they are. Because this practice itself implies some account of these terms, a principle of religious freedom, prescribing governmental neutrality toward all convictions about justice as such citizens find convincing, may seem impossible. Given the implied claim, in other words, a democratic constitution may appear to take sides among the convictions to which the government is supposedly neutral.

But this reasoning fails to credit the difference between what a constitution stipulates or explicitly provides and what it implies. If that constitution establishes a full and free discourse in which all comprehensive views are welcome, what is thereby provided is explicitly neutral to all such convictions. Notwithstanding its implied claim to be itself morally authorized, then, the constitution provides for a political process in which that very claim may be assessed because the entire point of the discourse is to determine the valid ultimate terms of political evaluation in their pertinence to political decisions.[18] As long as the state is prohibited from stipulating by law or policy how any of its activities ought to be evaluated and, thereby, prohibited from stipulating whether any given view protected by religious freedom is true or false, the government is neutral to the diversity of comprehensive views in precisely the manner required by the way of reason.

It might be thought that Habermas and Rawls each presents his theory as a contribution to democracy's full and free discourse, that is, presents an account of democratic politics open to assessment in accord with a process constituted by the way of reason. As a contribution to the discourse, in distinction from an explication of its constitution, each purports to be one among the theories of justice protected by religious freedom and, moreover, to be the theory participants in the full and free discourse should find convincing. Thereby, this theory does not define how all citizens should understand religious or comprehensive doctrines within the public sphere but, rather, presents an argument for why all other theories of justice, although legitimized by the constitution, are false.

This reading strikes me as implausible. Neither Habermas nor Rawls so explicates a democratic discourse or process of public reason as to place his own account within it. Also, neither in fact argues for his theory against what would then be its competitors—which would include not only each other but also avowedly teleological accounts of justice, metaphysical or otherwise.[19] Placed within the discourse, moreover, each proposal would contradict what it asserts. In the case of Habermas, political decisions could not be "impartially justified in light of generally accessible reasons" and thus "justified equally toward religious and nonreligious citizens and citizens of different confessions" (122). To the contrary, such decisions would be justified in terms of a particular nonreligious account (namely, Habermas's postmetaphysical theory). In the case of Rawls, the principles of justice would not stand free from any given theory protected by religious freedom. To the contrary, they would be dependent on one among them (i.e., Rawls's politically liberal theory).

To the best of my reasoning, moreover, separating principles of justice from comprehensive doctrines or from ethics and religion—the right from the good—cannot be successfully defended by argument. Such principles are thereby defined as constraints on inclusive ends humans are assumed to have, so that, as with every nonteleological moral theory, the character of right or of justice evaluates alternatives for purpose in some respect or respects but not in their entirety. By implication, then, the respects in which alternative purposes are not so evaluated are morally or politically indifferent. But the implied assertion that purposes are in some respects morally or politically indifferent is itself a *moral* conclusion about alternatives for decision. Accordingly, that assertion depends on a moral comparison of the alternatives in those respects. Against itself, in other words, separating moral or political principles from an evaluation of alternatives for purpose in their entirety presupposes another principle in terms of which purposes as whole things are evaluated. In sum, neither the right nor the just can be separated from the good without implying an inclusive conception of the good—and alternative purposes in respects said to be morally indifferent are, by implication, evaluated as equally good.[20]

The problem may be restated with specific reference to religious freedom. If either Kantian republicanism or a set of freestanding principles is proposed as one among many answers to be assessed within the way of reason, there is the following consequence: those who advocate a nonteleological proposal must then assume some other kind of evaluative thinking in human decision making. This concerns, for Habermas, one's choice of a conception of the good and, for Rawls, one's decision for a comprehensive doctrine. Thereby, those advocates concede to adherents of a comprehensive orientation or conception of the good possible validation by this alternative kind of thinking.

In defense, to be sure, nonteleologists will respond that such alternative thinking is irrelevant to justice. On their account, conceptions of justice or comprehensive doctrines are specific to diverse individuals and groups and concern the inclusive purposes of which justice is independent. Perhaps, moreover, such specific beliefs are allowed in political decision making in respects consistent with nonteleological justice—as Habermas suggests in discussing the "authentic, collective self-understanding" of a community (1996, 108; see also 96–97) and Rawls suggests in speaking of political issues in which the basic structure is "not at stake" (see, e.g., Rawls 2005, 235). Nonetheless, the supposed separation between morality and justice, on the one hand, and ethics and comprehensive doctrines, on the other, assumes rather than demonstrates the validity of nonteleology. Thus, adherents of a religion on which "the good enjoys epistemic primacy over the right" (263)—that is, of a metaphysical or other teleology—can rightly call this defense of nonteleology tendentious because the nonteleologists can only stipulate the irrelevance to justice of the teleological kind of thinking they themselves must posit.

In sum, nonteleology placed within a public discussion and debate becomes incoherent precisely because, as the proposals of Habermas and Rawls illustrate, any such theory assumes diverse conceptions of the good or comprehensive doctrines of which justice is said to be independent. On its own account, the theory entails denial of the presupposition essential to democracy as a full and free political discourse, namely, that differing convictions about the ultimate terms of political evaluation are open to validation and invalidation by public reason. The objection previously considered and set aside by asserting that religions answer a rational question cannot now be dismissed, that is, a nonteleological theory permits some such convictions consistently to call constitution by the way of reason an alien imposition on them, one that fails to legitimize their alternative form of validation.

In its own way, I believe, this critique simply repeats the previous one, namely, that nonteleological evaluation of purposes presupposes another principle in terms of which purposes are evaluated in their entirety. Denial of that presupposed principle is the positing of evaluative thinking about the good. My sense is that both Habermas and Rawls are aware of crediting this other kind of evaluative thinking. Accordingly, each assumes conventional religious beliefs to be, at least for purposes of democratic theory, immune to or outside of assessment by public reason, whereby this supposed fact becomes a condition for the proper constitution of public reason on which political decisions are based. In other words, each purports to advance an account of public reason, postmetaphysical or freestanding, that is said to be what democratic participants, whatever their religious beliefs or comprehensive doctrines, should explicitly share—and thus an account of public reason that belongs to the constitution of democracy with religious freedom. Given their common assumption about religious beliefs, in any event, those theorists have grounds to take that course, even if it, too, fails to provide a coherent account.

But if public reason has no need of either a Rawlsian or a Habermasian proviso, the alternative proposed here, along with all democratic theories, cannot be fully convincing without explicating why democratic citizens might agree to live together democratically. As mentioned earlier, Habermas asks this question of his own proposal, and his answer includes possible learning processes experienced by both religious and nonreligious citizens. His discourse principle as exemplified in democratic politics can, he says, itself be more or less easily defended. But "theories of justice that have been uncoupled from ethics [i.e., from conceptions of the good] can only *hope* that processes of socialization and political forms of life meet them halfway" (2003, 4)—which at least includes, on my understanding, hope that both religious and secular citizens experience the learning processes Habermas thinks are required. If his account is unconvincing, and the way of reason is proposed, the problem nonetheless remains: what, if anything, might move "citizens of a democratic polity" who "disagree about the principles of their living together" (2003, 4) to honor the democratic process, that is, to accept its outcomes and to pursue justice in solidarity?

THE ATTACHMENT TO DEMOCRACY

To this question, I will now pursue an answer—although its relation to the constitution of a full and free political discourse should be clarified at the outset. Any explicit account of how humans generally are or might be moved to act is part of a substantive theory about the moral enterprise and insofar explicates a particular religious belief of the kind to which a democratic constitution is properly neutral. Accordingly, no account of why citizens might be moved to honor the democratic process can be stipulated constitutionally. Hence, what I will here pursue are relevant *implications* of the way of reason, and I propose that a sufficient account of democratic commitment is possible if we credit two such implications. In the present context, I will do little more than assert them, although I hope to say enough about each to clarify what is being asserted and to show summarily how an argument for each might proceed. In other words, I will seek to answer the question based on what I take to be implied by a democratic constitution, recognizing that my answer depends on sustaining those implied premises.

The first relevant implication is this: because the religious question is rational, the ultimate terms of political evaluation specify to politics a principle present in common human experience. In calling the experience *common*, I intend those aspects of a person's relation to self and other reality that must be present whatever else she or he may experience. Some will, perhaps, deny the necessity of a principle commonly experienced, saying that ultimate terms of political evaluation may be completely contextual. Were that the case, however, the absence of a universal principle anywhere would imply that absence everywhere; in other words, this absence would be commonly experienced. Against the denial, moreover, a positive principle would be thereby experienced, namely: all humans ought to evaluate political possibilities in terms completely specific to their own context. Without such a commonly experienced principle, in any event, politics could not be constituted as a full and free discourse. In whatever respects a principle is contextual, it is insofar deniable without self-contradiction and thus cannot be validated by argument without another evaluative premise. Unless ultimate terms of evaluation are authorized by something undeniable—that is, a principle no person can deny without denying, at least by implication, what she or he also experiences—different convictions about those ultimate terms would have no court of adjudication. Every assertion about the basis of political evaluation could be defended only by appeal to a prior assertion of the same kind, and every supposed validation of a political claim would depend on positing some or other ultimate terms.

In calling the common experience a common *human* experience, I intend what is distinctive to existence with understanding, so that what is experienced by all is commonly understood, at least implicitly or inchoately. Having conceded a universally experienced principle, one may yet question whether all humans understand it. Perhaps this principle can be validated by reflection on human experience as such but is understood only if and when one has learned the principle. But this supposition ignores that what is commonly present whenever anything else is experienced is a *moral* principle, and moral principles are not given to an individual unless they are understood. A person cannot be subject to any moral prescription, that is, cannot be moral or immoral, if she or he is ignorant of the obligation. This is, on my understanding, one meaning of "ought implies can." One cannot decide morally unless one understands what ought to be decided and decides because (or for the reason that) one is so obligated—and immorality is the decision not to act morally. On the present proposal, then, proper political evaluation depends on a moral principle understood, if only implicitly or inchoately, in every moment of every person's experience. Religious formulations (in both the extended and conventional sense) include so many differing attempts to give explicit expression to what all humans already believe. All humans, we may say, are finally after the same thing, namely, to exemplify with integrity in all they do the truth about human life they commonly affirm or originally believe whenever they live with understanding at all. Religious representations are attempts to aid this vocation.

Postponing for the moment the second relevant implication, I wish to propose the following: the relation between common human experience and the religious beliefs or comprehensive doctrines in which we seek to make ultimate terms of political evaluation explicit provides a source for democratic commitment. Because we are all after the same thing, no religious belief can be valid unless it accords with a belief all humans already have. Recognition of this fact allows each democratic citizen to enter the political discourse with a religious reservation, namely, that one's own belief can be valid only if argument can sustain it. Thereby, what Habermas calls the "motivational deficiency" (2013, 355, emphasis removed) may be overcome; each citizen may be prepared at least to accept outcomes of the democratic decision-making process so long as there is a sufficient or, at least, tolerable measure of genuine discourse about the good that politics as such ought to pursue. Notwithstanding one's own comprehensive view, in other words, one's religious reservation is the commitment to political action-as-one bound by ultimate terms of evaluation reason can establish, and there is no political process consistent with that commitment except decision by way of full and free discourse.

For readers of Habermas, democratic motivation so understood may seem nothing other than what he elsewhere calls the "weak force of good reasons" (Habermas et al., 75; see also Habermas 1996, 113–14). But the point is thereby misunderstood, at least if reason is here said to be a weak force because justice, said to be nonteleological, is separated from ethics or conceptions of the good and thus, with Kant, from desire. Nonteleology requires the separation, in other words, insofar as desire defines inclusive ends to be pursued and, in that sense, is teleological. But nonteleological principles of justice are, on the criticisms presented earlier, inconsistent with a full and free political discourse, whether such principles are asserted as a constitutional stipulation or an account within the public discussion and debate. Hence, the separation of reason from a desire for the good by which human purposes in their entirety ought to be directed cannot be implied by religious freedom.

Here, then, is the relevant second implication of politics by the way of reason: the principle present in common human experience must be teleological, that is, must define moral and immoral in relation to an inclusive good. A democratic constitution, we noted earlier, itself implies a comprehensive doctrine; the practice constituting the political community claims to have a sufficient moral reason, even if the constitution has no business stipulating the ultimate terms of political evaluation by which it is authorized. Further, I will here assert Kant's view of the alternatives, with which I take Habermas to agree: either morality's universal principle is nonteleological or common human experience includes awareness of reality as such and thus a telos defined metaphysically. We may then say, against Kant, that politics by the way of reason itself implies a metaphysical good, and pursuit of its maximal realization is the vocation common to all humans.

This inclusive good is not merely ethical, in Habermas's sense, that is, not simply the realization of one's own good life or happiness. Our common human desire is, rather, to serve a purpose and, insofar as possible, realize a good that transcends the human adventure. Although I will not pursue the argument here, this is why, for many theists, moral and political principles implicate a divine or all-inclusive individual, in which all good realized in the world is unified and whose "happiness" is the overriding thing we all finally seek. In any event, our original belief in the truth about human life is an original desire for the good, and this affection not only gives "force" to the religious reservation but also overcomes what Habermas calls the "political deficiency" (2013, 356, emphasis removed), that is, evokes active engagement for the common good or for life together in solidarity. In both respects, our most profound attachment yields also an attachment to politics by the way of reason.

Still, this accounting, as mentioned, depends on implications that, when made explicit, are themselves aspects of a religious conviction in the extended sense. Hence, the explication of democratic commitment, along with the theory of democracy as a whole, can only be consistently intended as itself a contribution to the political discourse in which all religious convictions or comprehensive doctrines are legitimate. Some of those beliefs or doctrines may not explicitly affirm the religious reservation or human solidarity, and insofar explicit adherence to or inculcation of those beliefs will rival and, in consequence, sap our original attachment to the good and, thereby, to democratic politics. In this, as in other ways, democracy is always fragile. In the end, as far as I can see, there is no avoiding something like Habermas's hope that "processes of socialization and political forms of life" will meet democratic politics "halfway" (2003, 4)—even if what that hope anticipates is now quite different than what he describes. Habermas seeks learning processes through which all religions or conceptions of the good agree on an institutional threshold after which only secular reasons count, that is, agree on the postmetaphysical account of constitutional liberalism. In the present context, the hope is for a culture that cultivates the religious reservation and desire for the common good always already present within all who make political claims.

But the state is not permitted to teach this hope. Neither the rational character of answers to the religious question nor the teleology on which democracy depends is something a democratic constitution or the government it establishes properly stipulates, in distinction from what it implies. This is because, as mentioned, some beliefs about the ultimate terms of justice may deny one or both implications, and however false those denials may be, they, too, are legitimized by the constitution. Accordingly, the hope for a sustaining culture is that nongovernmental associations and institutions will be sufficient to the task. Among the relevant nongovernmental organizations, religious associations, at least on the conventional meaning of "religious," have a distinct importance. Because each religious conviction claims to represent explicitly the truth about our most profound attachment, one may especially hope for—and urge—recognition within these specific communities that all humans share an original desire, namely, to live in full commitment to the inclusive telos all humans experience. Religious associations would then serve both our common human vocation and the democratic pursuit that gives it political expression.

CHAPTER FIVE

ON THE HUMANITARIAN IDEAL

The Promise of Neoclassical Metaphysics

Alfred North Whitehead's book, *Adventures of Ideas* (originally published in 1933), has that title in part because he interprets therein the adventure a few very general ideas have had within Western history. Sociologically, the principal idea pursued is "freedom" and thus "the humanitarian ideal." Given ancient expression in Plato's notion of the human soul's inherent worth, this ideal smoldered throughout the medieval period, "nerving the race in its slow ascent" (Whitehead 1961, 18). Whitehead does not mean that history is solely the product of "consciously formulated ideals"; to the contrary, the course of events also waits on a complicity of "senseless agencies," by which he means both events devoid of conscious purpose and human actions insofar as they yield unintended consequences (Whitehead 1961, 16). Thus, a social or institutional embodiment of the humanitarian ideal could occur only when aided by the senseless agencies of modern science and its technological applications in economics, whereby release from immediate want could be substantially extended. The adventure of freedom then reached a kind of triumph with the birth of modern democracy—even if a triumph compromised by, as Whitehead puts it, "evil associates and disgusting alliances" (Whitehead 1961, 18).

But "the success," Whitehead continues, "came only just in time. For before and during the nineteenth century, several strands of thought emerged whose combined effect was in direct opposition to the humanitarian ideal" (Whitehead 1961, 28). Theories of political economy carried into social thought what he elsewhere calls the "historical revolt" of modernity: "the return to the contemplation of brute fact" (Whitehead 1925, 15). This persuasion rejected the metaphysical project and culminated philosophically in "Hume's criticism of the doctrine of the soul" (Whitehead 1961, 36). "On the other side of the account" (Whitehead 1961, 36), Bentham and Comte embraced the humanitarian ideal and its democratic expression. But they, too, "recurred to the scientific revolt against metaphysics" by taking the "supreme worth" of humans as an ultimate moral intuition "requiring no justification and requiring no ultimate understanding of . . . [its] relations to the rest of things" (Whitehead 1961, 37–38). In their own ways, then, these moral and political theories joined the opposition, and, Whitehead concludes, democracy divorced from metaphysics "lost its security of intellectual justification" (Whitehead 1961, 36).

Living more than eighty years after Whitehead looked back, we now look forward, sensible that Western civilization cannot be divorced from the human community as a whole. As part of its legacy to us, the twentieth century created a world in which virtually all humans have become consequential neighbors of each other. The senseless agencies whose unintended effects have largely produced this change include prodigious scientific advance; its expression in technological power of massive scope; and, aided by the latter, the emergence of global systems of interaction, especially the world economy. Summarily speaking, potential effects everywhere from activities occurring anywhere are now of such gravity that we begin the new millennium with heightened awareness of humanity as a common adventure.

In significant measure, attention to the global context commends itself to the enlightened self-interest of all, since some newly wrought threats to human well-being—for instance, those to our environment's integrity and those posed by unspeakable weapons of war—are largely indiscriminate as to victims. Without a common moral commitment, however, multiple aims at merely strategic advantage are themselves senseless agencies relative to the larger community, and a convergence of self-interests alone is easily fractured because each knows that all seek to exempt themselves from the common purpose whenever their self-interest is thereby served. To all appearances, the human community as a whole will be determined by the accidents of fate unless there is, in truth, a humanitarian ideal—and humanitarian in a twofold sense: on the one hand, it should affirm the flourishing of all humans, and on the other, all humans, simply by virtue of being human, should have reason to affirm and thus act on this ideal.

In this context, the present essay seeks to sustain Whitehead's conclusion. Unlike modern modes of thought that divorce human life from ultimate reality, I will argue, the promise of neoclassical metaphysics includes its backing for a humanitarian ideal in the twofold sense mentioned. As noted in the preface, I will in this discussion speak of "metaphysics," unless otherwise noted, in a strict sense, that is, to designate critical thought about reality or existence as such, the characteristics or features common to strictly all things—and "metaphysical" may also be used to designate those characteristics or features. This sense may be distinguished from "metaphysics" in a broad sense, whereby it designates critical thought about subjectivity or existence with understanding as such, whose characteristics, on a neoclassical account, include but are not exhausted by the features common to all things. In that broad sense, neoclassical metaphysics might be said to assert a humanitarian ideal. Whitehead's point, however, is the loss of "intellectual justification" that occurred when human existence was divorced from the rest of things. Accordingly, the discussion here will argue that neoclassical metaphysics provides the needed *backing* for a humanitarian ideal.

But redeeming that conclusion requires facing two important philosophical challenges. The first denies or simply refuses the possibility of any universal moral principles and thus, *a fortiori*, those based on neoclassical or any other account of ultimate reality.[1] The second, often expressed in modern theories of human rights, affirms an a priori and thus a universal moral principle or set of principles but denies its dependence on ultimate reality.[2] For the present discussion, the latter is best understood to antedate the former, even if both claim contemporary adherents. An a priori ground of morality independent of metaphysical implications (in the strict sense) is widely and properly associated with the achievement of Immanuel Kant, and theories of human rights illustrating that account typically understand themselves to be within the Kantian ethical tradition in something like a strict sense. In contrast, the refusal of moral universality is, on the whole, more recent and may be called post-Enlightenment because it steps away from both the metaphysics Kant criticized and from his universality in ethics.[3] To be sure, Kant understood his own constructive position to be "a prolegomena to any future metaphysics," but in doing so, he redefined "metaphysics." Against the pursuit of knowledge about reality as such, he confined the term to designation of those transcendental conditions specific to human subjectivity, that is, to theoretical and practical reason independently of any implication about ultimate reality.[4] The post-Enlightenment view, then, sees no need for metaphysics in either the Whiteheadian or the Kantian sense.

In seeking to show why a humanitarian ideal depends on ultimate reality, the present discussion can be only programmatic. Against the two challenges, I will offer summary arguments, and the explication of an alternative ethics and politics will have the same summary character. Still, I hope that enough will be said to commend more thorough attention to the promise of neoclassical metaphysics.

KANTIAN AND POST-ENLIGHTENMENT CHALLENGES

I begin with the more recent, post-Enlightenment view because, as far as I can see, it commands wider endorsement in contemporary thought. Its challenge to a humanitarian ideal is one aspect of a more or less comprehensive critique of universal subjectivity, on which the meaning and truth of our understandings are in all respects dependent on conditions limited to some or other location within the human adventure. During the past century in the West, it seems, increasing familiarity with the profound diversity of human experiences has occasioned, paradoxically, an increasing sense that understandings of ourselves and the world to which we belong are entirely circumscribed by peculiarities of context. But even if this historical perception is correct, the critique is principally philosophical and challenges neoclassical metaphysics because every metaphysical project, Platonic or Kantian, is indicted. Accordingly, no metaphysics can be sustained unless the philosophical indictment can be turned aside. Contemporary or recent accounts on which universal subjectivity is doubted or denied are sophisticated and vary among themselves, and I will not attempt explicitly to address their specific arguments. Although most philosophical terms mean different things to different people, the discrediting of metaphysics altogether, including its redefinition by Kant, finds expression more often than not when subjective existence is said to be inclusively "tradition-constituted," "neopragmatic," or "hermeneutical"—and, on my understanding, that critique is also the common ground for most proposals claiming to be "postmodern."[5]

For my purposes, the critique's importance derives from what I take to be its most compelling source, namely, sustained attention to the dependence of human understanding on participation in language, a focus with which much of Western philosophy has been occupied since the so-called subjective turn of earlier modernity was transformed by the so-called linguistic and hermeneutical turns. All understandings, many have concluded, are linguistically constituted or mediated by language—or, more generally, by a lifeworld. A language is a particular historical creation, and the more general term "lifeworld" here means a setting of interpretations and associated practices that, however inclusive of differing and overlapping expressions and however permissive of transformation, is nonetheless always a historically specific creation circumscribing meaning and truth. Hence, no understanding of self in relation to the larger reality can be meaningful or true universally, that is, for all subjects whatever their historical setting.

At least insofar as this analysis marks its source, the contemporary challenge to moral universality may be a legacy above all from Heidegger and Wittgenstein, each of whom, writes Karl-Otto Apel, "discovered the lifeworld in his own way" and for each of whom "this very lifeworld assumes the role of ultimate bedrock." On Apel's reading, this discovery yields, in Wittgenstein, "a critique of the meanings involved in metaphysical pseudo-problems, meanings which result from the non-reflection upon the linguistic *a priori* of language games" or result when "language 'goes on holiday,'" and in Heidegger, "the corresponding existential-hermeneutical insights into the dependence of our positive understanding of worldly significance upon human being-in-the-world and, in connection therewith, upon the worldly disclosiveness of historical language(s)" (Apel 1998, 139, 140). In either case, there is no getting beneath the lifeworld. Those who see our subjectivity in this way do not deny our capacity to think and speak about all humans or all things, but the meaning and truth of what is said are nonetheless circumscribed by our context. No thinking or speaking can have meaning or validity that transcends historical setting, however generously that setting itself may need to be understood.

I will formulate the principal conviction this critique articulates as follows: *reality presupposes understanding*. What is real and thus may be an object or objects of human experience is mediated by language or lifeworld, and in that sense, what is understood is constituted by understanding. This is not a collective kind of solipsism, as if there were no reality other than subjects; hence, one may also say, perhaps, that understanding depends on reality. Still, the point is this: it is nonsense to suppose that realities are differentiated from each other or have a given general character independently of the terms in which they are understood, and this is because the meaning and truth of understandings are circumscribed within a given historical location. The identity of things, their similarities and differences and thus their relations to each other within the encompassing whole, have no character beyond the definitions of a given lifeworld, a given linguistic or cultural and social context. Hence, there can be no aspect of understanding that is universal.

Notwithstanding how widely persuasive this critique may be, a minority voice in recent thought finds a denial of universal subjectivity pragmatically self-contradictory. Whether meaning and truth are said to be entirely dependent on a "thrown projection" of "being-in-the-world" or on "life-forms" and associated language games or, in some other way, on a historically specific background of culture or practice or power or interest, the argument required to redeem this self-understanding and thus the truth one claims for it cannot themselves be dependent in all respects on such a background. To make the truth of *this* understanding contingent on the peculiarities of a given context is to imply that, in some other subjective context, what one has said about all subjects may not be true. Denying any universal subjectivity, one would imply that elsewhere a subject may validly affirm what one has denied, and this implication contradicts one's denial.

Karl-Otto Apel makes the point with characteristic precision: "Whoever seriously speaks of the conceptual meaning of 'meaning' and 'truth' as being in the last instance dependent on events or fate—that is, [asserts] that the *logos* of our discursive claim to meaning and truth is subordinate to time—thereby cancels the claim to the meaning and truth of their discourse" (Apel 1996, 178). Or again and more summarily, reason cannot function "as object and no longer as subject of critique" (Apel 1998, 164).

To the best of my reasoning, this criticism of the critique is convincing, and it might be reformulated by way of the following recognition: if understandings in any specific historical location do not imply a universal principle of meaning and truth, then the absence of universal subjectivity must itself characterize subjectivity universally. Were there no universal conditions of human existence, the absence could not depend on a specific context because this would imply the possible presence elsewhere of one or more such conditions—and if present anywhere, universal conditions must be present everywhere. Hence, the absence of all such conditions must be, absurdly, a universal condition of subjectivity—and the character of understandings as circumscribed by historical location would itself be implied by all locations in the human adventure. In other words, the critique of universal subjectivity can only claim to be universally true, so that those who advance it must be exempt from the critique—and this repeats that making a claim for the critique is pragmatically self-contradictory. Attending to Wittgenstein's formulation, Apel makes the point this way: whatever may be said about historically specific life forms and associated language games, saying it implies a transcendental language game, in which one can make meaningful claims to truth (see Apel 1980, 1–45).

But if a denial of moral universality is problematic, that alone does not warrant a humanitarian ideal authorized by ultimate reality or by metaphysics. Stepping back from the critique of universal subjectivity, one encounters differing expressions of Kantian metaphysics, on which an a priori or transcendental moral law implies nothing about the nature of all things or reality as such. Kant himself formulated such a law—"So act as to treat humanity, whether in thine own person or in that of any other, in every case as an end withal, never as means only" (Kant 1949, 46, emphasis removed)—and some Kantians since have, in one form or another, sought to offer what they consider more sound formulations. These successors include Apel himself, who seeks to reconceive as intersubjective (or transcendental-pragmatic) what he takes to be Kant's solitary self and, accordingly, redefines Kant's moral law as the "meta-norm" (Apel 1979, 335) of communicative respect. "All beings who are capable of linguistic communication must be recognized as persons since in all their actions and utterances they are potential participants in a discussion" (Apel 1980, 259).

Thinkers like Apel are Kantian in something like a strict sense because, with him, the moral principle or set of principles they defend is both transcendental or a priori and nonteleological in character. I call a norm or principle or moral theory nonteleological when it purports to define moral in distinction from immoral action independently of any inclusive good, that is, a good to which all purposes in their entirety should be directed. A nonteleological theory differentiates right action in terms of some partial or abstract aspect that ought to be present—for instance, respect for certain human rights. Moral obligations, then, serve as side constraints or limiting conditions on proper human pursuits. Jürgen Habermas aptly formulates the point: a nonteleological principle "acts like a knife that makes razor-sharp cuts between evaluative statements and strictly normative ones, between the good and the just" (Habermas 1990, 104)—that is, between statements about some inclusive good to be sought and those about moral constraints on its pursuit.

Kantian nonteleology, moreover, is directly related to Kant's discrediting of traditional metaphysics. On my reading, Kant held that a good to which all purposes in their entirety ought to be directed could be defined only by the character of reality as such. But the longstanding Western metaphysical project he inherited was, he became convinced, futile. Summarily speaking, the attempt to know ultimate reality or, in Aristotle's phrase, "being qua being" had typically asserted, however different such metaphysical proposals might otherwise be, that worldly substances, which are finite and temporal and contingent, imply a realm or being or substance in all respects infinite and eternal and necessary—whether or not this eminent reality was called God. What is eminent, then, cannot be designated except by negation, namely, as not finite and not temporal and not contingent—or, in sum, as having nothing in common with the things of this world. On my understanding, it is this metaphysical account Kant discredited. What can be designated only by negation, he held, cannot be known, even if he allowed that it can be thought. Because the metaphysical project in question said that being qua being includes or depends on what is designated only by negation, Kant concluded, reality as such cannot be known. Hence, nothing known about what is the case can be knowledge of things-in-themselves or ultimate reality, and nothing about what ought to be the case can be derived therefrom.

I see no way successfully to redeem the metaphysical project Kant discredited. Still, asserting that knowledge of ultimate reality is impossible is something else—or what comes to the same thing, it does not follow that possibilities for knowing reality as such are confined to the longstanding Western project Kant denied. Neoclassical metaphysics, as I will subsequently seek to clarify, also rejects any knowledge of some eminent reality having nothing in common with worldly things and thus designated only by negation. Kant, however, took the typical metaphysics he inherited to exhaust metaphysical inquiry in the strict sense, even while for him, only a good defined by ultimate reality could direct all possible purposes in their entirety. Thereby, his *Critique of Pure Reason*, which restricted possible knowledge of what is the case (i.e., of objects, actual and possible, in time and space) to things-as-they-appear in distinction from things-in-themselves, became a negative condition of his *Critique of Practical Reason*, which defended a duty independent of any object to be pursued.

In any event, Kantian nonteleology is, I believe, also pragmatically self-contradictory—precisely because it defines moral and immoral in terms of some partial or abstract aspect of action. Thereby, moral and immoral evaluation compares alternatives for purpose in one or more respects but not in their entirety. Were this definition correct, the alternatives in other respects would be morally indifferent. Right and wrong actions would be distinguished by some partial feature (e.g., respect or disrespect for what are said to be the rights of all subjects) only because other aspects of alternative purposes (e.g., their service or disservice to other interests of affected individuals, or their consequences for creatures who are not subjects) make no difference to a moral comparison of those possible choices. But calling alternative ends in certain respects morally indifferent is itself a moral evaluation, and moral conclusions imply moral comparisons. Thus, a nonteleological principle implies a moral comparison of possible purposes in all respects. A principle said to be nonteleological, in other words, implies another moral principle in terms of which the moral relevance of alternatives for purpose in their entirety are compared—a principle by which the inclusive good is defined. A nonteleological theory implies, against itself, a teleological principle, and for this reason, claiming to define moral and immoral in terms of some partial feature of human purposes commits what we may call the partialist fallacy.[6]

The point is emphasized by Hume: "In moral deliberations we must be acquainted beforehand with all the objects and all their relations to each other; and from a comparison of the whole, fix our choice or approbation. No new fact to be ascertained; no new relation to be discovered. All the circumstances of the case are supposed to be laid before us, ere we can fix any sentence" (Hume, 290). A moral evaluation can only be between or among the alternatives inclusively, and a conclusion that some aspects of them are morally indifferent is part of an inclusive comparison. Hume's elemental point, on my understanding, is this: Human decisions can choose among their alternatives only as whole things. Because a moral evaluation, if it occurs, compares alternatives *with respect to choosing*, not with respect to their descriptive similarities or differences, it compares those alternatives in their entirety.

I speak of a moral evaluation "if it occurs" because, as is well known, Hume concludes that "this great difference between a . . . [matter] of *fact* and one of *right*" means that "after every circumstance, every relation is known, the understanding has no further room to operate, nor any object on which it could employ itself. The approbation . . . which then ensues cannot be the work of judgment, but of the heart; and is not a speculative proposition or affirmation, but an active feeling or sentiment" (Hume, 290). In other words, Hume denies that alternatives for decision can be compared with respect to choosing; the consciousness in decision making is exhausted by understanding descriptively the similarities and differences between or among possible purposes. Something similar to this conclusion has been advanced by thinkers for whom supposed moral utterances are solely "emotive" or, in any event, neither true nor false; that is, they are not claims to validity. On this view, a supposed moral question about the decision to be taken, such that alternatives could be understood or compared with respect to choosing, is, in truth, senseless.

Against that view, Kant argues—rightly, I believe—that Hume's assertion of nonconscious decision making is itself a moral understanding. Some humans, as Hume recognizes, may understand their approbation or disapprobation as if it were bound by some or other criterion in terms of which alternatives should be evaluated—a recognition expressed when he criticizes systems of morality for their failure to show how what is the case can imply what ought to be. Thereby, on Hume's account, these people compare their alternatives falsely because, in truth, choice cannot occur with understanding. But *that* supposed truth is itself an understanding of all decision making. The descriptive comparison of alternatives having been completed, Hume's supposed absence of consciousness from choice—or any other account on which understanding with respect to choosing cannot occur—can only be itself an understanding of the alternatives with respect to choosing. This conclusion is confirmed by the claim to truth for this understanding, which implies that all decisions *ought* to be consistent with it or *ought not* to be consistent with any false understanding of one's decision making.

The denial that choice is understood is, against itself, a certain understanding of choosing as such, namely, an evaluative understanding on which there is no moral difference between or among the alternatives, so that each is morally permitted. This outcome illustrates what I take to be Kant's singular insight and why he affirmed an a priori condition of practical reason, "the property of the will to be a law to itself" (Kant 1949, 63): every assertion about decision with understanding as such in relation to its available alternatives is a putative moral principle, precisely because it asserts that all comparison with respect to choosing ought to be consistent with it. The point is repeated in underscoring that all such assertions belong to theories of *practical* reason, so that each, in claiming to be true, is a principle for how humans ought to think about or understand choosing among their alternatives for decision.

With Kant, then, moral evaluation is inescapable for subjectivity or self-conscious life, but against Kant and with Hume, such evaluation can only concern the alternatives for purpose in the way that one among them must be chosen, namely, in its entirety. It is to the point that Kantian principles, prescribing side constraints or limiting conditions, assume that humans have alternatives for purpose, the decision among which ought to be constrained. Because the principles are nonteleological, in other words, those alternatives include features beyond respect or disrespect for, say, human rights, and given Hume's point, those additional features must also be morally assessed. Hence, they could be morally indifferent only if the alternatives are insofar morally equal or equally good—and this repeats that a nonteleological theory implies a principle of moral evaluation more inclusive than the principle it asserts.[7]

Having in mind that Kant's conception of morality antedates post-Enlightenment accounts, I suspect that his denial of an inclusive good contributed to the subsequent critique of all universal moral principles. For many subsequent thinkers, Kant's convincing conclusion is his discrediting of metaphysics in the strict sense and thus the impossibility of any inclusive good that is universal. For some of these thinkers also, nonteleological principles, universal or otherwise, are impossible; they imply a conception of the inclusive good from which they claim to be independent. Ethics, such thinkers conclude, requires an inclusive good even while no conception of it can be universal. Because entirely dependent on historical location, ethics must be post-Enlightenment.[8]

If these arguments against both post-Enlightenment and Kantian accounts—the critiques of universal subjectivity, on the one hand, and of moral universality that is nonteleological, on the other—can be given convincing explication, both proposals are, by implication, self-refuting. They also exhaust, I will now assume, the alternatives in moral theory to metaphysical teleology, that is, to a moral theory on which all purposes in their entirety are morally evaluated in terms of a good defined by reality as such. I recognize that some moral theories have affirmed a universal nonteleology even while denying to its principles the a priori character Kant asserted (see, e.g., Dworkin 2006; 2011). To the best of my reasoning, however, Kant properly equated moral universality with an a priori imperative or moral law: every supposed account of how decision with understanding as such relates to its alternatives is a transcendental moral theory. Hence, nothing is "more fatal to morality than that we should wish to derive it from examples" (Kant 1949, 26); that is, an obligation by which subjectivity as such is bound cannot be defined by any understanding one or more humans might consistently deny but, rather, must be transcendental to subjectivity as such.

Also, some moral theories have affirmed a universal teleology—that is, have asserted a telos, a priori or otherwise, in terms of which purposes are evaluated in their entirety—even while denying metaphysics. Perhaps Aristotle's account of happiness, certain expressions of utilitarianism, and John Dewey's definition of good as growth in experience are examples. But Kant, having rightly equated moral universality with an a priori law, was also lucid, as far as I can see, in believing that teleology requires a good defined by reality as such, and thus his discrediting of metaphysics entailed moral nonteleology.

On my reading, he reasoned in the following way: Because the moral law must be transcendental, teleology requires a transcendental telos, that is, a telos implicitly affirmed by every possible exercise of practical reason, so that denial of it is pragmatically self-contradictory. Because a telos is not a character of purposive action but, rather, a state of affairs or character of existence at whose realization purpose aims, teleology requires a good to be pursued that is implied by anything else at whose realization rational freedom might aim, even if one decides to pursue some contrary good. But, then, that telos cannot be anything whose realization would be empirical or logically contingent, for instance, cosmopolitan democracy (as a state of affairs) or the happiness of all humans (as a character of existence). Any such realization can be denied without pragmatic self-contradiction, and thus no such realization could be affirmed by every possible exercise of practical reason as a good to be pursued. For instance, neither cosmopolitan democracy nor the happiness of all humans is affirmed as a good to be pursued if one acts in pursuit of, say, aristocratic supremacy. Hence, one's decision to pursue any supposed good you please would affirm something as the transcendental telos only if the latter were a metaphysical good, a good defined by reality as such and thus realized whatever else is realized. Given the futility of metaphysics, then, moral teleology seeks to derive the moral law from examples.

To be sure, a turn from Kantian and post-Enlightenment accounts to metaphysical teleology as the remaining viable alternative for moral theory requires extended defense beyond the brief references here to Kant's arguments.[9] Still, if this turn can be sustained, we may endorse Whitehead's conclusion, namely, that moral ideals in the West lost their intellectual backing when divorced from any "ultimate understanding of their relations to the rest of things" (Whitehead 1961, 37–38). What I will now propose is a positive formulation of metaphysical teleology; that is, I will seek to outline how neoclassical metaphysics explicates a comprehensive good and thus a comprehensive purpose, after which I will return to the backing for a humanitarian ideal.[10]

METAPHYSICS AND HUMAN PURPOSE

For post-Enlightenment accounts, I have asserted, reality presupposes understanding—because what is real and thus may become an object or objects of experience is mediated by the language or lifeworld of some specific historical location. On neoclassical metaphysics, to the contrary, *reality is prior to understanding*. Existence as a subject, in other words, exemplifies in a specific way features common to all existence and, therefore, features independent of whether they are understood. The specific character of subjectivity is, indeed, existence by way of understanding, so that humans consciously decide what they will become and, thereby, what they will add to reality as a difference by which the future will be affected. But distinctions and relations among realities of the past and thus the general character of reality as such are given to a subject prior to understanding. "Prior" here does not mean temporally prior but, rather, prior in constituting the subject, so that understanding is a subject's relation to its own prior relations to distinct things and their inclusion within an encompassing whole. As Whitehead says, "consciousness presupposes experience, and not experience consciousness" (Whitehead 1978, 53). This metaphysics, then, backs a nonconscious experience of ultimate reality common to all individuals who also live with understanding.

Still, the importance of cultural and social context to human subjectivity is transparent. It seems undeniable that we realize and develop our subjective capacities through communication and, thereby, learning that is inseparable from a language community and its particular tradition or traditions. Hence, neoclassical metaphysics will not be credible if it prevents proper appreciation of the linguistic and hermeneutical turns so central, on my reading, to post-Enlightenment accounts. Due credit can be consistently given, I believe, through a distinction generally acknowledged by those who analyze our participation in language or lifeworld, namely, between understandings in the foreground and those in the background of self-conscious activity. Habermas, for instance, speaks of the lifeworld as something largely "taken for granted" (Habermas 1984, 335; see also Searle 1983, 141f; 1992, 175f.; Taylor, chapter 4). "Even at its brightest," as Whitehead puts the point, "there is [in our consciousness] a small focal region of clear illumination, and a large, penumbral region of experience that tells of intense experience in dim apprehension" (Whitehead 1978, 267).

Let us call understandings explicit when they are perspicuous or occupy the focus of attention and implicit when they occur in the dim background of consciousness. Here "implicit" means "contained in the nature of something although not readily apparent" (American College Dictionary). The surrounding level of understanding not in focus provides the indispensable backdrop for our interest in whatever dominates our consciousness. Even our explicit attention to mundane matters, for instance, preparing breakfast in the kitchen, depends on a vast array of understandings not readily apparent during the activity in question—in this case, the properties of various foods, how the stove works, and so forth. On other occasions, the point becomes more obvious. For instance, a reader of Abraham Lincoln's Second Inaugural would be lost without understandings of American history, religion, politics, war, English rhetoric, and the language itself (to name a few) that are effective but not perspicuous in consciousness when the reading occurs. Typically, the more extensive or complex the relevant implicit understandings one enjoys, the more profound the understanding of whatever occupies the center of interest—for instance, the more thorough one's appreciation of Lincoln's genius.

We may—and, I am inclined to think, should—agree that explicit understandings, at least beyond embryonic ones, are mediated by language and lifeworld. Moreover, many or most understandings in the background on any given occasion were previously acquired by the individual through her or his learning or reflection on learning; they were, in other words, the content of focused attention at some previous moment in the individual's life and are now implicitly remembered. We may further agree that no understanding occurs, at least beyond embryonic ones, unless there is or has been linguistic communication, so that something is or has been understood explicitly. What the critique of universal subjectivity asserts is, however, something further—namely, that every understanding present to a given subject is consequent on learning or reflection on learning, so that strictly all implicit understandings first occur explicitly, and any given subject's understandings are circumscribed by participation in a historically emergent linguistic community or lifeworld. Accordingly, understandings universal to subjects as such are impossible.

But this something further does not follow from what precedes it. Nothing in the recognition that every explicit understanding is mediated by a specific community requires the critique of universal subjectivity—and, indeed, it is, if the argument against it summarized earlier is sound, self-refuting. To the contrary, then, nothing in due appreciation of the linguistic and hermeneutical turns, including the recognition that something must be understood explicitly if there is to be understanding at all, excludes the following affirmation: human existence universally, as soon as its capacity for understanding is awakened, also includes a certain implicit understanding or set of understandings as the indispensable background for all others. That background is, in other words, necessary to subjectivity as such, even if that understanding or set of understandings is not now and never has been explicit in a given individual's life (or, for that matter, any individual's life), so that she or he is incapable of making it the express content of speech.

An implicit understanding or set of understandings necessary to subjectivity as such is what the assertion of neoclassical metaphysics requires. On that account, meaning and truth are not, as the post-Enlightenment view asserts, bound to the peculiarities of historical location; understanding is not in that way circumscribed. To the contrary, all subjects always are given in their experience and, further, understand the ultimate character of things, whatever learned understandings they may also have. The nonconscious relations always prior in constituting a subject, namely, to distinct things and their inclusion within a whole, allow an understanding of what is always included in those relations, namely, the general character of reality. This understanding and any others necessary to subjectivity as such may be called prelinguistic, because they are not constituted by language or do not depend on learning.

We may note how the self that understands is always present in subjectivity; perhaps we will also agree that an understanding of oneself as a subject is also always present because anything else understood is understood as distinct from the self having that understanding. Given a prelinguistic awareness of reality as such, we can now say that self-understanding cannot be in all respects learned. This follows because the discrimination of self must be from strictly all other things and, in that respect, also prelinguistic. On this account, in other words, understandings of *specific* similarities and differences by which subjects and other things are distinguished from each other, at least beyond an embryonic presence, are indeed mediated by learning, but subjects could not be subjects absent the inescapable awareness of themselves as subjects in relation to ultimate reality. Accordingly, Whitehead writes: "The primitive stage of discrimination . . . is the vague grasp of reality, dissecting it into a three-fold scheme, namely, the Whole, That Other, and This-Myself" (Whitehead 1938, 150)—and this is rightly called the primitive stage because it is presupposed by any other discrimination at all.

In speaking of "the Whole," Whitehead expresses his concept of God, the "chief exemplification" (Whitehead 1978, 343) of metaphysical characteristics. Although some have sought to develop neoclassical metaphysics without God, most who take their bearings from Whitehead either endorse his theism or, notwithstanding revisions they advance, affirm a concept of God profoundly indebted to him. Taking this majority view to be correct, we can say that, on neoclassical metaphysics, our prelinguistic discrimination of reality as such is also the implicit understanding of a differentiation between God and all others. But this theism does not include reference to a realm or being or substance having nothing in common with things of this world because completely eternal or changeless. For neoclassical theism, at least on what I take to be its most convincing formulation, God is the eminently temporal individual, not eternally complete—such that the whole of reality has been and will be forever changing as it fully includes whatever has become actual in the world. While God is indeed the one necessary individual, this whole of reality can never begin or end or fail to include in all detail all other real things, and thus the realization of God's individuality is always contingent because what is thereby included depends on contingent realizations in the world.

In contrast to many other proposals in Western history, it will be useful to note, this metaphysical account does not mark concrete singulars or, in that sense, actual things as substances, at least if "substance" designates something concrete that remains once we abstract from relations to other things. The final real things are here said to be relativities; each is constituted by unifying its relations to other actual things, its efficient causes. At the same time, unification or singularity is never completely a product of the past but, rather, is achieved in some measure, however trivial, as an act of self-creation or by its own decision and thus its final cause. Upon unification, then, the new relativity becomes another object in the past by which successor relativities in what is now its future will be determined—the future being, at present, merely a set of possibilities. Hence, a present moment *is* this act of self-creation. We may also call each such unification a metaphysically singular actualization of what had been merely possible—or simply call it an actuality, meaning thereby a metaphysically final real thing—that "arises as an effect facing its past and ends as a cause facing its future" (Whitehead 1961, 194).

In this sense, a present moment of human experiencing, which is nothing other than the emergent singularity of relations to things experienced, is taken to be our most immediately available exemplification of the relativity characterizing all actualities. Accordingly, a human individual, meaning thereby the enduring existence of self-consciousness (which may vanish, as in dreamless sleep, and then reappear) in the human brain, is a series of experiencing actualities—an enduring series distinguished at least in part because each member actuality experiences in an especially intimate way the particular brain and, through it, the larger human body in which it is set. "Here am I, and I have brought my body with me" (Whitehead 1938, 156). Typically, Whitehead notes, we do not speak this way, but it clarifies what "I" can mean in designating an experiencing individual. Other individuals are also relativities in a distinct sequence—and the divine reality is the metaphysical individual, the one necessarily existing individual that is distinguished from all others solely by its metaphysical characteristics and whose sequence of actualities is the ever-changing whole.

The difference between divine and worldly actualities, then, is that between all-inclusive and fragmentary relativity. Each divine relativity includes in complete detail all that has been realized in the temporal world, and the divine individual will include whatever becomes realized as the worldly future becomes present. In contrast, the relativities of each worldly existence are fragmentary, each typically including an immensely limited measure of what is completely included in the whole, as the limitations evident in human experiencing illustrate. The inescapable presence of actual relativities and the possibilities for others—ordered by relations of successors to predecessors and including self, others, and the whole—is the content discriminated in a subject's primitive stage or understood implicitly by subjects as such.[11] The presence of this understanding is what constitutes the pragmatic self-contradiction in every subject who denies universal subjectivity; the denial contradicts what the subject in question also necessarily understands and thus affirms.

Because it rejects the post-Enlightenment critique, this neoclassical outline agrees with Kant's moral theory in its defense of universal subjectivity. But this agreement with Kant and Kantians does not include a nonteleological moral law. To the contrary, neoclassical metaphysics affirms a metaphysical good. "The many become one, and are increased by one" (Whitehead 1978, 21) is Whitehead's metaphysical characterization of a final real thing or concrete singular. This summary formulation is, moreover, itself a variable in terms of which actualities can be greater or less and thus differ in value. What varies is the unity-in-diversity realized as relations are unified, whereby each actuality adds itself to the past to which subsequent things will relate.

The past, then, creates possibilities for the present, and the measure of value a given actuality may realize depends on the ordered diversity it inherits. Where this past is more favorable, the present enjoys greater freedom and the greater chance to be distinctive. Again, human experience, now in its variable unity-in-diversity, illustrates the point. Our subjectivity may be boring or trivial (e.g., when hearing an especially vapid political speech) or, alternatively, marked by complex intensity (e.g., when relevant learning opens appreciation of Lincoln's Second Inaugural)—and other things equal, the latter is more valuable because the past inherited was more valuable (e.g., was created by Lincoln's genius, which relevant learning made available). Whitehead calls his summary characterization—the many become one, and are increased by one—the category of creativity (see Whitehead 1978, 21), and thus we may speak of concrete moments exemplifying greater or lesser value because they realize greater or lesser creativity. On his meaning, in other words, creativity defines both actualities as such and the good.

I will call the understandings common to all subjects our original understandings, the content of which includes the character of ultimate reality. If this character also defines the good, our original understandings also include a moral principle—prescribing the aim at maximal creativity. Kant, too, I believe, affirms an original understanding of his categorical imperative. On the most familiar meaning of his formula, "ought implies can," a person cannot be obligated to perform an impossible deed. On its equally important meaning, however, the dictum says that one cannot act as one ought unless one can so decide because (for the reason that) morality requires. "Ought" marks a precept for conscious decision, and the relevant consciousness would be absent were action in accord with the moral law to occur by mere accident, that is, without awareness of what is required. One cannot be moral or immoral while ignorant of one's obligation. But moral obligation as such is and could only be defined by an a priori principle, a principle implied by every exercise of freedom, and this could not be so were any exercise of freedom ignorant of it. Hence, all subjects are originally aware of the practical self-legislation of reason, and any denial of it is pragmatically self-contradictory because the agent then denies what she or he also affirms. Indeed, the most compelling argument for the presence of original understandings may be this moral argument—namely, humans are bound by an obligation that must be transcendental to subjectivity, which is possible only if subjects as such are aware of the moral law.

In *Religion within the Limits of Reason Alone*, if I understand it rightly, Kant explains radical evil through a fundamental exercise of will, the choice for or against the categorical imperative as one's fundamental maxim. Accordingly, the moral law originally understood entails an original decision, namely, to act in accord with its imperative or to act in self-contradiction, that is, to choose against it even while one is aware of what ought to be decided. Perhaps for Kant—I am simply not clear—each person takes this immoral choice only once and subsequently exemplifies radical evil, so that redemption is a temporal process overcoming the consequences of this "fall." If so, his explication may betray his account of time and space as solely forms of phenomena rather than noumenal freedom. But whatever Kant's intention, the original decision occurs, on a neoclassical accounting, in every present decision with understanding—and, as already discussed, the moral law originally understood becomes, against Kant, a teleological principle. It is properly formulated as a comprehensive purpose: so act as to pursue maximal creativity, or so act as to maximize creativity—and because time and space are metaphysical and the metaphysical value of creativity does not depend on when or where it occurs, pursue maximal creativity in the long run or the future as such.[12]

Reflection on this teleology, moreover, may include arguments for the implied reality of God, and one such argument is this: Absent an all-inclusive or divine reality, moral activity would seek a multiplicity of realizations— because the worldly future as such will be realized in many fragmentary creatures. The human creativity one seeks to enhance, for instance, will occur in a multiplicity of women and men. Were the future confined to fragmentary actualities, however, the imperative to maximize would make no sense. That imperative implies the summation or consummation of the many realizations into a whole, whereby speaking of greater or lesser consequences overall has meaning, and all-inclusive relativity is implied by the teleological principle because this composition is implied.

The same conclusion can be reached, I believe, from the premise that creativity is always the becoming of unity-in-diversity and thus of greater or lesser value. This metaphysical conception implies a comparison of any and all actualities, instances of "the many become one, and are increased by one," whereby some are of greater value than others (and, perhaps, some are of equal value with others)—and because value is realized in fully concrete singulars, the comparison must be in a fully concrete singular. If one asserts of two past moments in one's experience a difference in value, one implies a concrete comparison of the two, for instance, in one's present experience in which the two are remembered. But no fragmentary relativity could compare all past actualities; indeed, no fragmentary present could compare any two past actualities in their full concreteness. To the contrary, this metaphysical conception of value requires an actuality in which all other concrete unifications are included in all of their detail—a divine relativity, that is, a divine individual whose actualities again and again unify and thus compare all other concrete things.

If arguments such as these are (or, with revisions, can be) sound, the moral obligation to make the comprehensive purpose one's own prescribes the aim at maximal creativity in the future as such because this is also the future of God, that is, of the all-inclusive whole. The metaphysical good implies the metaphysical individual, the one who is the best possible being and thus worthy of worship. Things in the world have whatever value they have because all in their entirety make a difference to the creativity of God, and the moral law can be stated: so act as to maximize the divine good.

Assuming this comprehensive purpose, we may now posit what I expect will be noncontroversial, namely, that human existence enjoys dramatically increased possibilities for creativity in comparison with other known creatures—possibilities occasioned by its capacity to understand the world and itself. A human individual, let us say, may flourish; that is, she or he flourishes in the measure her or his distinctively human activities are creative. It then follows that one's chance to flourish is greater or lesser depending on the ordered diversity to which one relates, and the dramatic difference characterizing subjective creativity means that a suitably ordered world of other human achievements inherited is, other things equal, especially important to human flourishing. Inherited achievements include one's own past experiencing and decisions. But even these, as the present ones, depend especially on inheritance from other persons. In sum, the possibilities for human realization of the good will be especially enhanced insofar as each person is empowered by others and by communities of others.

To be sure, human flourishing does not exhaust the realization of value. Because the good has a metaphysical character, all worldly realization is, in some greater or lesser measure, good—and this recognition entails the intrinsic value of our nonhuman worldly environment. In the world as we know it, however, human communities are especially important not only to empower the capacity of persons for dramatically increased creativity but also, and just for that reason, as the locus of future good we should seek to maximize. In that sense, our comprehensive purpose calls for human interaction in which the achievements of each enhance the flourishing of all. I will express this special importance and seek simultaneously to affirm wider worldly value in the following formulation: with whatever due attention to the nonhuman world is required, the moral law prescribes our maximal common humanity. Here, "our common humanity" means the common world of human achievements, itself consisting of wider and more local patterns, insofar as it provides or promotes greater possibilities for the flourishing of all. The metaphysical account of final real things as relativities yields a moral law prescribing human relationships for their own sake, in accord with a telos of human life together on which, with whatever due attention to the nonhuman world is required, each individual is to the maximal extent both a beneficiary and a benefactor of all others and thus all flourish insofar as possible. Pursuit of this telos creates the best possible world for the divine relativity.

But if this teleological conclusion has been commended, it does not discredit completely the Kantian assertion of universal human rights. To the contrary, I believe, that assertion expresses an indefeasible aspect of ethics. If Kantian theories do, as I argued previously, commit the partialist fallacy because they presuppose the inclusive moral evaluation of purposes nonteleology denies, this indefeasible aspect alone cannot be sufficient to moral evaluation. Nonetheless, human rights may be advanced as a principle or principles to be honored whatever the consequences—and, on my accounting, prescriptions having this character, which I will call deontological, are not necessarily nonteleological. Nonteleology denies a comprehensive good, but deontological principles may be consistent with teleological ethics because through them a comprehensive purpose is applied to human actions indirectly. It is one thing to apply the ethic directly to each human action, such that all other norms are at best provisional and can be overridden by one's obligation to maximize good consequences—and something else to assert indirect application, that is, to prescribe pursuit of the good through social practices and institutions that require reciprocal roles or duties to be honored whatever the consequences.[13]

As Brian Barry has explicated, deontological norms are necessary just insofar as human cooperation and coordination are essential to maximizing the good—because, absent social practices and institutions, no one could have settled expectations about what others will do (see Barry, 217–21).[14] The practice of promise making, for instance, would be undermined if the recipient of a promise knew that overall pursuit of the good may permit or require the promiser, at the time when fulfillment is due, to break her or his vow. This unpredictability, then, is cumulative. Once all actors must decide without settled expectations regarding the actions of others, what any given actor can anticipate from others becomes radically indeterminate, and the probability that a given actor is permitted or required to set aside rules that are merely provisional escalates. Whatever may be the case with other teleological ethics, the telos of maximal creativity requires human cooperation and coordination. This is transparent given a comprehensive purpose prescribing, with whatever constraints our responsibilities to the nonhuman world may involve, our maximal common humanity, a common world of human achievements that maximally provides or promotes the flourishing of all.

That recognition, I suggest, is sufficient to show why the good as defined by neoclassical metaphysics cannot be maximized without deontological norms. Naturally, one may still question whether any teleological ethic can consistently be applied indirectly. Perhaps teleology as such self-destructs precisely because it both requires and nonetheless prevents human cooperation and coordination. Maximal good, it may be said, is impossible without indirect application even while the comprehensive obligation must be directly applied and thus contradicts social practices whose norms one is bound to observe whatever the consequences. To the contrary, I am persuaded, such norms will be consistently prescribed if all human activity implies not only the comprehensive purpose but also a deontological principle and thus a universal social practice. If that is so, both the comprehensive purpose and the deontological principle are necessary presuppositions of subjectivity as such and imply each other, and the principle is an indirect application of the purpose. On my accounting, this is the abiding significance of Kant's legacy. Kantians in something like a strict sense have, with Kant, typically defended some or other deontological principle as a priori or transcendental to human freedom, and the teleological ethic of maximal creativity has good reason to appropriate that conclusion.

Given the metaphysics outlined here, a universal social practice is implied by subjectivity as such because every human activity, upon unifying its relations, conditions what its successors will become. Each, to repeat Whitehead's formulation, "arises as an effect facing its past and ends as a cause facing its future" (Whitehead 1961, 194). Every human decision is, in other words, a self-expression or is pragmatic—whereby each makes or implies a claim for its self-expression as morally valid, at least as morally permissible, and thus consistent with pursuit of maximal good. Insofar as other subjects are affected by the activity, moreover, the decision also claims validity for a moral prescription applicable to them, namely, that each should evaluate the effects received in accord with the same understanding of comprehensive good. This is because all subjects are bound by the comprehensive purpose with which the self-expression claims to be consistent. But, now, "ought implies can," a dictum whose relevant meaning here is, as mentioned previously, that recipients are morally bound by a prescription only if they can decide to act accordingly because it is valid. It then follows that every human activity, in making or implying a moral claim for its self-expression, imposes on itself an obligation to respect the moral freedom of all recipient subjects, that is, their capacity to decide what is morally valid. What follows, in other words, is a deontological principle, prescribing that every subject respect the equal moral freedom of all others. I take this principle to be substantially similar to Apel's "meta-norm" of communicative respect (Apel 1979, 335), and this paragraph is indebted to his Kantian argument. Indeed, we may appropriate the name—the principle of communicative respect—to designate this principle of human rights.[15]

In contrast to Apel, however, the deontological principle is here asserted as the indirect application of a comprehensive purpose, such that the former is an aspect of the latter because both are implied by subjectivity as such, and the purpose cannot prescribe any direct application overriding communicative respect. The moral character of human life, in other words, includes an inviolable obligation to respect human rights—although it should be noted that human rights constitute a community of rights, a universal social practice, so that some may be released from its constitutive obligations if others have violated them. I will not here pursue the details of such release. Nor will I seek here to articulate specific rights implied by this account except to note the following: the universal practice constituted by this deontological principle requires, at least wherever it is possible, a democratic political community, wherein those who are ruled are also the sovereign rulers; that is, the governing order is determined through discussion and debate among the people it governs.

Democracy is, wherever possible, implied by the universal social practice and thus is itself a human right because communicative respect includes political respect for those subject to the same political rule. In claiming the moral validity of one's effects on other subjects, one's communicative respect for their moral freedom is a pledge that one's claim can be, if contested, redeemed by argument or in discourse. A political claim, moreover, potentially affects all other citizens, because politics is a second-order social practice, through which the governance of all action and interaction in the community is determined. Hence, respect in politics—political respect—both recognizes the right of every other citizen to contest one's claim and pledges that, if contested, it can be redeemed in discourse, and this entails one's agreement that governing activities should not be determined by the claim unless it can be so redeemed. Wherever conditions permit, a full and free political discourse is the social practice a political constitution should establish. Given these conditions, a democratic political process is the political expression of communicative respect.

If human rights indirectly apply the pursuit of maximal creativity in the future as such and democracy is, given enabling conditions, implied by communicative respect, we can say that democracy is then implied by the comprehensive purpose. That conclusion can be confirmed, I believe, by showing how, given due attention to the nonhuman world, pursuit of our maximal common humanity and thus the flourishing of all prescribes democratic politics. Although here I will do little more than assert the point, the prescription follows from the telos for the following reason: being the recipient of political respect, being treated as an equal member of "we the people," empowers human flourishing and, moreover, does not conflict with any other conditions of flourishing politics may properly seek to provide. Accordingly, the neoclassical backing for democracy is itself an account finding its rightful democratic place only within the full and free discourse. When this metaphysical proposal in its application to politics prescribes democracy, it carries the pledge that, if contested, it can be redeemed by argument, so that governance should be determined by this proposal only if convincing reasons can be given for it in the public discussion and debate. Affirmation of this telos, in other words, can never be the express business of a democratic constitution.

Nonetheless, the proposal claims to be the valid account of what is implied by the constitution and what ought to be convincing among "we the people." Given due attention to the nonhuman world, political order rightly seeks human creativity, and thus the democratic task is to provide or promote general patterns of interaction among citizens in or through which the achievements of human activity enhance the flourishing of all. Wherever democracy is possible, in other words, pursuit of maximal comprehensive good prescribes indirect application through social practices defined by valid democratic law and, thereby, prescribes the social and political rights to flourishing properly secured by democratic politics. By enjoining and enforcing such practices, politics will do what it can to honor the comprehensive purpose. If and when conditions do not permit democracy, moreover, it remains as a political telos. Other forms of political community, if required or permitted in some circumstance, should include the aim at providing or promoting patterns of interaction in which the flourishing of all is so honored that conditions under which democracy becomes possible are created.

MAKING THE HUMANITARIAN IDEAL EXPLICIT

Maximal creativity as the comprehensive good cannot aid specific private and public decisions without extensive further discussion. But my intent here is a programmatic response to our now heightened sense of humanity as a whole and our need for a humanitarian ideal in the twofold sense: on the one hand, it should affirm the flourishing of all humans, and on the other, all humans, simply by virtue of being human, should have reason to affirm and thus act on the ideal. In the context of this need, I seek to assert the promise of neoclassical metaphysics.

On the one hand, that metaphysics does affirm the flourishing of all humans—and this, we may say, for both moral and religious reasons. Morally, the pursuit of our maximal common humanity seeks, with due attention to the nonhuman world, to maximize the measure in which all humans are empowered to flourish. The deontological principle by which this telos is indirectly applied prescribes human rights to flourishing—including the right, wherever conditions permit, to a democratic political community—such that these rights cannot be overridden by direct application of the comprehensive purpose. Religiously, the flourishing of every human not only enhances others in the world but also makes a difference to the divine or metaphysical individual, which constitutes the ultimate worth of all creativity and without which there could be no worth at all. On the other hand, all humans, simply by virtue of being human, have reason to affirm this ideal, because awareness of the comprehensive purpose is original in human existence. Subjectivity as such believes implicitly, as an inescapable common human experience whenever we understand anything at all, that decisions have worth only because they contribute to the divine good, and one's difference to God is maximized by pursuing maximal creativity in the future as such. In this sense, all humans are finally after the same thing—and all humans know it.

Still, the need in our contemporary context is not adequately addressed by a humanitarian ideal whose ground is implicitly affirmed in common human experience. The course of human events more or less obviously depends on the ends women and men, as individuals and in associations, deliberately or explicitly pursue. Thus, our hope for the human future waits on the explicit representation of this ideal in ways that are effective in human life throughout the world and might increasingly inform deliberate decisions, including especially political decisions, about specific purposes and policies. But we have already acknowledged—or, at least, posited—that all explicit understandings are mediated by the concepts and symbols of an inherited setting or horizon, and the contemporary global community is characterized by a diversity of cultural systems or lifeworlds. How, then, is it possible to have an *explicit* humanitarian ideal by which the human community as a whole can be united?

Nothing makes this question more pressing than our religious diversity. Here, I intend "religion" to designate in what I call its strict sense, namely, the form of culture in terms of which a conviction about human life in relation to its ultimate context is so expressed as thereby to mediate implicit commitment to that belief. A religion, in other words, is a system of concepts and symbols, including symbolic practices, through attention to which a community of people seeks to persuade their own original decisions. Accordingly, a religion includes some or other explicit belief about authentic human life, what all humans ought to be or do—and insofar as differing religions express substantively different convictions, at least some will be at odds with the conclusions of neoclassical metaphysics. Moreover, the differing religious systems in our world are transparently so different that some doubt whether adherents of one can so much as understand the beliefs and practices by which adherents of at least some others are distinguished, and this is why our religious diversity is a special challenge to the need for an explicit humanitarian ideal. On my understanding, the explication of neoclassical metaphysics is not religious in this strict sense, although it purports critically to clarify the understanding religions ought to mediate. Nonetheless, that explication remains a representation whose terms are culturally specific to the Western lifeworld and its philosophical "language game." How, then, can the humanitarian ideal be explicit in the way required to unite the human community as a whole?

The severe difficulties notwithstanding, what we should underscore here, I believe, is the relation between explicit and implicit understandings of human life. If subjective existence as such includes an awareness of one's relation to ultimate reality, religious or philosophical representations of human authenticity can be assessed as valid or invalid through appeal to reasons authorized by common human experience—reasons that determine whether a given religious or philosophical formulation indeed represents what is implied by any understanding at all and thus makes explicit what is original to subjectivity. Because all humans are finally after the same thing, every language and lifeworld must include concepts and symbols, or at least the potentiality for concepts and symbols, in terms of which our original relation to ultimate reality can be made explicit. Thus, differing religious and philosophical language games are best understood as diverse ways in which differing communities express, communicate, and critically assess explications of what all humans commonly know implicitly—and because each such explication seeks to express the same understanding, it follows that each lifeworld includes the possibility of representing in its own terms the same humanitarian ideal.

It also follows that participants in a given lifeworld may, with sufficient effort, understand how those in others explicate the character of human existence as such and its relation to the entirety—precisely because all have the same experience these differing explications claim to represent. Accordingly, participants in differing lifeworlds may engage in argumentative assessment of the adequacy with which differing religions and philosophies represent the human condition. At present, I expect, effective approach to a common ideal within the human adventure waits in part on far greater and more pervasive capacities within the human community for communication with others who inherit very different forms of being-in-the-world. Similarly, discourse about our common human experience waits on the emergence of lifeworld formations more of less global in scope.

In this respect, perhaps changes during the past century, effected principally by the senseless agencies of economic and technological development and through which all humans have increasingly become consequential neighbors of each other, will make an important contribution. At the same time, genuine discourse about the human condition depends on far greater realization of our common humanity and thus commitment to the humanitarian ideal, especially in politics, by those who are presently the principal beneficiaries of economic and technological interaction. That discourse will not occur, in other words, given the massive disparity in economic and social resources available to people in differing countries and, most especially, the abject poverty so much of the human community continues to suffer. Discussion and debate that reaches to religious and philosophical difference in order deliberately to determine our life together is itself a practice dependent for its success on all participants enjoying a significant measure of security and at least relative equality in social and economic conditions. But even then, effective entertainment of a comprehensive end all humans may affirm simply as humans will not occur without the increased presence of what is now all too rarely found in our contemporary world, namely, a willingness to submit differing religious and philosophical claims to the final sovereignty of discursive assessment. Whitehead called it simply "the appeal to reason," to "that ultimate judge, universal and yet individual to each, to which all authority must bow" (Whitehead 1961, 162)—the appeal to reasons authorized by our common human experience.

Whether these possibilities for the human future will be increasingly recognized and embraced is, naturally, uncertain. But they are so much as possible only because all humans originally understand themselves in relation to others and the whole and, thereby, have an attachment to the comprehensive good, pursuit of which seeks the flourishing of all. On my accounting, then, the promise of neoclassical metaphysics is this: it exemplifies—in contrast to any alternative expressing classical metaphysics, Kantian nonteleology, or a post-Enlightenment critique of universal subjectivity—a critical interpretation of the human condition on which the humanitarian ideal may reclaim what Whitehead called its "intellectual justification" (Whitehead 1961, 36), and all humans have the best of reasons to embrace our common humanity.

CHAPTER SIX

REINHOLD NIEBUHR'S THEISTIC ETHIC

The Law of Love

Richard Fox, one of Reinhold Niebuhr's biographers, is surely right in saying, as have many others, that Niebuhr "immersed himself" in "the passing flux of history." He wrote and spoke "with at least one eye firmly fixed on social and political forces" (Fox, 295). We have, then, special reason to note that Niebuhr is not our contemporary. The years in which his major systematic work, *The Nature and Destiny of Man* (1941–43), was published are now decades farther in the past for us than the nineteenth century was then for him. Still, Fox may be hasty when he consigns the significance of Niebuhr's social and political thought to Niebuhr's own time: "He was not a man for all seasons. His social and political views cannot be ripped out of their context and pressed into service today" (Fox, 295). In fact, something like a revival of interest in those views has occurred more recently. As one example, his book, *The Irony of American History* (1952), republished in 2008, seems to many especially pertinent in view of current undiscriminating claims for America's virtue or America's exceptionalism. Also, the forty-fourth president of the United States, Barack Obama, has called Niebuhr one of his favorite philosophers.

NIEBUHR'S SYSTEMATIC PROJECT

In any event, Fox errs dramatically in saying or implying that Niebuhr did not, as did "a Tillich, a Barth, or a Richard Niebuhr . . . mount sustained theological inquiries" (Fox, 295). To be sure, Reinhold Niebuhr never accepted the name "theologian," understanding himself to be a Christian social ethicist, just as his chair at Union Theological Seminary was in "Applied

Christianity." His writings are replete with analyses of communal dynamics, especially their political expressions, thereby understanding the contemporary context against the sweep of Western history by which current problems were conditioned. He excelled in reading and revealing the "dramas of history" (see Niebuhr 1955). At least in this respect, one is challenged to find a thinker whose purchase on the Western inheritance, up to and including his own time, is more instructive today. Still, all of his intellectual power was in service to Niebuhr's principal intent as a Christian social ethicist, namely, to show the abiding importance of Christian faith for understanding history and, thereby, our contemporary problems and possibilities.

Toward that end, he exposed how other abiding views of life's ultimate meaning are not only mistaken but also implicated in the failures of human life and, especially, in its pursuit of justice, and this "negative proof of the Christian faith" or negative apologetic (Niebuhr 1949, 152) was preparation for his Christian theological account of human life in relation to God. In presenting the latter, I believe, Niebuhr mounted a sustained theological inquiry that merits continuing critical assessment far beyond the context of his time. On my accounting, moreover, his achievement is distinguished because he both addressed systematically the central questions about Christian faith and articulated his answers in a way important to current public practitioners. As far as I can see, no thinker during the decades between Niebuhr and our own time has rivaled the comprehensive account of politics and Christian self-understanding his legacy offers.

Niebuhr's proposal may be understood, at least in large measure, as a response to two imperatives: a) to show how human life and history imply a transcendent reality, and b) to show how the transcendent reality requires justice and, therefore, politics rightly pursued. This description of his thought may be repeated in terms he used: Niebuhr advanced a political alternative to those he came to call "the foolish children of light" and the "cynical children of darkness" (Niebuhr 1944, see especially chapter 1), the adherents of differing but commonly nontheistic political positions. On Niebuhr's account, the human self relates to something "beyond itself and the world" (Niebuhr 1941-43, I, 14)* because one cannot act without some "overt or covert presupposition" regarding "the totality of things conceived as a realm of meaning" (1942, 44; see also I, 13–14).

In making this point, Niebuhr intends to explicate the character of every human activity and, specifically, a decision that occurs, to cite one of his formulations, "as an overtone" present at "the outermost rims

---

*Subsequent citations from Niebuhr 1941-43 will be by volume number and page number or numbers alone. References to others of Niebuhr's works will be henceforth by year of publication and page number or numbers.

of . . . consciousness" (I, 127). He speaks, in other words, of an existential experience, which is, at least typically, implicit or in the dim background of consciousness and in which one decides for some understanding of oneself in relation to the totality of which one is a part—or decides about "the center and source" (1942, 45) of the meaning or worth every human activity inescapably claims for itself. This decision of faith, as we may call it, is either to trust in the truth about human life (and, for Christian faith, the true source of our worth is God, the eternal totality) or to rebel against the truth by embracing a false self-understanding, affirming something else as if it, too, could define the realm of meaning.

Moreover, the choice, with integrity or duplicity, of one's source of worth informs or is implicated in the simultaneous decision of how in the given situation to act within the world (see I, 179). The decision of faith is also a decision about how to add oneself to the world here and now. Because it may be or is typically implicit, Niebuhr continues, the existential character of self-understanding should be distinguished from what one may say or think about it explicitly, that is, when one attends to religious or moral questions in the focus of one's consciousness. Naturally, he cannot discuss the two types of political views or "children" mentioned earlier except explicitly, but he intends to mark thereby the existential decisions each type takes to be authentic or true, and in contrast to Christian faith, both are, he says, secularistic because they presume the center and source of meaning to be within the world. More succinctly, then, his project sought to purge twentieth-century political thought of secularistic convictions.

On my understanding, the "foolish children of light" are not secularistic because they are "children of light," that is, because they "seek to bring self-interest under the discipline of a more universal law and in harmony with a more universal good" (1944, 10). Indeed, Christians are, on Niebuhr's account, wise children of light (see 1944, 9, 41). But affirmation of a universal law or good becomes foolish when its center and source are taken to be within history. Children of light then have "a touching faith in the possibility [not to say inevitability] of achieving a simple harmony between self-interest and the general welfare" (1944, 7). The "children of darkness," in contrast, "know no law beyond their will and interest" (1944, 9)—or, at best, the will and interest of a particular community. If they are cynical because they deny any universal law, they, too, are secularistic because that denial implies a particular source of meaning within the world. A political alternative to both, Niebuhr concludes, vindicates democracy against both its defense by optimistic and thus foolish universalists and its discounting by pessimistic and thus cynical particularists. "Man's capacity for justice makes democracy possible; but man's inclination to injustice makes democracy necessary" (1944, xiii). Moreover, such optimism and pessimism exhaust the possibilities open to political theory within secularistic convictions. Hence, the vindication is necessarily a theistic political theory, using "theistic" here in a broad sense, whereby it designates any understanding on which the center and source of meaning is said to be beyond or transcendent to the self and the world (see I, 14).

For Niebuhr, however, conceptions of a transcendent reality—and thus theistic convictions, in this broad sense—are not always consistent with the vindication of justice and, thereby, politics rightly pursued. To the contrary, the transcendent or theistic source of meaning is sometimes understood to be exclusive of history. "Classical idealism and mysticism" deny the meaning of politics in particular and the world in general in the name of a rational or nonrational eternity that "swallows up all particularity" (II, 11, 13). Hence, Niebuhr distinguishes such accounts of eternity, which we may call inclusively those of "classicism," from his intended alternative to both secularism and classicism, and we may call this alternative "authentic theism," which is, for Niebuhr, expressed in the Christian faith. The latter, then, affirms a source of meaning not only transcendent to but also inclusive of the world and, thereby, of history—and thus affirms the meaning of politics. Because the religious alternatives are, for Niebuhr, exhausted by secularism and theism, his own religious conviction may be defined negatively as neither secularistic nor classical.[1]

> Without the presuppositions of the Christian faith, men run into the Charybdis of life-denial and acosmism [classicism] in the effort to escape the Scylla of idolatry [secularism]. Either they make some contingent and relative vitality or coherence into the unconditioned principle of meaning [secularism] or they negate the whole of temporal and historical existence because it is involved in contingency [classicism]. (I, 166)

This typology of religious convictions may be summarized schematically in Figure 6.1.[2]

The purpose of this essay is to examine Niebuhr's thought at a point where his theism and political theory are systematically related—specifically, to examine his theistic ethic.[3] Because he did not consider himself a theologian, he did not, as some have noted, give extended attention to explicating a concept of God (see, e.g., Stone, 225–26). It is nonetheless eminently clear that a proper account of the ethic included in or implied by Christian faith and the reasons why that ethic is superior to alternatives were, for him, a central intellectual concern. At least in large measure, moreover, his constructive political theory was an attempt to articulate the relevance of that ethic to the problems of human communities. Thus, Niebuhr's theism

	source of meaning is			
	transcendent to history THEISM		not transcendent to history SECULARISM
	transcendent source of meaning is		historical source of meaning is
inclusive of the world	not inclusive of the world	universal	particular
AUTHENTIC or CHRISTIAN THEISM	CLASSICISM	"FOOLISH" UNIVERSALISM	PARTICULARISM

Figure 6.1. Niebuhr's typology of religious convictions.

in relation to his interpretation of political life cannot be clarified absent an analysis of his ethic. But if neither his theism nor his political theory will be the principal focus of discussion here, his ethic and its application to politics nonetheless depend on the divine reality. In due course, therefore, it will become important to show how his apparent understanding of God is implicated in his formulation of what he calls the norm of human existence.

The next section will seek to explicate that norm and Niebuhr's argument for it; the following section will offer an assessment. His formulation, I will argue, is compromised by classical implications and thus does not do justice to his own transparent intentions. But I am convinced by his intent to defend authentic theism, and thus the final section will propose a modest reformulation through which his constitutive pursuit of meaning in politics and history as such is, I believe, given its required theistic backing.

NIEBUHR'S ETHIC: HARMONY AND SACRIFICIAL LOVE

Because authentic theism understands transcendent reality to be the center and source of "the totality of things conceived as a realm of meaning" (1942, 44), Niebuhr frequently speaks of "the norm of human existence" as "harmony"—that is, a total or perfect harmony. A human person "knows that he ought to act so as to assume his rightful place in the harmony of the whole" (1937, 295–96; see also 1944, 9, 73). Thus, the "original righteousness" of human existence is said to be "a harmony between the soul and God . . . , a harmony within the soul . . . , and a harmony between the self and neighbor" (I, 286; see also I, 288–89). Or, again: "It is . . . not the highest perfection of man to achieve a unity of being from which all natural and historical vitalities have been subtracted. The highest unity is a harmony of love in which the self relates itself in its freedom to other selves in their freedom under the will of God" (II, 94–95).

Because Christian theism is, for Niebuhr, authentic, he also sees the character of divinity and the norm of human existence disclosed through the special events decisive for the Christian faith—and when his focus is Jesus as the Christ, he speaks of the norm as "sacrificial love" (II, 68). The sacrificial life and death of Christ represent both "the perfect disinterestedness of the divine love" and, simultaneously, "the ethic of . . . *agape*" or "conformity to the will of God" (II, 72, 84). As the divine will to which it conforms, sacrificial love is "disinterested," a definition sometimes replaced in Niebuhr's exposition by the terms "heedless" and "non-calculating" (e.g., II, 72; 1953b, 160–61; 1949, 184). On occasion, these terms can suggest an activity that is "ecstatic" or "spontaneous" in a sense to which discursive thinking is alien (see, e.g., 1949, 184); in the main, however, Niebuhr understands this norm in contrast to all imperatives that affirm attention to one's own self-interest. *Agape* is "a love 'which seeketh not its own'"; "what is demanded is an action in which regard for the self is completely eliminated" (II, 72; I, 287). Sacrificial love is disinterested in, heedless to, or non-calculating of the consequences to self.

For this reason, the Christian ethic is one of "pure non-resistance" (1940, 9–10; see also II, 72). Indeed, Niebuhr's identification of *agape*, "as taught in the Sermon on the Mount" (II, 72, n. 2), with the ethic of non-resistance belies any presumption that he means by sacrificial love simply the willingness to sacrifice the self whenever such is required for the greatest good of all. In his polemic against pacifism, for instance, he is quite clear that self-assertion is *always* a compromise of the Christian ethic.

> The pacifists . . . are forced to recognize that an ethic of pure non-resistance can have no immediate relevance to any political situation; for in every political situation it is necessary to achieve justice by resisting pride and power. They therefore declare that the ethic of Jesus is not an ethic of non-resistance, but one of non-violent resistance; that it allows one to resist evil provided the resistance does not involve the destruction of life or property . . . There is not the slightest support in Scripture for this doctrine of non-violence. Nothing could be plainer than that the ethic uncompromisingly enjoins non-resistance and not non-violent resistance. (1940, 9–10)

The "final goodness," to repeat the point again, "stands in contradiction to all forms of human goodness in which self-assertion and love are compounded" (II, 89).

These two formulations of the authentic norm—"perfect harmony" and "sacrificial love"—complicate a reading of Niebuhr's ethic because, at the least, the sense in which both can designate the same thing is not immediately apparent. On the one hand, perfect harmony seems to include some affirmation of the self, simply because the self is included within the totality. On the other hand, that affirmation seems to be proscribed by sacrificial love. At first blush, in other words, one is led to ask whether Niebuhr in fact presents one or two theistic norms.[4] Whatever the merit of that response, however, it is important to recognize that no such question exists for Niebuhr himself. Indeed, nothing seems clearer in his ethical discussion than his intention somehow to mark with both terms the same essential character of human existence.

Not only does he use both to define the norm of human existence, but also his phrase "the law of love," which refers to the same norm, appears in some contexts as synonymous with "*agape*" (see, e.g., II, 96; 1949, 173–79) and in others as synonymous with "perfect harmony" (see, e.g., I, 16; II, 246; 1938, 70). In more than one passage, moreover, he explicitly asserts a union of the two: "The 'essential,' the normative man, is thus a 'God-man' whose sacrificial love seeks conformity with, and finds justification in, the divine and eternal *agape*, the ultimate and final harmony of life with life" (II, 81). Or, again:

> The principle of equal affirmation of all life is closest to the ideal of sacrificial love, in which each life is subjected to the necessities of life as such. Yet equality is only an approximation of love. The ideal of love fulfills and transcends all law. It fulfills it in the sense that it completes what every high moral law implies. It transcends it in that it presupposes a harmony of life with itself and all life which man in history never realizes. (1938, 94)[5]

Further, his statement that sacrificial love demands "an action in which regard for the self is completely eliminated" (I, 287) occurs within an extended discussion of perfect harmony. As far as I can see, Niebuhr's intent to designate the same ultimate imperative in both ways is beyond informed dissent—and there are, I think, reasons for his doing so, which I will now try to explain.

The unity affirmed by Niebuhr is rephrased in saying that both sacrificial love and perfect harmony are, for him, neither classical nor secularistic.

For this reason, both refer to the same norm. Classical ethics assume a transcendent source of meaning exclusive of history and thus call for "escape from history" either through "contemplation of" and/or "final incorporation into" an "undifferentiated unity of life in eternity" (II, 91, 90, 70). To the contrary, perfect harmony "fulfills rather than negates the historical process," and sacrificial love "is an act within history" (II, 291, 68). Secularistic ethics deny a transcendent source of meaning. To the contrary, sacrificial love "presupposes a harmony . . . which man in history never realizes" (1938, 94). As one might expect, it is principally through the contrast with secularistic ethics that Niebuhr develops his own—and that contrast, therefore, provides an approach to clarity regarding the normative unity of *agape* and perfect harmony in his thought.

More especially, Niebuhr's theistic ethic may be better understood in distinction from the ethic of "mutual love" which is the term he frequently uses for "the highest good" known "from the standpoint of history" (II, 68–69; see also 81–82), that is, within secularistic convictions. Obedience to this norm appears to be defined by the aim at reciprocity of advantages between the self and another or others. "Only in mutual love, in which the concern of one person for the interests of another prompts and elicits a reciprocal affection, are the social demands of historical existence satisfied" (II, 69; see also 247). One must not infer that Niebuhr here defines an activity in which the agent's concern for another is a means toward serving her or his own interest—an activity informed by, at best, "a prudent regard for the interest of the self" (II, 96). A few of his formulations may make this inference plausible (see, e.g., 1949, 176). On the whole, however, he clearly considers prudential self-interest a corruption of mutual love, and the two are easily confused, perhaps, because, as we shall presently discuss, Niebuhr holds that human activity inevitably degenerates into this corruption when mutual love is assumed to be the ultimate norm. Nonetheless, the norm prescribes an activity that aims at *mutual* advantages through reciprocity or cooperation. The self is simply one among the more than one whose interests are pursued. "Coherence and consistency in the whole realm of historical vitality" demand that "all claims within the general field of interests must be proportionately satisfied and related to each other harmoniously" (II, 69). For mutual love, then, the interests of all relevant individuals are equal in merit. "In mutual love and in distributive justice the self regards itself as an equal, but not as a specially privileged, member of a group in which the rational self seeks to apportion the values of life justly or to achieve perfect reciprocity of advantages" (1953b, 160).[6]

Mutual love is secularistic, on Niebuhr's understanding, because activity that takes this as the ultimate imperative presumes to be "justified by historical consequences" (II, 247). To the best of my reading, he never explains precisely what he means by the term "justification," but his intention in the present context can be plausibly inferred. Consider the following citations: "Only in mutual love, in which the concern of one person for the interests of another prompts and elicits a reciprocal affection, are the social demands of historical existence satisfied" (II, 69). "The Christian faith in its profoundest versions has never believed that the Cross would so change the very nature of historical existence that a more and more universal achievement of sacrificial love would finally transmute sacrificial love into successful mutual love, perfectly validated and by historical social consequences" (II, 87). If the "social demands of historical existence" require a reciprocal response to one's concern for another, and if only this successful mutuality provides validation by historical social consequences, we may plausibly conclude that mutual love is justified or validated when its historical consequences include the fulfillment of the agent's interests.

This conclusion is strengthened when we note Niebuhr's assertion that "non-Christian conceptions of love . . . seek to justify love from the standpoint of the happiness of the agent"—or, what appears to be the same, that "mutual love . . . seeks to relate life to life from the standpoint of the self and for the sake of the self's own happiness" (II, 84, n. 16, 82). To consider mutual love the ultimate imperative, then, is to assume that mutuality as intended will be realized, whereby the historical consequences of one's action will include one's own interest fulfillment. In sum, mutual love is secularistic, for Niebuhr, because it assumes a historical coincidence of meaning and fulfillment—or, in the traditional terms, a historical coincidence of virtue and happiness. Activity in obedience to the norm is assumed to be activity that will, as a result in part of reciprocal action by others, maximize the satisfaction of one's own interests. It may be worth repeating here that Niebuhr does not intend to identify mutual love with prudential self-interest. The point is not that an agent's concern for others is simply instrumental; to the contrary, she or he intends the proportionate or reciprocal fulfillment of all relevant interests and assumes that this mutuality will be realized, so that such action is or will be coincident with her or his own happiness.

But this ethical intention inevitably "degenerates from mutuality to a prudent regard for the interests of the self; and from the impulse towards community to an acceptance of the survival impulse as ethically normative" (II, 96; see also II, 70; 1953b, 166). If Niebuhr is correct in this accounting, it warrants his conclusion: "mutuality is not a possible achievement if it is made the intention and goal of any action" and must, therefore, "be the unintended rather than purposed consequence" (II, 69, 84). Moreover, his argument here confirms that he understands mutual love to assume the coincidence described above: degeneration into prudential self-interest is inevitable because the response of the other is unpredictable. Mutuality "is too uncertain a consequence to encourage the venture of life towards the life of the other," so that "actions are dominated by the fear that they may not be reciprocated" (II, 84, 69). If the intention of mutual love cannot be maintained because reciprocity is uncertain, the suppressed premise about this intention can only be its assumed guarantee of realized mutuality. The agent takes her or his action to be meaningful only because, on her or his belief, the intended mutuality inclusive of her or his own interest fulfillment is assured.

Secularism, as noted earlier, is a conviction that the source of meaning is within the world—and, for Niebuhr, this belief is implicit in the presumption of historical "justification." Because a guarantee of the agent's historical fulfillment is then the *sine qua non* of meaningful activity, Niebuhr reasons, the ultimate telos of mutual love must be a community within history—that is, some historical community made particular by the inclusion of just this historical fulfillment. Mutual love seeks historical "harmony with other human interests and vitalities"; the "strategies of mutual love" are those "in which the self, individual and collective, seeks both to preserve its life and to relate it harmoniously to other lives" (II, 74, 96). And where the ultimate telos of activity is presumed to be within history, a historical or secularistic source of meaning is implied.

Some secularistic beliefs, we should recognize, evoke loyalty to a cause to the point where individuals relinquish their own interests and, indeed, their very existence. This is often true of nationalistic commitments and was also true of dedicated communists in Niebuhr's own time, who, on his account, assumed the source of meaning to be the classless society to which they dedicated themselves. As another example, one may well admire all those in the American Civil Rights Movement, including those without any traditional religious belief, who risked their own lives. Attention to these examples suggests that secularistic commitment to mutuality cannot require the self's aim "both *to preserve its life* and to relate it harmoniously to other lives" (II, 96, emphasis added), whatever may be the case in more intimate or local human interaction.

On my reading, Niebuhr's general characterization of mutual love intends to include commitment aimed at some future historical community to which one's present action contributes but in which one may not or will not participate. Hence, the assumption that reciprocity will assure one's own fulfillment is one form of mutual love, and the defining character of all such forms is not a historical "justification" of one's action (the coincidence of virtue and happiness) but, rather, the assumption that present action derives its meaning from a source within history. All forms of mutual love are secularistic. When the intended mutuality does not or does not necessarily include the self's participation, it remains that realization of this perfected community is taken as historically inevitable—because only so can present action have the meaning inescapably claimed for it. Even if realization demands one's own life or occurs subsequent to it, one's life has worth because it contributed to the final goal of history.

This implied affirmation of some historical source of meaning invalidates, Niebuhr argues, the ethic of mutual love. In part, this follows because historical possibilities are indeterminate, and thus no particular historical realization can be the source of meaning for human life, that is, can define the ultimate telos. No particular state of affairs can exhaust all possible value. "The achievements of justice in history may rise in indeterminate degrees to find their fulfillment in a more perfect love and brotherhood" (II, 246). Every historical achievement can be transcended or, to say the same, none can be completely perfect. "There are no limits to be set in history for the achievement of more universal brotherhood, for the development of more perfect and more inclusive mutual relations" (II, 85).

Given the ultimate meaning of historical achievements, this fact about them is, I expect, sufficient to defeat any claim for some historical telos as the source of meaning; that is, action can always be aimed at something better, so that no historical community could provide worth for action as such. In addition, however, secularistic ethics are, for Niebuhr, incoherent because all historical achievements are invaded by immoral activities, pursuits of narrow self-interest. "There is . . . no development towards larger realms of brotherhood without a corresponding development of the imperial corruption of brotherhood. There is . . . no historical development which gradually eliminates those sinful corruptions of brotherhood which stand in contradiction to the law of love" (II, 95–96; see also 1944, 16–17, 48–50). Or, again: "all historical realizations [are] partial and incomplete" in part because "sinful egoism" (II, 74) makes them so, and thus "all such realizations contain contradictions to, as well as approximations of, the ideal of love" (II, 247).

If asked how one knows each of these things—namely, that historical possibilities are indeterminate and, moreover, historical realizations are corrupted by sin—Niebuhr answers: the former follows from the essential human capacity for self-transcendent freedom, and the latter follows from the inevitable misuse of this freedom. On the one hand, "man's freedom over the limits of nature in indeterminate regression means that no fixed limits can be placed upon either the purity or the breadth of the brotherhood for which men strive in history" (II, 244). On the other hand, "sin is natural for man in the sense that it is universal but not in the sense that it is necessary." It "proceeds . . . from a defect of the will, for which reason it is not completely deliberate; but since it is the will in which the defect is found and the will presupposes freedom the defect cannot be attributed to a taint in man's nature" (I, 242).[7] Accordingly, "the Christian view of human nature is involved in the paradox of claiming a higher stature for man and of taking a more serious view of his evil than any other anthropology" (I, 18)—and this paradox is the basic conviction informing Niebuhr's political realism.

But even if one doubts Niebuhr's account of "original sin," in which human decision is inevitably at fault, it remains that all historical communities at least include the possibility of immorality or injustice, that is, of people whose freedom is exercised in pursuit of narrow self-interest and thus without commitment to reciprocity. That fact alone entails the uncertainty of any historical mutuality at which one might aim; its realization cannot be guaranteed, and thus it cannot be the source of meaning. Indeed, the optimism required to affirm history's inevitable perfection of the human community and, thereby, to believe in historical progress, however fitful, toward that consummation is why, for Niebuhr, those who take mutual love as the norm of human existence are *foolish* children of light. When the optimism becomes difficult to sustain in face of historical facts to the contrary, the only secularistic option remaining is one's retreat into a narrow community and, eventually, a prudent regard for the interests of the self as what gives meaning to one's life—presumably because one's own life is that over which one has the most control. The idealist joins the "cynical children of darkness."

The proper end of human activity, Niebuhr concludes, must transcend history; the source of meaning must be transcendent to the world: "the moral and spiritual culmination of the meaning of history, is not within history itself" (1949, 235). Or, again: "Against utopianism the Christian faith insists that the final consummation of history lies beyond the conditions of the temporal process" (II, 291). Perfection "can neither be simply reduced to the limits of history nor yet dismissed as irrelevant because it transcends history. It transcends history as history transcends itself. It is the final norm of a human nature which has no final norm in history because it is not completely contained in history" (II, 75; see also 1958a, 141). It is this perfect community or state of affairs to which Niebuhr refers with the symbol "Kingdom of God" and which he variously describes as "perfect brotherhood" and "perfect harmony" (see, e.g., II, 85; I, 288–89).

We may now return to the unity of perfect harmony and sacrificial love in Niebuhr's thought. Because an ultimate norm prescribing equal but not specially privileged affirmation of the self is secularistic, he reasons, only complete disregard for self (i.e., sacrificial love) is conformity with a harmony transcendent to history. But if this is so, then the imperative to disregard self completely must follow from the meaning of perfect harmony—and Niebuhr so believes. As representing the indeterminate possibilities of human freedom, the argument runs, perfect harmony requires of each individual an indeterminate or limitless love that is compromised whenever self-assertion and thus the interests of the self are introduced. This indeterminate love has, we might say, both intensive and extensive dimensions. Intensively, "there are no exact limits to the degree of imagination with which I may enter into the needs and consider the interests of the neighbor. The love commandment is therefore always a challenge which stands vertically over every moral act and achievement. It defines the dimension, ending in a transcendent Kingdom of God, in which all moral actions take place" (1938, 81). Because at some point the interests of the self will conflict with the fulfillment of the neighbor, attention to the former precludes indeterminate love for another person. "There is always the possibility of sacrificing our life and interest" (II, 74–75; see also 1953b, 159).

Extensively, perfect harmony calls for "a universal love which finite man is incapable of giving" and thus "can only be regarded as a reminder of the indeterminate possibilities of freedom which exist for man despite his finite and parochial loyalties" (1958a, 122; see also 117–18). Because an individual "can set no limit to what he ought to be short of the character of ultimate reality" (I, 163), the admonition of Jesus, "'Be ye therefore perfect as your Father in heaven is perfect,' means, for Niebuhr, "Let your love be therefore all-inclusive as God's love includes all" (1958a, 116, 117). But attention to one's own interests precludes love for those whose fulfillment conflicts with one's own or those who will not reciprocate. "'If ye love them that love you, what thanks have ye?'" is, Niebuhr holds, the biblical expression of the fact that universal love is sacrificial (1953b, 155–59; 1958a, 118; 1938, 75). In short, nothing less than indeterminate love, intensive and extensive, conforms to perfect brotherhood, and nothing less than complete disregard for self is consistent with such perfect love.

The authentic norm, then, "dispenses with historical justification" (II, 247). But conformity with the law of love is not, for that reason unjustified. To the contrary, "the *agape*, the sacrificial love, which is for Christian faith revealed upon the Cross, has its primary justification in an 'essential reality' which transcends the realities of history, namely, the character of God" (II, 96). Given the meaning of "historical justification," it seems fair to conclude that Niebuhr here means to assert a coincidence between authentic activity and *transcendent* fulfillment. Although one's interests may be sacrificed, precisely in sacrificial love the meaning of one's life is coincident with genuine fulfillment—because one is thereby a participant in the Kingdom of God. In other words, the biblical assurance that to lose one's life is to gain it means for Niebuhr that disregard of one's own interests is the purchase of one's true self or transcendent self-realization. "Such a gain cannot be measured in terms of the history which is bound to nature. The gain can only be an integrity of spirit which has validity in 'eternity.' It can have meaning only when life is measured in a dimension which includes the fulfillment of life beyond the present conditions of history" (II, 75; see also 1949, 175–76).

This does not say that humans can live in this world without attention to self or can withdraw from participation in the rivalries of self-interest: "a love which seeketh not its own is not able to maintain itself in historical society. Not only may it fall victim to excessive forms of the self-assertion of others; but even the most perfectly balanced system of justice in history is a balance of competing wills and interests, and must therefore worst anyone who does not participate in the balance" (II, 72). Within history, then, humans are called to seek patterns of mutuality or justice. But these pursuits will achieve more if those who seek mutuality do not assume its inevitable realization, that is, do not make this end "the [ultimate] intention and goal" (II, 69) of their action and thus the source of their meaning. "The grace of *Agape* prevents self-seeking love from degenerating into a consistent egoism and thus has a creative relationship to the whole range of human experience" (1949, 178). In other words, "achievements of justice in history" (II, 246) will be "higher" when those who pursue them recognize that perfect harmony transcends history or—what, for Niebuhr, comes to the same thing—recognize their own account of the good to be partial and likely biased in favor of their own interests and, in any event, understand "that all such [historical] realizations contain contradictions to, as well as approximations of, the ideal of love" (II, 246–47). In that spirit, humans take their action for imperfect harmony to be justified by their relation to God and will, in certain circumstances, sacrifice their interests or even themselves because they live affirming their "tangent towards 'eternity'" (II, 69). Thereby, the impossible norm is relevant to history.

The meaning of this transcendent justification or fulfillment may be explained through the identity of sacrificial love and perfect harmony. In the Kingdom of God, authentic activity conforms to a state of affairs in which "all men are perfectly related to each other, because they are all related in terms of perfect obedience and love to the centre and source of their existence" (1937, 16). If one's interests are sacrificed, one is nonetheless assured of transcendent fulfillment because God's eternal kingdom is "the plane upon which all distinctions between mutual love and disinterested and sacrificing love vanish (II, 86),[8] and Niebuhr can also speak of this transcendent state of affairs as "perfect mutuality" (see, e.g., II, 87, 83). Indeed, fulfillment in God's kingdom is assured—notwithstanding history's pervasive corruptions, including one's own inevitable sin—because, for Niebuhr, the God whom Christians worship is not only the ultimate judge of human fault but also the ultimate redeemer, who forgives all, and this is precisely the point in saying that authentic theism affirms a God who is the totality or includes the world in its entirety.

As a consequence, Niebuhr can affirm the "idea of a 'general resurrection,' in which all those who perished before the fulfillment of history, are brought back to participate in the final triumph," because this symbol "does justice to both the value of individual life, without which the fulfillment of history would be incomplete; and to the meaning of the whole course of history *for the individual*, without which his life cannot be fulfilled" (II, 311, emphasis added; see also II, 36). For Niebuhr, then, the norm of sacrificial love, which prohibits regard for the self, is the same as the norm of perfect harmony, which implies some self-affirmation, because the self that is disregarded is not the same as the self that is affirmed. In the first instance, fulfillment of the historical self is proscribed; in the second, fulfillment of the eternal self is assured.

NIEBUHR'S ETHIC: A CRITIQUE

If the preceding discussion does explicate how Niebuhr understands the ultimate norm of human existence, we might express the conclusion as follows: perfect harmony is the eternal totality or state of affairs in which each individual is characterized by limitless sacrificial love—or, again, such "sacrificial love" designates the intending of each individual and "perfect harmony" designates what each intends. Assuming the appropriateness of this reading, we now have reason to doubt whether Niebuhr has succeeded in formulating the ethic of authentic theism. Because this alternative to both classicism and secularism affirms a source of meaning *inclusive of history*, the ethic of authentic theism should endorse (although, clearly, not be exhausted by) the self's historical realization or fulfillment. But precisely this endorsement is excluded by the imperative to disregard one's own interests completely.

The point may be rephrased: For Niebuhr, we may recall, secularistic ethics are fallacious because they require activity that affirms meaning in history by reason of a historical source, and classical ethics are fallacious because they require activity that denies meaning in history by reason of a transcendent source. If we assume, with Niebuhr, that only authentic theism remains among the logical possibilities, this third alternative must require activity that affirms meaning in history by reason of a transcendent source. For Niebuhr also, however, the norm of human existence requires activity that completely disregards one's own interests, which implies a transcendent source exclusive of them. Because this norm is universal, defining the proper character of all human existence, it follows that fulfillment of every self's interests is excluded from totality as a realm of meaning—and this contradicts the call for activity that affirms meaning in history.

It does not help when Niebuhr says, as he sometimes does, "the highest form of self-realization is the consequence of self-giving, but . . . it cannot be the intended consequence without being prematurely limited" (1944, 19). We may readily agree that self-giving cannot be intended as instrumental to fulfillment of one's own interests, and perhaps Niebuhr's formulation is a wise counsel given our temptation to consider ourselves inordinately important. But he cannot here refer to a "form of [historical] self-realization" and consistently assert a norm of human existence that logically requires complete disregard for the self's interests. Were historical self-realization endorsed, self-giving might well be required because the historical interests of everyone, with no special privilege for one's own, would be the proper intended consequence; but this aim could not logically exclude the self. Moreover, to repeat a point from the previous paragraph, such complete disregard cannot define the norm proper to authentic theism because, given the norm's universality, everyone's highest self-realization would then be exclusive of their own interests, and there would be nothing within history at which self-giving could aim. If your historical interests define a good for all others to pursue, why are they, along with those of all others, not a good for you to pursue? Perhaps, to be repetitious again, there is wisdom in the counsel to live heedless of self, at least for some people in some situations, but no universal meaning of "good" and thus no norm of human existence could consistently include the interests of all others and exclude one's own.

Because perfect harmony is said to imply sacrificial love, in other words, Niebuhr's theistic ethic is not consistently authentic but, rather, compromised by classical implications. I do not mean that he intends this outcome. To the contrary, he unites the two norms because both are, he believes, necessary to an ethic on which a transcendent reality gives meaning to all of history. For this reason, he often contrasts his ethic and those of classicism. "It will be noted that the Christian statement of the ideal possibility does not involve self-negation but self-realization. The self is, in other words, not evil by reason of being a particular self and its salvation does not consist in absorption into the eternal" (I, 251). Or, again: "The Christian ethical norm has little relation to mystical concepts according to which the particularity of egohood is regarded as an evil and redemption is equated with the absorption of individual consciousness into universal consciousness. In contrast to such schemes of redemption from self, the Christian faith does promise self-realization" (1949, 175). These assertions do not, however, mitigate the force of this essay's argument. If the particularity of egohood is not regarded as an evil, then the ethical demand of complete disregard for self must be qualified. If the Christian faith does involve or promise self-realization, then the ultimate imperative calls for something less than indeterminate and thus sacrificial love.

The argument here concludes, in other words, that Niebuhr's formulation of the ultimate imperative violates his own intentions. His ethic is, in that respect, internally inconsistent, and citations like those in the previous paragraph merely confirm this conclusion. The inconsistency is also expressed, I believe, when Niebuhr calls "the *agape* of Christ" a "disclosure of both the divine love which bears history and the human love which is history's 'impossible possibility'" (II, 76). His norm of *agape* is indeed impossible because life within time cannot love indeterminately; history is not the eternal "plane upon which all distinctions between mutual love and disinterested and sacrificial love vanish" (II, 86). Strictly speaking, therefore, a person in whose action "regard for the self is completely eliminated" (I, 287) does not embody the love with which one's essential nature is realized in the Kingdom of God—because the latter is an indeterminate or limitless love impossible within history. Although Niebuhr calls sacrificial love "an act in history" that "transcends history" because "it cannot justify itself in history" (II, 68), a historical individual cannot exemplify the eternal completeness of such sacrificial love. Hence, *agape* in history is, perhaps, better characterized as an act that "symbolizes" or represents—is a disclosure of—the Kingdom of God because "the perfection of man is not attainable in history" (II, 68).

Accordingly, all attention to historical interests, whether one's own or those of others, is a distortion of God's Kingdom and thus of who or what one ought to be. Principles of justice, which prescribe for historical communities, are applications of the law of love only in the sense that application also means incomplete conformity—contradiction to as well as approximation of the norm—and Niebuhr can call this norm a possibility only to say that recognition of one's failure and that of history generally is conducive to higher realizations of justice. In truth, however, an impossible norm cannot express what an exercise of freedom ought to be; that is, "ought implies can"—and the arresting term "impossible possibility" also betrays the classical implications of Niebuhr's ethic.

Candor requires one to note another important implication of Niebuhr's ethic, namely, that moral evil is consequent in part on finitude. Here, too, Niebuhr's intentions are, I believe, violated. The justly celebrated discussion of original sin in his Gifford Lectures takes pains to make clear that moral evil is *always* a misuse of freedom, actualizing a "defect of the will" (I, 242). Still, the relation of that discussion to his theistic ethic is clarified, I think, by attention to his earlier writings, especially *An Interpretation of Christian Ethics* (1935; but see also 1938, 72–79, 94–95), in which the misuse of finite freedom is reconciled with an impossible moral demand.

In that book, the point is signaled when he associates "the Kantian axiom, 'I ought, therefore I can'" with a liberal Christian mistake on which "human nature has the resources to fulfill what the gospel commands" (1935, 65)—a mistake because:

> The human spirit is . . . able to apprehend, but not to comprehend, the total dimension [that is, the eternal God] . . . The consequence is that it is always capable of envisaging possibilities of order, unity, and harmony above and beyond the contingent and arbitrary realities of its physical existence; but it is not capable (because of its finiteness) of incarnating all the higher values it discerns . . . Thus when life is seen in its total dimension, the sense of God and the sense of sin are involved in the same act of self-consciousness; for to be self-conscious is to see the self as a finite object separated from essential reality. (1935, 66–67)

"In the Christian interpretation of moral evil," Niebuhr continues:

> guilt is attached not only to actions in which the individual is free to choose a higher possibility and fails to do so, but in which higher possibilities, which the individual is not free to choose, reveal the imperfection of the action which he is forced to take. Thus the simple moral guilt of conscious evil is transmuted into a sense of religious guilt . . . Even though the highest moral possibility transcends the limits of his imperfect freedom, there is always an immediately higher possibility which he might take. A general sense of religious guilt is therefore a fruitful source of a sense of moral responsibility in immediate situations. (1935, 75–76)

Or, again:

> A significant portion of human wrong-doing is due to human finiteness. This finiteness includes both the imperfect vision of human reason and the blindness of human impulse. . . . It is, nevertheless, a different order and level of evil from the spiritual evil which is the consequence of trying to make the self the center of existence. It is this latter type of evil which is sin in the strictest sense of the word. (1935, 87–88; see also chapter 3 generally)

Here, Niebuhr appears to assert the following: although the full moral demand is impossible, humans also fail to decide for the best possibility genuinely available. All "sin in the strictest sense of the word" *is* a misuse of freedom. Nonetheless, the moral demand transcends the possibilities of a finite will—and this is important because the impossible demand yields a sense of religious guilt that intensifies recognition of the simultaneous misuse.

Later in life, Niebuhr wrote in reflection on An *Interpretation of Christian Ethics*: "I was only dimly feeling my way in this book toward a realistic and valid Christian ethic. I disavowed some of my ideas and amended others in later works, which roughly represent my present position" (1958b, 434–35). In keeping with this judgment, attention to Niebuhr's earlier formulation does not alter a proper reading of his considered or mature position. His incisive analysis of human wrongdoing in the Gifford Lectures equates it, to all appearances, with what he previously called "sin in the strictest sense"; that is, moral evil is so understood as to preclude any implication that finitude is involved therein. This apparent change in his view occurs, we have every reason to believe, in order to preclude any implication that God, creator of finite individuals, is responsible for evil. Nonetheless, the earlier treatment is significant because, notwithstanding a subsequent change, there is no substantial indication that his ethic is reformulated accordingly. To the contrary, only if the demand for indeterminate love is maintained can one make sense of the union between perfect harmony and sacrificial love that pervades Niebuhr's mature position in the Gifford Lectures and beyond (see 1949, 178–79; 1953b, 154–55; 1958a, 122).

Moreover, Niebuhr appears to leave his ethic unaltered for the same reason that his understanding of moral failure is revised, namely, that each is, he believes, required by authentic theism. Just as this religious conviction is incompatible with evil entailed by finitude, so the same theism, he believes, requires an ultimate imperative to which historical activity cannot conform. If the impossibility of Niebuhr's theistic norm is inconsistent with his mature account of human wrongdoing, in other words, this does not count against the reading of his ethic offered here. Rather, the inconsistency is explained by the evolution of his thought—is a consequence of his attempt to correct an error perceived in his earlier account without sacrificing what he held to be essential to his theistic ethic. Either he is not aware of the resulting dilemma or, what is far more likely, he takes it to be the most adequate account of the human condition.

In any event, the classical implications of Niebuhr's ethic are present, I suggest, because his reasoning includes an illicit deduction. Having argued from both the indeterminate possibilities and inevitable corruptions of history to a transcendent end (perfect harmony), he further derives from this telos the demand for indeterminate love of which every affirmation of self-interest is a compromise (sacrificial love). But this further assertion involves a non sequitur. It overlooks—and, therefore, unwittingly collapses—the difference between an *ideal to be pursued* and an *ideal to be illustrated*. It is one thing to prescribe pursuit of perfect harmony; it is quite another to prescribe illustration of this ideal.

This distinction should be clarified: An ideal to be pursued defines proper activity in terms of its telos; an ideal to be illustrated defines proper activity in terms of its character. The two may well be related because the proper character of activity may be defined as pursuit of the telos. But as *pursuit* of the telos, this definition of activity's proper character simply confirms the difference between an ideal to be pursued and an ideal to be illustrated. Let us suppose, for instance, a belief that world peace—understood, say, as commitment by all nations to nonviolence and mutual respect—is a prescribed telos of activity. Accordingly, relevant present activity should seek to promote that state of affairs. World peace is an ideal to be pursued; the pursuit of world peace is an ideal to be illustrated. It is, then, something other to prescribe pacifism, to hold that always acting nonviolently and with respect toward other nations is the proper character of activity or an ideal to be illustrated. Perhaps in some situations, so acting is the best way to promote what one pursues. But that is a further decision requiring further deliberation and is not, therefore, simply synonymous with saying that world peace is the telos of one's activity. Indeed, Niebuhr himself underscores the distinction when he argues with considerable determination that pacifism may be destructive of achieving peace among nations—for instance, in response to the aggression of Nazi Germany (see 1940, chapter 1).

Let us now suppose that someone committed to pursuit of world peace neglects the difference between an ideal to be pursued and an ideal to be illustrated. Having affirmed world peace as the proper telos, she or he infers the imperative always to act as if world peace were realized, as if there were peaceful mutuality, whereby pacifism is prescribed because it illustrates this ideal state of affairs. In a similar way: when Niebuhr argues for a transcendent source of meaning, he defends perfect harmony as an ideal to be pursued; when he infers that perfect harmony requires indeterminate and thus sacrificial love, he transforms this telos into an ideal to be illustrated. In sacrificial love, on Niebuhr's understanding, one acts as if the Kingdom of God were realized and thus illustrates that state of affairs. Having affirmed the Kingdom of God as the proper end, Niebuhr improperly prescribes this kingdom as normative for character.

> Man is self-determining not only in the sense that he transcends natural process in such a way as to be able to choose between various alternatives presented to him by the processes of nature but also in the sense that he transcends himself in such a way that he must choose his total *end*. In this task of self-determination

he is confronted with endless potentialities and he can set no limit to what he *ought to be*, short of the character of ultimate reality. (I, 162–63, emphasis added)[9]

As this critique suggests, a similar problem seems present in Niebuhr's appeal to the indeterminate possibilities of human existence. From the premise of human freedom, one may well conclude that "achievements of justice in history may rise in indeterminate degrees to find their fulfillment in a more perfect love and brotherhood" (II, 246), and thus "no fixed limits can be placed upon either the purity or the breadth of the brotherhood" (II, 244) humans in some distant future might realize. As an ideal by which human freedom is bound, then, perfect harmony or perfect brotherhood is a transcendent telos. It is something other, however, to assert indeterminate possibilities for the freedom of any given activity or any given individual. "The love universalism of the gospels . . . demands a universal love which finite man is incapable of giving. It can only be regarded as a reminder of the indeterminate possibilities of freedom which exist for man despite his finite and parochial loyalties" (1958a, 122). Or, again:

> In so far as man has a determinate structure, it is possible to state the "essential nature" of human existence to which his actions ought to conform and which they should fulfill. But in so far as he has the freedom to transcend structure, standing beyond himself in every particular social situation, every law is subject to indeterminate possibilities which finally exceed any specific definition of what he "ought" to do. Yet they do not stand completely outside of law, if law is defined in terms of man's essential nature. For this indeterminate freedom is a part of his essential nature. (1953b, 154–55; see also I, 170)

Niebuhr's failure to distinguish clearly "indeterminate" as used in relation to history's telos from "indeterminate" as used in relation to the demand on any given individual reflects his transformation of the ideal to be pursued into an ideal to be illustrated.

Because this transformation makes possible the union of perfect harmony and limitless sacrificial love, one has reason to ask whether Niebuhr's argument against mutual love is sound. As the norm of human existence, Niebuhr holds, the aim at mutuality is inherently secularistic because it presupposes a historical location for the source of meaning—either in a reciprocity whereby one's decision is "justified," so that one's meaning is coincident with one's historical fulfillment, or in the inevitable perfection of historical mutuality to which one contributes. On the face of it, this assertion seems peculiar. There is no apparent reason why pursuing fulfillment of "all claims within the general field of interests . . . proportionately" (II, 69) must assume that one's meaning comes from either a guarantee of one's own fulfillment or the eventual historical realization of what is pursued. Indeed, that assumption is inconsistent with that aim—and this for reasons Niebuhr himself gives: all historical realizations are incomplete, in part because they always can be, not to say inevitably will be, invaded by immoral activities, so that reciprocity is always, at best, uncertain.

Thus, Niebuhr has good reason to assert that one can aim at mutuality only if the meaning of one's activity does not depend on realizing what is pursued. If one assumes a guaranteed reciprocity, activity will degenerate into a prudential aim at self-interest, so that one can pursue mutuality only if willing to sacrifice one's own interests. "Love, heedless of the self, must be the initiator of any reciprocal love" (1958b, 442) is, *in this sense*, correct. And when the mutuality to be pursued is universalized, so that all present and future individuals are included, sacrifice may be a frequent consequence, and the grounds on which one is willing to forego the fulfillment of one's own interests may become a pressing matter in ethical theory. But all of this does not mean, as Niebuhr believes it does, that mutual love is self-defeating because it cannot be sustained if taken as the norm of human existence. To the contrary, what follows is the inconsistency of mutual love with historical justification or a historical source of meaning. Indeed, given a pursuit of mutuality that is universalized—whereby the aim in question may be defined as maximal mutuality and, by implication, in the long run—one may argue that mutual love presupposes theism. This argument, too, might call on the very considerations Niebuhr urges against secularistic ethics: "There are no limits to be set in history for the achievement of . . . more perfect and more inclusive mutual relations" (II, 85), and all historical communities include (or, at least, may include) "sinful corruptions of brotherhood" (II, 96).

But if Niebuhr implicitly affirms the theistic entailment of mutual love, why does he explicitly deny it? A possible account might start with his transformation of an ideal to be pursued into an ideal to be illustrated. His neglect of the difference may lead him to read the New Testament dictum, "He that loseth his life for my sake shall find it" (Matthews 10:39; see I, 251; 1944, 19), as expressing the norm of indeterminate love and thus the requirement to illustrate perfect mutuality.[10] If authentic theism calls for sacrificial love, in other words, it follows that mutual love must be secularistic. Already convinced that human nature's "tangent towards 'eternity'" (II, 69) is ethically defined by sacrificial love, he might then conclude that mutual love as the norm of human existence assumes a source of meaning within history, either through a reciprocity in which one's own interests are satisfied or an inevitable perfection of the human community.

Still, that explanation also raises another question, namely, why does Niebuhr, in this understanding of the ultimate imperative, collapse the distinction between an ideal to be pursued and an ideal to be illustrated? This question seems the more apt, perhaps, because we have already mentioned in passing his polemic against pacifism, which depends on something very like a distinction between pursuing and illustrating world peace. Moreover, this polemic is simply a specification of Niebuhr's belief that conditions of higher justice are always something unrealized in history and, therefore, something to be *pursued*. To note this last, however, suggests a reason for his failure to credit the same distinction in reference to transcendent reality. If the distinction applies within history because conditions of higher justice—or, more generally, ends to be pursued—are future and hence remain unrealized, the collapse may occur because Niebuhr understands transcendent reality to be without unrealized states of affairs. For him, to the best of my reading, the Kingdom of God is, always has been, and always will be eternally realized.

More precisely, the distinctions among past, present, and future are, for him, inapplicable to divinity. In saying this, I mean in no way to deny that he intends without evasion to include history within the divine. That the world is good and human life has meaning because God includes them in all of their temporal contingency and particularity is utterly fundamental to his account of authentic theism. But his vision of God who includes the world is, I think, finally determined by the traditional assumption that God is not temporal; for Niebuhr, eternity is the inclusive category for the divine reality. Any attempt by theists to avoid this understanding is, Niebuhr seems to believe, inconsistent with the divine transcendence and thus compromises the Christian faith with secularistic implications or fails to affirm authentic theism with full integrity.

So understanding Niebuhr's concept of God is sustained when he concludes his Gifford Lectures speaking of "two dimensions in the relation of eternity to time," namely: "Eternity stands over time on the one hand and at the end of time on the other." It then becomes apparent that eternity is identical in both dimensions: "The eternal is the ground and source of the temporal. The divine consciousness gives meaning to the mere succession of natural events by comprehending them simultaneously, even as human consciousness gives meaning to segments of natural sequence by comprehending them simultaneously in memory and foresight" (II, 299). In other words, the totality to which every exercise of human freedom is forced to relate itself is eternally complete—including past, present, and future events in all of their detail in one nontemporal reality. Hence, "we are . . . confronted with the formidable difficulty of asserting what seems logically inconceivable, namely, that eternity will embody, and not annul, finiteness, or, in the words of Baron von Hügel, that the 'total abidingness of God' will not destroy our 'partial abidingness'" (II, 297).

To all appearances, Niebuhr does indeed mean that a literal statement designating God's nature is logically absurd or contrary to human reason. A later essay, entitled "Coherence, Incoherence, and the Christian Faith" contrasts "strictly rational terms of coherence" with the "suprarational character" of the divine and thus the "final coherence of life" (1953b, 183, 181, 184)—and in a later book, he reformulates von Hügel's point: "This picture of fulfillment involves the rational absurdity of an eternity which incorporates the conditions of time: individuality and particularity" (1949, 137).[11] The absurdity occurs, if I understand rightly, because "there will be time in eternity" (1953b, 181) asserts literally that something completely changeless (eternity) includes changes (the conditions of time). Niebuhr is entirely clear, in other words, that change in any part of a whole is, literally speaking, change in the whole. Accordingly, his arguments against alternatives to authentic theism notwithstanding, "it is not possible for finite minds to comprehend that which transcends and fulfills history" (II, 289). To the contrary, "knowledge of the true God . . . can not be supplied by a further rational analysis of the human situation" (1949, 165) but, rather, "involves a definition of God which stands beyond the limits of rationality" (1953b, 184). Or, again: "The only principle for the comprehension of the whole (the whole which includes both himself and the world) is therefore inevitably beyond his comprehension. Man is thus in the position of being unable to comprehend himself in his full stature of freedom without a principle of comprehension which is beyond his comprehension" (I, 125). The paradox in this statement is clarified, I think, if Niebuhr's intention is so understood that his last sentence asserts an ultimate comprehension beyond the limits of rational comprehension.

This is why, for Niebuhr, "the finite mind can only use symbols and pointers to the character of the eternal," and "the Biblical symbols, which deal with the relation of time and eternity, and seek to point to the ultimate from the standpoint of the conditioned [or temporal]" cannot be taken "literally" but should be taken "seriously." If the symbol is understood literally, eternity and thus God's transcendence is reduced to temporality or given a secularistic meaning, and if the symbol is "dismissed as unimportant," history is not taken seriously and "eternity . . . annuls rather than fulfills the historical process" (II, 289). Niebuhr's "ultra-rational" (I, 16) understanding of God's character is expressed, I think, by how consistently he formulates the meaning of Christian faith and thus of Biblical symbols by stating what they do not mean—and these formulations are, at least more often than not, differing ways of saying that authentic theism is neither secularism nor classicism.

As far as I can see, Niebuhr's conviction that God's character is suprarational and thus can be designated only by symbols or myths led him to formulate a dialectical relation between general and special revelation of the divine—both of which he understood to occur existentially. Special revelation is required for a positive awareness of our eternal source of meaning and thus a full understanding of our own nature precisely because that divine source is beyond our rational comprehension. But for the same reason, general revelation—and thus a common human experience of standing somehow in relation to a reality the world cannot contain—is required if something suprarational is to be received. "Nothing is so incredible as the answer to an unasked question" (II, 6). Absent general revelation, therefore, the special revelation of God's character, preeminently in Jesus as the Christ, "would not gain credence" (I, 127). But absent special revelation, the "unconditioned ground of existence, this God, can be defined only negatively," and the common human experience of standing "too completely outside" of both self and world to understand oneself "in terms of either without misunderstanding" oneself (I, 14, 15) "would remain poorly defined and subject to caprice" (I, 127).

On my accounting, the mark of a truly systematic theist is this: her or his thought about any other theological issue implicates her or his understanding of God, because the divine reality is the primary source and final end of all things. In the case of Niebuhr, that understanding may not be something on which he focused his critical attention. Perhaps, therefore, he accepted without sustained examination the traditional assertion that God must be completely unconditioned or eternal—even while his abiding conviction about the goodness of creation and the meaning of history led him to speak of eternity including time and, thereby, to disagree with other theologians for whom a completely changeless God is also a divine simplicity. But if the character of God did not command Niebuhr's extended critical reflection, he was nonetheless a truly systematic theist who was lucid about the concept he affirmed—and thus his answers to all other systematic theological questions about human life implicate his understanding of the divine reality. In any event, his ethic, if I have understood it rightly, does so, and for that reason, it is compromised by classical implications. Accordingly, the traditional idea of God is not essential to authentic theism but is, to the contrary, itself compromised by classical implications.

The conclusions here, then, give reason to doubt that Niebuhr's theistic ethic will adequately serve his attempt to relate theism and political theory. Classical theism, as he defines it, denies the meaning of politics. Given that consequence, it is important to say again that his intention is unequivocally to the contrary. His constitutive purpose is so to understand politics in particular and history in general as to affirm both their meaning and their transcendent or theistic source. There is no more telling evidence of this reading than Niebuhr's account of "the most distinctive content of special revelation" (I, 143) in Jesus as the Christ—and, especially, in "the Cross of Christ" (I, 142). It discloses the divine mercy or forgiveness "as the final revelation of the personality of God" or "the revelation of God's freedom in the highest reaches of its transcendence," and the Cross, above all, is the assurance of divine mercy because it reveals that "God takes the sinfulness of man into Himself" (I, 142). God, we can believe, "has resources of love and redemption transcending His judgments" (I, 143) because Jesus reveals that God suffers. "It is God Who suffers for man's iniquity" (II, 46). As far as I can see, nothing expresses more fully Niebuhr's intent to affirm that God includes all the distinctive deeds of history than the suffering of God for the abiding misuse of human freedom. It is, then, this constitutive affirmation to which, on my reading, his conceptions of God and ethics give compromising formulation.

If this judgment is correct, one is not surprised to find Niebuhr preoccupied throughout most of his theological writings with the "application" of the ultimate imperative to political activity—or, as he also puts it, "the relation of Christ's perfection to history" (II, 76f.). The pivotal chapter of his early systematic work is entitled "The Relevance of an Impossible Ethical Ideal" (1935, 97). He writes in 1940s: "It is no easy task to do justice to the distinctions of good and evil in history . . . and also to subordinate all these . . . to the final truth about life and history which is proclaimed in the gospel. Every effort to do it involves the whole paradoxical conception in Biblical faith" (II, 198). And he asserts in the 1950s: "There is, in short, no social ethic in the love universalism of the gospels" (1958a, 118), so that "the problem of the application of the law of love to the collective relationships of mankind contains within itself the whole possibility of a Christian social ethic" (1953a, 237). Precisely because his ethic is compromised by classical implications, in other words, the question of its relevance to political activity is, for Niebuhr, continually seeking adequate formulation.

NIEBUHR'S INTENTIONS REVISITED

I wish now briefly to offer a revised account of the ethic dependent on authentic theism. To be sure, the previous conversation with Niebuhr does not necessarily commend a discussion in this direction. One is led to secure Niebuhr's intentions only if the arguments about human existence on which his constitutive purpose depends are credible. As the reader may have surmised, however, I find convincing his general account of our existential decision and his reasons for denying both meaning in history without a transcendent reality and a transcendent reality without meaning in history.

Summarily stated: secularism is, I think, incredible because the worth every self-conscious decision necessarily affirms for itself is ultimate worth, such that nothing within history can be its source; classicism is, I think, incredible because the worth every self-conscious decision necessarily affirms for itself is the ultimate worth of something contingent and particular, such that the source cannot be exclusive of history. Accordingly, Niebuhr's achievement includes a sound *negative* argument for authentic theism as the source of meaning for politics.[12] This alone counsels attention to his political realism if one seeks an adequate understanding of political problems and possibilities in our own time. Still, his negative argument—or negative apologetic—calls for a convincing positive formulation of authentic theism and the comprehensive norm by which all human activity is bound, a formulation on which Niebuhr's theistic ethic is purged of its classical implications.

That formulation, I believe, will deny that "eternity" is the inclusive designation of our theistic source and, thereby, remove Niebuhr's transformation of the ideal to be pursued into an ideal to be illustrated. Authentic theism then properly conceives of God as the eminently temporal whole of reality, which again and again has unified everything that has occurred in the world, thereby giving to it everlasting worth, and which will again and again add to this whole everything that does occur in the world when it occurs. On this account, the existence of some world or other is as necessary to God as God is to the world, although only God is the necessary individual whose activities continually unify all of the world and thus again and again constitute "totality . . . as a realm of meaning" (1942, 44). The divine reality is indeed eternal, in the sense that God's character as the individual inclusive of strictly all that has happened is independent of strictly everything that so much as could happen—but this eternal divine character is only the most abstract feature of the concrete whole or series of concrete wholes that always has and always will change with whatever changes do occur in the world.

Against Niebuhr's apparent belief, moreover, God as eminently temporal is not inconsistent with divine transcendence because the necessary individual is infinitely different from any possible worldly or contingent thing and transcends the world in the way a concrete unity transcends its diverse parts. Some decades ago, Schubert M. Ogden argued for secular but not secularistic Christian theology, that is, a critical explication and assessment of Christian faith on which unqualified human concern for this world and its affairs can be and is affirmed only because the world depends on the God decisively represented in Jesus as the Christ (see Ogden 1966, 1–70). The affirmation of an eminently temporal individual is, as Ogden shows, secular but not secularistic. Loyalty to the entire world is affirmed because and only because all worldly achievements are ultimately significant through their inclusion within the divine temporality. In saying this, I mean to propose that neoclassical theism, for which the systematic proposals of Alfred North Whitehead and Charles Hartshorne are the classic resources, is far more promising than the traditional understanding inherited by Niebuhr.

Reconceiving Niebuhr's eternity inclusive of time as a temporal totality inclusive of its eternal character would require changes elsewhere in his theological formulations, and this is simply to repeat how thoroughly systematic Niebuhr's theism is. Among other things, I expect, the revised concept would commend revisiting the relation between the meaning of one's life and, to use Niebuhr's term, its "justification." To be sure, he does not, to the best of my reading, ever define his use of that term, and perhaps one could take him to mean simply the ultimate worth of one's self-conscious decisions. As I discussed previously, however, he seems more often to imply that one's activity is justified when a decision for it is coincident with one's own, at least eventual fulfillment or self-realization. Thus, mutual love, at least in some instances, assumes what cannot be the case, namely, the historical inevitability of one's fulfillment; in contrast, sacrificial love is justified by its "tangent towards 'eternity'" (II, 69). Fulfillment or self-realization is truly assured only in the Kingdom of God, where "all distinctions between mutual love and disinterested and sacrificing love vanish" (II, 86). This accounting accords with Niebuhr's apparent belief in an eternal totality, which is, while unchangeable in all respects, both above time (the vertical dimension), whereby our lives have meaning, and at the end of time (the horizontal dimension) symbolized in Christian faith by the "idea of a 'general resurrection,' wherein "all those who perished before the fulfillment of history, are brought back to participate in the final triumph, . . . without which his [the individual human's] life cannot be fulfilled" (II, 311)—and eternity is both above and at the end because, while nontemporally complete, it nonetheless includes time.

If that concept of God is untenable, and if God is properly understood as the necessary individual who again and again unifies the totality, a coincidence between meaning and fulfillment is, I think, debatable. That the divine whole receives strictly everything in the world and gives to it everlasting worth—what we may call metaphorically, the vertical relation of God to our every deed—is indeed the irrevocable assurance that our decisions and our lives have ultimate meaning. But whether our lives as persons or individuals will be fulfilled is, I expect, a horizontal question about what occurs in the world, and because worldly events depend in significant measure on what creatures do with their freedom, God could not possibly vouchsafe such fulfillment.

To be sure, critical attention to this issue should consider possibly different meanings of "fulfillment" or "self-realization" as part of a substantially extended discussion. Still, I am troubled that an ultimate coincidence of meaning and fulfillment seems to deny the possibility of genuine sacrifice for the sake of maximizing the good; whatever appears to be sacrifice is said to be canceled by eternal fulfillment. Further, evil in the human community—for instance, wanton cruelty or injustice—is in truth without ultimate consequence because, given God's transcendent mercy, both perpetrators and victims are eternally fulfilled. Finally, what Niebuhr appears to mean by justification in eternity seems to imply that living for God is coincident with living for self, since the former has as its ultimate consequence the self's realization. As far as I can see, to accept the gift of ultimate meaning is also to claim the privilege of maximizing our worth by living not for ourselves but, rather, for the divine good, whereby we embrace our distinctively human vocation by loving God and all God loves, whether or not our good or fulfillment is simultaneously served.

This is not to qualify in any way what divine love means, namely, that each person is precious to God, and each person's flourishing is the object of God's purpose. The question is whether any conceivable divine goodness could possibly assure to all humans the fulfillment so apparently denied to some by conditions and events of history—or whether instead, as Niebuhr himself implies at the outset of his Gifford Lectures, what God's all-embracing love provides is rest for the "essential homelessness of the human spirit," that is, the "meaning of life" that cannot be found in ourselves or the world and thus defines our true self-understanding (I, 14). In the end, notwithstanding Niebuhr's assertion of "justification in . . . the character of God" (II, 96) and "the fulfillment of life beyond the present conditions of history" (II, 75), I am not entirely sure how he wishes to be understood. All talk of God or the Kingdom of God is, he says, symbolic or mythological, to be taken seriously but not literally, so that fulfillment beyond history is not something he claims to comprehend and, rather, may be a different reality than whatever "fulfillment" means within history. In that respect, Niebuhr's account of "fulfillment" in eternity may be similar to Kant's noumenal account of "happiness" in the condition where all agents are holy (see Kant 1956, 114–36); in either case, the designation of the term is not its designation in the straightforward or literal sense. Hence, one cannot be sure about Niebuhr's intention in speaking of "an integrity of spirit which has validity in 'eternity'" (II, 75).

Still, he would, I expect, be willing to revisit his formulations of our "tangent towards 'eternity'" (II, 69) because, as I am inclined to think, he would have endorsed neoclassical theism had he understood the alternative it offers. Had he been given to think of God as eminent temporality without implying that totality is a final event in history, and thus to think of totality as the realm of meaning without implying God's suprarational character, he would have embraced the general revelation of God as redeemer of the whole world—because that understanding of authentic theism does justice to so many of his theological affirmations.[13] Indeed, his address to other central theological questions often begs for an understanding on which the divine character is present in common human experience and, therefore, can be validated, as classicism and secularism can be invalidated, by reasoned reflection on what is implicitly understood by all women and men.

This is the case, for instance, when he presents his classic treatment of original sin as a rebellion against God. One cannot decide for something defined only by negation and thus cannot be responsible for a failure to do so, but sin is, on Niebuhr's analysis, universal in human existence; accordingly, he implies an understanding of God's character present in our existential situation as such. Indeed, at one point, Niebuhr himself appears to recognize this implication, notwithstanding his formulations to the contrary in his account of special revelation: "Experiences of repentance . . . presuppose some knowledge of God. They may not be consciously related to Biblical revelation but yet they do presuppose some, at least dim, awareness of God as redeemer as well as God as judge" (I, 257).[14] Again, his discussion of our essential nature and thus the norm of our existence, which is nothing other than conformity to God's law of love, at least suggests a universal awareness of its character: "Christian thought has consistently maintained that the law must be regarded not simply as something which is given man either by revelation [he means here, I think, special revelation], or for that matter by the authority of society, but as written on the heart. This can only mean that the requirements of action, dictated by man's essential nature, are a part of his real self" (I, 274–75). Accordingly, his political realism calls for due attention to both our "self-regarding and social impulses," recognizing "that the former is stronger than the latter" (1965a, 39), because our essential nature is not lost even when we inevitably sin—and he often so speaks of humans quite independently of whether they confess Jesus as the Christ. "Man's capacity for justice makes democracy possible; but man's inclination to injustice makes democracy necessary" (1944, xiii).

Moreover, these anthropological accounts (of original sin and our essential nature) are differing expressions of Niebuhr's thoroughly existentialist analysis of common human experience, the experience of finite freedom: self-conscious existence in its every moment decides at least implicitly or inchoately for an understanding of its meaning in relation to the totality to which we belong. Accordingly, human existence is constituted by some "overt or covert presupposition about the meaning of life" (1942, 44). Above all, then, Niebuhr would, I am persuaded, recognize neoclassical theism as the proper completion of his project simply because his most fundamental conviction, namely, that God is the source of worth every human asks about in every existential decision, and thus God suffers to redeem history in its entirety, would be so thoroughly vindicated—without the logically incoherent assertion that time cannot be ultimately real because all of history is somehow eternally realized.

Whatever the merit of that speculation, the consequence of this neoclassical revision for the norm of human existence is the theistic backing for mutual love. In relation to the eminently temporal reality, our essential nature is defined by an ideal to be pursued, and the ideal to be illustrated is pursuit of that telos. The comprehensive or divine purpose, at least insofar as the human future is significant, prescribes the aim at maximal mutuality among all persons in order to maximize what God includes and, thereby, the divine good. We may agree that "man's inclination to injustice makes democracy necessary"; that is, wisdom with respect to human nature counsels the widest possible distribution of political power in order to protect against political domination. Still, this form of government is also vindicated because democratic politics is the political form of human mutuality, the political process whereby politics itself exemplifies the aim at maximal human mutuality, the telos wherein each individual flourishes through her or his appreciation of and contribution to the fulfillment of all. Because God is the source of meaning in history, however, so understanding the ultimate imperative does not imply a historical justification or threaten degeneration into prudential self-interest. To the contrary, a person's pursuit of maximal mutuality is willing to sacrifice interests of the self because meaning is not derived from a guaranteed historical outcome but, rather, from the God who assures that "fine action is treasured in the nature of things" (Whitehead 1961, 274).

CHAPTER SEVEN

ON THE LOSS OF THEISM

A Conversation with Iris Murdoch

Iris Murdoch was a reserved friend to theistic religion. In that relationship, she was obviously reserved, because she was not herself a theist. Given the contemporary Western philosophical setting, however, those who affirm the reality of God might well be tempted to feature her friendship in a manner that neglects the circumspection with which it was offered. After more than a century that has been, on the whole, decidedly unfriendly to metaphysics and, especially, has massively denied its necessity for moral theory, her articulation of "metaphysics as a guide to morals," the title of her 1993 book based on her 1982 Gifford Lectures, is, at least for philosophical theists, a welcome exception—and they should be the more grateful by virtue of the comprehensive scope, argumentative force, and insight into the human condition with which her proposal is advanced. When one adds her insistence that morality is necessarily related to religion and, further, her reassertion of fundamental importance in the ontological argument, the fact that Murdoch herself was not a theist is of little consequence with respect to widely accepted alternatives in which philosophical theism is currently discredited. But just because they have the best of reasons to appreciate and admire her achievement, theists cannot ignore her considered refusal to affirm a divine reality. In this essay, then, I will pursue an understanding and assessment of her reservation.

EMPHATIC MORAL REALISM

Because philosophy and, specifically, moral theory have so long been unfriendly to metaphysics, it will be useful first to clarify what Murdoch means by metaphysical thinking. This is clearly something other than empirical science and, moreover, something other than empirical thought generally—where the latter includes any thought about the variable conditions of human life and the world of which it is a part. In contrast, metaphysics seeks "to promote understanding of very general features of our lives" (Murdoch 1993, 212).* We may take this to mean the *most* general or abiding features of the human condition, because she also says that metaphysical systems offer "huge general *pictures* of what 'must be the case' for human being to be as it is" (259). Metaphysics attends to what is "essential" and what "must be built into the explanation at the start" (55)—and for this reason, seeks to show us "the internal relations between concepts of great generality" (434).

Because "good metaphysical arguments" (395) "make models of the *deep* aspects of our lives" (55), they "are successful appeals to experience" (395). The enterprise is possible, in other words, because "levels and modes of understanding are (somehow) levels and modes of existence. My general being coexists with my particular being" (146). Metaphysics "sets up a picture which it then offers as an appeal to us all to see if we cannot find just this in our deepest experience" (507). Thus, Murdoch can also write that metaphysical thought is "partly circular" because "determined to *argue* for something which it already *knows*" (435; see 511). For her, we might even say, metaphysics "leaves everything as it is"—except explicit ignorance or self-deception.

Still, that description alone permits misunderstanding, because the same might be said of Kant. His "prolegomena to any future metaphysics," which limits the most general features of our lives to those specific to human subjectivity, theoretical and practical, also intends, in its own way, to explicate the essential characteristics of human being. Notwithstanding other ways in which Kant is important to her, however, Murdoch is, in this respect, Platonic rather than Kantian. Adequate concepts of the greatest generality are not limited to those about subjectivity, much less about our language or about our historically specific form of life. They may also picture the deep or fundamental character of reality, because what we already know in our deepest experience is our encounter with a real world that transcends us, in distinction from what merely appears. Metaphysics, some have said, includes both a broad and a strict sense of its task. On the former, one seeks to explicate the conditions specific to possible subjectivity or existence with understanding as such, and on the latter, one seeks to explicate the conditions of possible existence as such—and the two are systematically related

---

*Subsequent citations from Murdoch 1993 will be by page number or numbers alone.

because the broad sense implies or includes the strict sense. Subtleties aside, I judge, Murdoch reaffirms this understanding, and this essay will, contrary to the general practice in previous essays, use "metaphysics" and "metaphysical," in her twofold sense.

Whatever else she offers in her picture of the deep character of reality, surely its most important aspect is what she calls "the ubiquity of value" (250) or "the omnipresence of value" (259). With Plato, "goodness is connected with reality" in the profound sense that Murdoch implies with the assertion: "the supremely good is the supremely real" (398). This does not mean that all reality is good, at least not in the sense that all real things are equally good. Rather, the ubiquity of value is the omnipresence of "an opposition between good and bad" (259) in the world we encounter. If I understand her rightly, the reality to which we are related *is* its value—good or bad, better or worse—and for this reason, Murdoch's project includes a persisting and powerful critique of all philosophical proposals that assert, in one way or another, the separation of fact and value. She is, on my reading, in full accord with Whitehead's affirmation: "Our enjoyment of actuality is a realization of worth, good or bad. . . . Its basic expression is—Have a care, here is something that matters!" (Whitehead 1938, 159).

The separation of fact and value, Alasdair MacIntyre has written, is "the epitaph" of the Kantian or Enlightenment project—and, for MacIntyre, the modern dissolution of moral theory derives from the dominance of this separation in thinking subsequent to Kant (MacIntyre, 56). On my reading, MacIntyre does not credit metaphysics in Murdoch's sense, and for this reason, she finds more to affirm in Kant's critique of practical reason, especially in the religious character of the categorical imperative. But she also agrees that "most recent [moral] philosophers" are "neo-Kantian" (46) because they sever the connection between goodness and reality and do so for reasons that may be traced to Kant's critique of theoretical reason and, thereby, his separation of knowledge and morality. Resisting this dominating picture of our cognition, she reaffirms that consciousness as such "is a form of moral activity" (167). "Value, valuing, is not a specialized activity of the will, but an apprehension of the world, an aspect of cognition, which is everywhere" (265). Or, again: "It is certainly often worth saying: Look at the facts! . . . But what we look at, and attempt to clarify and know, are matters in which value already inheres. . . . Value goes right down to the bottom of the cognitive situation" (384). Because reality is its value, apprehension or cognition must be an evaluation, and this view is so far from a fact/value separation that she can say: "Perception itself is a mode of evaluation" (315).

It follows that the good life should be inclusively understood as a quest to apprehend or be conscious of reality—or, if we may speak redundantly, to apprehend reality truly. Morality is identified in terms of reality; "the good man perceives the real world, a true and just seeing of people and human institutions" (475). Murdoch is, we might say to characterize her position as a whole, a moral realist in an emphatic sense. Not only are moral values real because they transcend our explicit interpretation or construction of them, but also all of reality as the object or possible object of human attention is good or bad in a morally relevant sense. With Plato, then, we should understand human life as "a spiritual pilgrimage from appearance to reality" (10), a metaphysical fact given unsurpassed expression in his myth of the cave. "Life is a spiritual pilgrimage inspired by the disturbing magnetism of *truth*, involving *ipso facto* a purification of energy and desire in the light of a vision of what is *good*" (14).

Cognition or apprehension as a moral good is something for which we must quest because human consciousness is prone to distort the world egoistically and, thereby, to see the world through prejudices, illusions, and fantasies that accord with our own unrealistic evaluations of ourselves. "The human mind is naturally and largely given to fantasy" (322), and our energy is "naturally selfish" (Murdoch 1970, 54). Murdoch would not, I expect, object to saying that human illusions can take the form of self-debasement as well as self-aggrandizement—as, for instance, in the possibility that victims of racism internalize the prejudice of their victimizers and, insofar, see the world with the same debasement of themselves. In any event, "the world is not given to us 'on a plate,' it is given to us as a creative task" (215). What we require, or what is required of us, then, is "a progressive redemption of desire," a movement that is "patiently and continuously a change of one's whole being in all of its contingent detail," that is, the detail of one's cognition or consciousness, "through a world of appearance toward a world of reality" (25). Moral advance *is* the movement toward reality.

This pervasive connection between cognition and morality is not an ethic that elevates the *vita contemplativa* over the *vita activa*, as Plato's thought has sometimes been accused of doing. Truthful cognition is internally related to or expressed in good action. "The whole of morality involves the discipline of desire which leads to instinctive good action" (384). Another way to make the point is to underscore the incurably personal character of the moral pilgrimage, "and belief in this person is an assertion of contingency, of the irreducible existence and importance of the contingent" (349). A contemplative understanding of human life in some sense that depreciates action cannot consistently include the importance of particularity. In contrast, Murdoch's moral realism affirms the significance of human life in all of its contingent detail.

GOOD WITHOUT GOD

Enough has already been said to confirm that Murdoch is, at least in the contemporary philosophical setting, a friend to theistic religion. If it departs from the dominant consensus of moral theory after Kant, her emphatic moral realism is also a conviction to which theists, at least those who have sought metaphysical formulations, have traditionally adhered. "Goodness and being," says Thomas Aquinas, "are really the same, and differ only in idea" (Aquinas, 34). But the concert between Murdoch and the theistic tradition is the more profound because, for her, too, emphatic moral realism implies an idea of something that is beyond us and all else in the world, an idea of perfection.

"We *know* of perfection as we look upon what is imperfect" (427)—above all, the imperfection of people and human institutions. Human life as a moral pilgrimage implies an ideal of *the* Good, "a distant moral goal, like a temple at the end of the pilgrimage, . . . glimpsed but never reached" (304), to which or by which this quest is oriented. This implication may also be expressed through noting that contingency is "irreducible incompleteness." Given "the essential contingency of human life" (490) and its world, the connection of goodness and the things in our experience is always more or less incomplete, and thus we also "*experience* both the reality of perfection and its distance away" (508), an absolute or complete good through which incompleteness is identified. Moreover, "the idea of the perfect object is one with its reality" (400), because the moral character of reality "is not one empirical phenomenon among others. . . . [It] cannot be 'thought away' out of human life" (412), and showing this is the abiding significance of the ontological argument. We experience, in Paul Tillich's words, the "unconditional element in the structure of reason and reality" (cited, 432).

Just this unconditional element of morality makes it essentially religious, because religion is concerned with "the absolute in a specifically moral way" (140). "Religion is a mode of belief in the unique sovereign place of goodness or virtue in human life" (426)—"the *attachment* to an ultimate and fundamental demand," indeed, "the *love* of that demand" (146). Morality is religious because the essence of the former is orientation or attraction to the unconditioned Good that "exerts a magnetism which runs through the whole contingent world," and "the response" to which "is love" (343). Of this religious reality also, unsurpassed expression occurs in Plato's myth of the cave. The idea of perfection or Form of the Good is the sun to which all consciousness is attracted because in its light alone do we see what is real, and in this respect, Murdoch repeats in her own way the characteristic theistic assertion that we see "everywhere in the world" (398; see also 474) the God who is beyond or above all of the world.

But the Good is not God. Murdoch's metaphysics moves "from 'God' to 'Good,' taking 'religion' along too" (426). This is the central respect in which her proposal occupies common ground with those who pursue a demythologized theology, and she can say: "the 'demythologisation' of religion is something absolutely necessary in this age" (460). Notwithstanding that some may "extend the meaning of our word 'God' to cover *any* conception of spiritual reality," including the idea of perfection, in truth "'God' is the name of a supernatural person" (419; see also 425), and God and the Good differ because the latter may be loved but is not loving, while the former means a supreme person or Thou who is responsive to us. "God is love" is, perhaps, the identifying conviction of theistic religion (see 342–43).

We need a "theology that can continue without God" (511) not simply because the picture of a loving, supernatural Thou is increasingly inaccessible to or unpersuasive within modern modes of thought. The concept of God is also problematic for more profound metaphysical reasons. A supreme person must be a supreme individual. But a supreme being, if it is not totalizing in a sense that implicitly denies all differences, "becomes one more contingent thing among others, even if the grandest one" and, therefore, cannot be "the 'unconditional element in the structure of reason and reality'" (432), the perfection beyond all else that our moral pilgrimage includes or implies. As *a* being, the ultimate could not be ultimate, and for this reason, Murdoch holds, the ontological argument itself clarifies "the reasons for rejecting God" (425). "That than which nothing greater can be conceived" is not a sensible combination of words if it refers to a contingent individual—and, therefore, God is impossible.

But "we can lose God" without losing Good (473). The idea of perfection is not a being or "a Person, it is *sui generis*. It is a 'reality principle' whereby we find our way about in the world" of beings (474). Although in this respect Plato and Kant, the two singular participants in the dialogue that underlies all of Western philosophy, speak with one voice (see 57, 407), we here again recur best to Plato. To identify the Form of the Good with a metaphysical individual or supernatural deity "would be absolutely un-Platonic" (475), because Plato recognized that Good is "above being" (342) or "above the level of the gods or God" (475). Hence, Murdoch also appreciates Paul Tillich, who spoke of the "God above God" (Tillich 1952, 186), even if she probably does not consider this the happiest formulation. Our experience of the "light in which the whole world is revealed" (39) "leads us to place our idea of it outside the world of existent being as something of a different unique and special sort" (508).

It is just because this something is outside the world of existent being that Murdoch, for all of her critique of philosophical separations of fact and value, can also write: "A proper separation of fact and value, as a defence of morality, lies in the contention that moral value cannot be *derived* from fact" (26). To that statement, a metaphysical theist is bound to take exception, at least if "fact" includes any statement about any being. If the idea of perfection is the idea of God, then a designation of the character of God entails a designation of the character of the good. Moreover, Murdoch's insistence that the Good is beyond beings explains why she departs from "philosophers [who] have sought a single principle upon which morality may be seen to depend" and, in that sense, to reduce the moral life "to a unity" (492). She certainly affirms that "Good . . . [is] absolute, above courage and generosity and all the plural virtues"; the Good is a "pure source, . . . which creatively relates the virtues to each other in our moral lives" (507). But as she wrote in *The Sovereignty of Good* (1970), "'all is one' is a dangerous falsehood at any level except the highest; and can that be discerned at all?" (Murdoch 1970, 56).

It cannot because it is in all respects unique, and it can because all of our consciousness occurs in its light. "The One who alone is wise does not want and does want to be called by the name of Zeus" (Heraclitus, cited 56). For this reason, the required demythologization of religion must be succeeded by a remythologization. Because metaphysics as a guide to morals must include reference to something real beyond existence, an adequate moral theory cannot finally escape formulations that are pictorial or figurative in character, just as Tillich insisted that all positive statements about the "God above God" (Tillich 1952, 186) are symbolic, and these pictures are offered "to see if we cannot find just this in our deepest experience" (507).

THE LOSS OF WORTH

If the foregoing will serve as a relevant summary of Murdoch's emphatic moral realism, I am now in a position to discuss the reservation in her friendship to theistic religion. "Often . . . when a general philosophical viewpoint loses its charm," she observes in another context, "something is lost" (221). If I understand her rightly, the supposedly outdated viewpoint included, however inadequately, some metaphysical insight that is neglected when philosophy turns generally in another direction. With the loss of theism, I now wish to argue, something in this significant sense is lost.

We may approach the issue at stake by making explicit what has been at least implicit above, namely, Murdoch so connects morality and the real that either may be defined in terms of the other. If moral advance is identified as the movement of consciousness from appearance to reality, reality is identified as the object or possible object of moral advance. More precisely, reality is that the apprehension of which, in distinction from ignorance or misapprehension, makes an individual better, and this simply repeats her definition of the real world as that which we see in the light of the Good. The two definitions are convertible because each marks metaphysically the possibility of human existence, "what 'must be the case' for human being to be as it is" (259).

Assuming that we do so with care, we may also formulate the point as follows: if Murdoch is an emphatic moral realist, she is also a pragmatist. For a pragmatist, on this usage, cognition of the truth about ourselves and the world of which we are a part insofar makes us better—or, in Murdoch's case, the apprehension of reality is never cognition of mere fact, independent of our orientation to perfection. Care is here required because she is clearly not an empirical pragmatist, in the sense often associated with the thought of John Dewey and in accord with which the method of empirical science is *the* method of intelligence; much less is she a neo-pragmatist, in the sense often associated with the thought of Richard Rorty and in accord with which true understandings are those that "pay their way" in relation to our historically specific interests. We can protect against these misunderstandings and underscore the distinctive character of her proposal by saying that she is, however irregular the term may seem, a Platonic pragmatist. If I understand rightly, she thinks that finally Plato was one, too (see 39).

This point is pertinent because it implies a criterion for the validity of statements about reality: no such statement can be true unless believing it makes us better. This, of course, is not to say that all true statements are about good things, as if this were the best of all possible worlds. Rather, a statement about reality cannot be true unless it involves, as previously mentioned, "an opposition between good and bad" (259), so that believing it orients us to the good. To be sure, this criterion may seem useless in the absence of some norm or principle of the good, and pragmatists are often accused of begging the question because they simply posit or define persuasively the putative character of the good life. But the pragmatic test, I judge, does serve us at least in this respect: no valid statement can be completely negative.

With the phrase "completely negative statement," I mean a negation that has no positive content, the assertion of absence that is not by implication the assertion of some presence. "The rose is not red" is, we may say, only partially negative because it implies the positive statement that a rose exhibiting some color other than red is present. In contrast, the Kantian assertion that things in themselves are unknowable is, I believe, a complete negation, devoid of positive content. To consider this statement also partially positive because it implies that all knowable things are only phenomena in distinction from noumena repeats the point because noumena can be identified only as not-phenomena, and therefore phenomena are said to be distinguished only from complete negation.

Notwithstanding her considerable appreciation of Kant, Murdoch rejects his distinction between phenomena and noumena because, as I have mentioned, her account of metaphysics rejects his limitation of the inquiry to specifically human features and thus, by implication, his separation of theoretical and practical reason. That she is, in this respect, Platonic rather than Kantian is, I now suggest, an expression of her pragmatism. Completely negative metaphysical statements could never be true because believing them adds nothing to our orientation and, therefore, cannot orient us to the good. Such a statement could be true, in other words, only were it to designate a sheer fact, separated from or independent of value. Whatever else pragmatism means, then, it asserts that all cognition is partially positive. We do not apprehend absence without apprehending some presence, and we know what is absent only because it is incompatible with what is present. In the light of the Good, sheer nothing cannot be seen.[1]

Now, Murdoch's denial of theism, I believe, is in truth a completely negative metaphysical statement because it asserts that our moral pilgrimage makes no difference beyond itself. This is not to say that she denies the difference, for better or worse, each of us makes to ourselves and other human individuals, including succeeding individuals, and to the nonhuman world by which we are sustained and enriched. What the denial of theism denies is that leading our lives makes an unconditional or everlasting difference, so that something about strictly all of the future is at stake in what we do. An unconditional difference requires an unconditional or everlasting reality to which the difference is made. If "God is love" is the identifying conviction of theistic religion, its central affirmation is that we ought to love God because all of our lives in all of their detail make an abiding difference to the divine reality. In contrast, the Good, as an Idea rather than an individual, is always to be loved but is never loving.

Precisely because her Platonic pragmatism is nontheistic, then, Murdoch could write in *The Sovereignty of Good*: "I can see no evidence to suggest that human life is not something self-contained" or "self-enclosed" and, therefore, has no "external point or *telos*" (Murdoch 1970, 79). At least this much is included when she says, "the Good . . . excludes the idea of purpose . . . The only genuine way to be good is to be good 'for nothing'" (Murdoch 1970, 71; see 1993, 312). "Our destiny can be examined but it cannot be totally explained. We are simply here. And if there is any kind of sense or unity in human life, and the dream of this does not cease to haunt us, it is of some other kind and must be sought within a human experience which has nothing outside it" (Murdoch 1970, 79).

But, we may ask, what positive content is implied by saying that human life is self-contained or self-enclosed—or, to rephrase the question, what presence could we possibly apprehend that would confirm the absence of any ultimate difference and orient us to the good? Some may reply that an absence of any everlasting difference implies the presence of a temporary difference, and it is this temporary difference that is better or worse. But this response has missed the question. We have assumed, with the pragmatists, that all we do makes a difference and, therefore, our lives are worth leading. At issue is whether that assumed difference is *only* temporary or *not* permanent, and this question is: what presence does this negation imply? Absent some positive content in this statement, it must be inconsistent with the pragmatic affirmation of our significance.

We may now be told that the indifference of our lives within their largest context is what makes them dear or gives to them their importance while we lead them. As far as I can see, this is a non sequitur. The statement that what we do here will be in the long run neither good nor bad neither implies nor is implied by the statement that what we do here is in the short run significant. To the contrary, the belief that value is constituted by its own eventual nullity is a confusion similar to the thought that moral responsibility is constituted by the absence of any transcending or real norm of the good. The absence of a real norm means only that there is nothing to be morally responsible to, and the absence of something ultimate at stake means only that ultimately there is nothing at stake in our decisions. To the best of my reasoning, the notion that human life is "good 'for nothing'" (Murdoch 1970, 71) is, at least if pragmatism is true, a thought with which we can do literally nothing and, therefore, purports to designate a condition of our lives the apprehension of which could not possibly make us better or be seen in the light of the Good. For a pragmatist, it could never be valid, because it is completely negative and, therefore, could only be a valueless fact.

Good metaphysical arguments, Murdoch rightly insists, successfully appeal "to us all to see if we cannot find just . . . [their conclusions] in our deepest experience" (507). If pragmatism is correct, then so far from sensing no external purpose or telos, our deepest experience and, therefore, all of our cognition includes the irrevocable affirmation or conviction that our lives are unconditionally significant. To assert the contradictory can only be a pragmatic self-contradiction, and were one truly to believe it, the consequence could only be moral immobility. "No matter what the content of our choices may be," writes Schubert M. Ogden, "we can make them at all only because of our invincible faith that they somehow make a difference which no turn of events in the future has the power to annul" (Ogden 1966, 36). What in truth does not cease to haunt us is, writes Whitehead, "that the immediate facts of present action pass into permanent significance for the universe. The insistent notions of Right and Wrong, Achievement and Failure, depend upon this background. Otherwise, every activity is merely a passing whiff of insignificance" (Whitehead 1941, 698).

THE NECESSITY OF GOD

My provisional conclusion is that Murdoch's religion without God is inconsistent with her emphatic moral realism because her philosophical proposal is also a pragmatism. On her own terms, the loss of theism is the loss of a deep aspect of human life. But this conclusion must be provisional because it cannot be sustained without a return to the ontological argument. Murdoch offers reasons to think that Anselm proved in fact, even if contrary to his intent, the necessary nonexistence of God. If she is correct in this assessment, then her statement that human life is "good 'for nothing'" (Murdoch 1970, 71) is simply a denial of the impossible. If she is right about Anselm, in other words, then either pragmatism does not imply theism or something is altogether amiss with metaphysics as a guide to morals.

On her accounting, the proof proves that God is impossible because an individual, even the best one, "becomes one more contingent thing among others" (432) and, therefore, cannot be perfect. Anselm insisted that perfection—"that than which nothing greater can be conceived"—cannot be conceived not to exist and, therefore, must exist necessarily. This conclusion is implied, he argued, because necessary existence is greater than contingent existence, a premise that is less than clear in the widely criticized second chapter of the *Proslogion* but unmistakable in the third and the reply to Gaunilo. On this premise, it is not existence but, rather, mode of existence that is said to be a property, and if perfection is conceivable, necessary existence is implied. "Anselm's principle," says Charles Hartshorne, asserts that "perfection could not exist contingently" (Hartshorne 1962, 51). Murdoch credits the judgment that Kant's objection, "existence is not a predicate," begs the question against this premise in *Proslogion*, chapter 3 (see 408–10). But, as Leibniz and, perhaps, Gaunilo before him pointed out, the argument is not sound unless the idea of a greatest conceivable thing can itself be conceived, is not a self-contradictory concept.

For Murdoch, this is not a genuine concept if it is taken to designate an individual, precisely because such an individual would thereby be said to exist necessarily, and all individuals exist contingently. Still, as we have seen, perfection *is* a genuine conception if understood to mean an Idea or Form of the Good "outside the world of existent being" (508) because the pervasive moral character of our cognition implies it. For this reason, Murdoch cites Tillich's contention that the ontological argument successfully displays the question of the unconditioned, even while it obviously fails as a proof of God's existence (see 391–92). It is, then, the logical choice between perfection as one contingent thing among others and perfection as an Idea or Form beyond existent being that precludes a theistic pragmatism. But I suggest that these alternatives are, in truth, logical contraries rather than contradictories; although both cannot be true, both may be false. There is, in other words, a third option that is something like a common contradictory of the other two: perfection designates an individual that is universal or coextensive with all other reality and, therefore, not simply one contingent thing among others, and this individual includes an Idea of the Good as its own essential and abiding purpose.

It may be objected that the concept of a universal individual implies a totalizing metaphysical system, and as Murdoch says, with Hegel's *Phenomenology of Mind* in view: "What makes metaphysical ('totalising') coherence theories unacceptable is the way in which they in effect 'disappear' what is individual and contingent by equating reality with integration in a system, and degrees of reality with degrees of integration," so that "'ultimately' or 'really' there is only one system" (196). But this objection also fails to consider all of our options because Hartshorne's achievement is principally directed to the formulation and defense of a nontotalizing concept of the divine individual. Definitive of this account is his distinction between the divine existence and the divine actuality, in accord with which only the former is necessary and means that strictly universal coextension is always actualized somehow. In contrast, the divine actualizations are contingent because they consist in completely adequate relativity to whatever else is in fact real, and contingency is in evidence everywhere in the world. This concept is nontotalizing, in other words, because temporality is a necessary characteristic of the divine existence. God is unsurpassable and also self-surpassing. At every time, the divine individual is perfectly related to all other actuality and necessarily will relate to all that is now only possible; it now includes all that has occurred, and succeeding divine actualities will add all that does occur as the future becomes present (see Hartshorne 1948). God is the light in which all is seen because God sees all of reality and reality alone.

On this account, then, perfection marks an individual that cannot be rivaled in its relations to reality or goodness and an individual that is also self-surpassing because its relations to goodness increase without end insofar as good is achieved by others. Its own everlasting telos, namely, that maximal good should be achieved by others in order to maximize what God includes, is the Form of the Good, the condition of the possibility of our own moral pilgrimage because the divine purpose is the telos of reality as such. Conversely, just because the moral good consists in so leading our lives as to maximize our contribution to the divine good, the choices we make "pass into permanent significance for the universe" (Whitehead 1941, 698). What we do in response to the "magnetic" force of this telos makes an everlasting difference, for better or worse, and because we have our being in God's sight, we live and move with an irrevocable confidence in the unconditional worth of our adventure.

As an alternative to Murdoch's Idea of the Good, Hartshorne's concept of the perfect individual counsels, I believe, a revisit to the view that metaphysics cannot escape pictorial or figurative formulations. I do not deny that symbolic language is inseparable from religious expression, because I take the function of religion to be the representation of perfection in a manner that cultivates or evokes our pilgrimage from appearance to reality. But Murdoch, if I understand rightly, holds to the necessity of pictorial representation even in critical metaphysics because, as Tillich also believed, the unconditioned is beyond beings. Given that perfection is completely unique, it cannot be designated literally by concepts that refer literally to existing things. Insofar as an account of metaphysical formulation depends on this putative uniqueness of the unconditioned, we may expect that a differing concept of perfection will have consequences with respect to philosophical expression.

A long tradition in philosophical theology, claiming especially distinctive representatives, has asserted that all positive statements about the divine reality are symbolic or analogical. But that view is, I believe, critically unacceptable—because it asserts a reality about which, literally speaking, we can say nothing. Whitehead says that philosophy has insofar failed when it pays "metaphysical compliments" to God (Whitehead 1925, 161) because it has "exempted [God] from all the metaphysical categories which applied to the individual things in this temporal world" (Whitehead 1961, 169). The concept of self-surpassing perfection, I am persuaded, pays no such compliment. To be sure, the divine reality is unique in the sense that only one individual can be coextensive with all else. But it is not completely unique in the sense that its difference from all others cannot be identified literally. To the contrary, the difference between some and all is a literal distinction implied by the term "some." If we can speak literally of human and other nondivine individuals as imperfect because they are related merely to some other reality and, thereby, capable of only some good, then we can also, absent some other reason to the contrary, speak literally of the divine as all-inclusive and, therefore, perfect.

This account of perfection is, I hope, sufficiently clear to confirm that it merits attention as a third alternative to perfection as simply another contingent thing, on the one hand, and perfection as solely an Idea or Form of the Good, on the other—and, therefore, another alternative for what the ontological argument, rightly understood, proves. Even if that is so, however, my summary characterization can hardly suffice to establish the validity of this theistic account. In the end, no such concept can be fully redeemed without a more or less comprehensive metaphysical proposal on the order Murdoch has pursued and that Hartshorne also has sought to formulate and defend. Moreover, we should, I believe, agree with her that our final appeal is to what we already know in our deepest experience because it " 'must be the case' for human being to be as it is" (259). Properly speaking, I hold, theists believe that the place of theistic arguments in our cognitive and moral life is precisely that which Murdoch attributes to the metaphysical enterprise. Successful proofs for the divine existence are not meant to create an experience of God where one is not already present and, in that sense, to argue us into religious faith. To the contrary, their purpose is critically to clarify the inescapable relation to perfection that constitutes our every thought and action. In that sense, they, too, leave everything as it is.

Some for whom Hartshorne's concept of divine perfection is or, at least, may be self-consistent still insist that it does not redeem the ontological argument but warrants only the conclusion: *if* God exists, God exists necessarily. On this reading, metaphysical necessity must be distinguished from logical necessity. Those who are persuaded to side with Kant against Plato in the matters that fundamentally divide the two will, I judge, credit this distinction. Because reality as such is unknowable, no existential denial is logically impossible. Thus, a divine individual, if it exists, is metaphysically necessary or coextensive with all other reality, but whether or not God exists remains logically contingent.

As I have suggested, this reading requires, against the pragmatic view, the logical possibility of valueless facts, because the claim that a perfect individual is possible but does not exist is a completely negative metaphysical statement or has no positive implication. It is solely the negation of any unconditional worth in what occurs and thus in what we do with the possibilities given to us. Precisely because a universal individual is one to which literally everything can and does make an everlasting difference, its existence must be strictly noncompetitive or consistent with anything else that could conceivably be present. Accordingly, there is no presence we could apprehend that would imply its absence, and conversely, its absence would have no implication about what is present.

There are, I think, convincing arguments against the logical possibility of any completely negative existential statement. They can be summarized by noting that any such statement purports to designate an object of thought different but indistinguishable from a merely putative thought that has no object at all, for instance, a thought whose supposed object is designated only by a self-contradiction. The two must be different because the first is said to be logically possible, but they are indistinguishable because, in either case, the supposed object is completely negative. Still, this summary argument begs for further explication that I will not pursue here.[2] Insofar, then, I have not offered a defense of pragmatism and, in that respect, defended the soundness of the ontological argument. Although I also find convincing

Murdoch's sustained argument for the "ubiquity of value" (250), the burden of my reflections has been to suggest that her emphatic moral realism implies a theistic metaphysics. Thereby, I have sought to recommend that her friendship with theistic religion need not have been reserved because it was, by implication, an embrace.

CONCLUSION

The title, *Adventures of Ideas*, Alfred North Whitehead tells us, "bears two meanings." On the one hand, his book traces "the effects of certain ideas ... in the history of mankind" and on the other, the name means "the author's adventure in framing a speculative scheme of ideas which shall be explanatory of the historical adventure." The two are related because "theories are built upon facts; and conversely, the reports of facts are shot through and through with theoretical interpretation." Or, more concisely: "our history of ideas is derivative from our ideas of history." Whitehead's point is not that theories properly determine the facts of history; general ideas never imply any given exemplification of them. Rather, "the historian in his description of the past depends on his own judgment as to what constitutes the importance of human life" (Whitehead 1961, vii, 3, 7, 4) and thus on an explicit or implicit conviction about the nature of human action and its relation to the entirety in which we are set. Whitehead's "ideas of history" were his specification of the neoclassical metaphysics that largely began with him and now is also especially indebted to Charles Hartshorne.[1]

On my reckoning, the promise of this metaphysics for interpreting US political history has not been sufficiently appreciated. Accordingly, the first three essays in this volume seek to illustrate that promise through their engagements with Thomas Jefferson on religious freedom, the US Constitution as read by David Strauss, and Abraham Lincoln on democracy and nature's God. Jefferson's tribunal of reason is given new significance; the Constitution's authority, which defines the US political adventure in history, is clarified; and Lincoln's ancient faith in a divine moral order specified to politics in the Declaration of Independence assumes special importance in his contribution to that adventure.

If these three essays offer historical interpretations, they also argue, as does the succeeding essay engaging a proposal from Jürgen Habermas, for an account of democracy with religious freedom. In doing so, however, those four essays do not claim explicitly to prescribe that democratic way. Their intention is, rather, to formulate clearly how religious freedom must be understood if the form of political community it marks is to be itself coherent and thus so much as possible. Later essays, then, seek to show, at least provisionally, why democracy with religious freedom is morally authorized—and they do so by defending the promise of neoclassical theism for moral and political theory. We may approach a summary statement of this relation between politics and its metaphysical backing by repeating why religious freedom requires that religious claims can be assessed by reason.

On the proposal advanced in this work, religious freedom protects from governmental interference the sovereignty of each citizen over the ultimate terms of political evaluation and thus over their authorizing ground. The government, therefore, may never explicitly affirm or deny any such conviction—so that "we the people," together as equals, can be the final ruling power. Given that democracy means popular sovereignty, in other words, the phrase "democracy with religious freedom" is, at least by implication, redundant. The people can be sovereign only if the constitution legitimizes any explicit belief about the character of justice as such and its authorizing ground any citizen finds convincing.

Still, that account is coherent only if the question to which a plurality of such beliefs offers alternative answers is rational, so that "we the people" can be politically united through full and free discourse. If, to the contrary, answers to this question are immune to argumentative assessment, democracy with religious freedom becomes an alien imposition on convictions it purports to legitimize—because the constitution stipulates adherence to a practice inconsistent with the way in which justice is, in truth, discerned. Thereby, popular sovereignty is an impossible form of political union. Differing beliefs about the ultimate terms of political evaluation that cannot be civilized through reasoned discussion and debate can be only asserted in conflict with each other. Barring a modus vivendi, they can only fight over the terms of their life together.

Given that religious freedom protects answers to a rational question, however, a democratic constitution imposes nothing on any citizen she or he does not self-impose in making a political claim, including a religious claim purporting to be immune to reasoned assessment. If beliefs about the ultimate terms of political evaluation can be, in truth, validated or invalidated in public discussion and debate, any citizen who participates politically in fact pledges that her or his political claim can be redeemed by convincing reasons. Discourse with its norms is then self-imposed as the practice in which she or he chooses to engage. On my reading, virtually all attempts to make sense of politics with religious freedom fail because they assume that religious differences, at least on the conventional understanding of what counts as a religion, are not properly objects of reasoned assessment. I am also impressed that thinkers who so assume rarely argue for this premise. Perhaps its mere assertion is their concession that one cannot establish by argument criteria of validation and invalidation beyond reason. As far as

I can see, in other words, those for whom religious convictions are nonrational or suprarational must posit this assumption as itself nonrational or suprarational and thus must beg the question of whether they have it right.

In any event, one way to show that religious freedom protects answers to a rational question is to explicate and establish an answer by rational appeal—and in doing so to explain why that answer and, more generally, reasoned assessment of all convictions about justice as such and its authorizing ground are patient of that appeal. As mentioned, later essays in this work argue, at least provisionally, that valid moral and political principles depend on the metaphysical backing clarified by neoclassical theism. In relation to politics, moreover, that authorizing ground prescribes, wherever enabling conditions exist, democracy and thus religious freedom—in part because the argument for principles of justice also explains why a practice of public discourse about religious claims is possible.

Chapter 5 explicates a humanitarian ideal—humanitarian because, on the one hand, it directs purpose to the flourishing of all humans and because, on the other, the ground for this ideal is present in the deepest awareness of all humans and thus necessarily affirmed by human subjectivity as such. By virtue of the latter, all explicit convictions about the ultimate terms of morality and justice seek to represent something all humans already know. Accordingly, any such conviction can be validated or invalidated by appeal to common human experience—and this is why all such convictions, including neoclassical theism and the humanitarian ideal it authorizes, are answers to a rational question. The ultimate terms of political evaluation backed by neoclassical metaphysics can prescribe democracy, wherever enabling conditions exist, because citizens who are sovereign over their explicit beliefs about justice already share an original belief in its ground and thus can be united by the way of reason.

On the presentation in chapter 5, democracy is indeed prescribed by our humanitarian ideal because it directs us to pursue, with due attention to the nonhuman world, our maximal common humanity as the context for the flourishing of all. This formulation simply restates, given noncontroversial assumptions about human life in this world, the comprehensive purpose prescribing aim at maximal creativity in the future as such—a purpose authorized by a divine reality because the future as such is nothing other than the future of God. Pursuit of our maximal common humanity, moreover, is properly applied indirectly through certain social practices, one of which is the universal practice ordered by the principle of communicative respect, a community of human rights to be honored whatever the consequences. Because that principle is also implied by human activity as such, its deontological prescription and the teleology of our humanitarian ideal imply each other—and this is why the former is an indirect application of the divine purpose. Within the process by which the state's activities are determined, communicative respect is political respect, and the latter can occur only when "we the people" are the final ruling power. Wherever possible, then, politics ought to be democratic—and this conclusion can be confirmed by consideration of the humanitarian ideal itself. In its own way, politics properly seeks our maximal common humanity because justice provides or promotes general conditions for the flourishing of all, and democracy is prescribed because democratic respect itself empowers human flourishing, regardless of any other empowerment politics properly provides or promotes.

Although the argument is incomplete, the backing of neoclassical metaphysics and the comprehensive purpose it authorizes are defended in these essays by pleading their greater coherence relative to other views of our moral responsibility and its political application—and special attention is given to some of those more widely credited among contemporary citizens, including contemporary theists. Two of the more persuasive accounts of democracy today, especially in the academy, are those that challenge metaphysics altogether. On one continuing expression of this challenge, moral theory takes its bearings from Immanuel Kant's supposed discrediting of attempts to know ultimate reality and his consequent formulation of a priori or transcendental imperatives that are nonteleological. But the metaphysical project has also been denied subsequent to Kant by post-Enlightenment thinkers who further challenge, as Kant did not, theoretical and practical principles universal to human subjectivity. To the contrary, these thinkers argue, meaning and truth are always circumscribed by some specific location within the human adventure, however generously conceived—so that reality presupposes understanding because understanding is impossible except as constituted by participation in some language or lifeworld.

In chapter 5, the humanitarian ideal is defended in part through a criticism of both challenges to metaphysics. The critique of universal subjectivity characteristic of post-Enlightenment thought is, I contend, self-refuting because itself an instance of universal subjectivity; reason cannot function "as an object and no longer as the subject of critique" (Apel 1998, 164). Kantian nonteleology is also problematic because it defines principles in terms of side constraints or limiting conditions on the ends humans are assumed to pursue. Thereby, moral evaluation is said to compare alternatives for purpose in one or more respects but not purposes in their entirety. By implication, differences among those alternatives in other respects are said to be morally indifferent—and such indifference is itself a moral conclusion. Hence, Kantian nonteleology, against itself, implies a principle comparing alternatives for purpose in their entirety, that is, a teleological principle.

Given that neither a Kantian nor post-Enlightenment challenge to metaphysics permits a credible moral and political theory, one may be led to consider the claim for metaphysical teleology. To be sure, some theorists have advanced alternatives to all three. Such theories—for instance, some expressions of utilitarianism—typically affirm a universal principle or set or principles but deny its transcendental character. For Kant, in contrast, every supposed account of how rational decision making as such relates to its alternatives is a transcendental moral theory. Moreover, he reasoned, a transcendental moral law must be nonteleological because a good by which all human purposes in their entirety would be directed requires the kind of metaphysical understanding he thought impossible. In chapter 5, I endorse Kant's reading of the universal options and thus consider metaphysical teleology required if Kantian and post-Enlightenment proposals fail.[2]

Still, a theory of moral responsibility dependent on metaphysics is common to differing metaphysical projects, among them not only neoclassical theism but also differing expressions of classical theism and of nontheistic metaphysics. The final two essays engage prominent representatives of those latter two alternatives. Among Western theologians, I judge, Reinhold Niebuhr's comprehensive account of politics in relation to a theistic ethic has not been equaled during the many decades since its appearance—and in any event remains extensively persuasive, at least among those who affirm or defend Christian faith. In Niebuhr's own original way, his proposal appropriates classical theism, on which the divine reality is in all respects eternal, and chapter 6 attempts to show why neoclassical theism provides a more coherent backing for his own account of human existence and his abiding affirmation of ultimate meaning in history. Among other thinkers, the possibility of nontheistic metaphysics as a guide to morals is well represented in Iris Murdoch's work, which asserts the reality of Good without God or, what comes to the same thing, of Good beyond beings. The conversation with her in chapter 7 is my attempt to redeem a better metaphysics.[3]

Critical discussion of these several alternatives is designed, as mentioned earlier, to commend the explication of morality and justice backed by neoclassical theism. If that metaphysics is valid, democracy and thus religious freedom are, wherever possible, required—and a democratic constitution *implies* a moral teleology indebted to Whitehead and Hartshorne, even while that constitution stipulates *explicit* governmental neutrality toward all convictions about the ultimate terms of political evaluation. I emphasize the implicit relation to this metaphysical good in order to underscore that a democratic state must never compromise the full and free discourse among such convictions through which governing decisions are properly determined. Within the process provided by the constitution, Kantian and post-Enlightenment, classical theistic and nontheistic metaphysics, and all other accounts of political evaluation as such, whether we call them religious or not and whether or not their public representation is clear or vague, are legitimate. Religious freedom protects the sovereignty of each citizen over her or his political evaluations, and the case for neoclassical metaphysics belongs to democratic politics only within the discourse among citizens. But if that account is valid, government should be, wherever possible, constituted by the way of reason because democratic practice itself implies and is authorized by the divine reality.

Thus, the principal constructive assertions informing the several essays in this collection—religious freedom as constituting the way of reason and neoclassical theism about human life in relation to ultimate reality—are inseparable. A coherent theism alone validates the ultimate terms of political evaluation, which prescribe democracy, wherever possible, because they also vindicate the way of reason. Democracy and thus religious freedom are thereby the political specification of the divine good.

NOTES

CHAPTER ONE

1. In calling the consent to the constitution about which this discussion asks "principled," I exclude any accidental common adherence that might occur because each individual or relevant group, for its own strategic reasons, finds democracy a means to its own ends, that is, common adherence as a modus vivendi.

2. In speaking of the shared commitment essential to republican government as based on moral principles, Jefferson is assuming or asserting a positive answer to the question this essay, as I said at the outset, will not address, namely, whether democratic or republican government is itself morally good or right. On this positive answer, common adherence to the democratic or republican form of government by all citizens is itself morally authorized. That Jefferson so assumed or asserted is not surprising; the Declaration of Independence asserted that government by consent of the governed is authorized by "the laws of nature and of nature's God."

3. As far as I can see, however, Mead was not entirely consistent about whether religious freedom depends on the common adherence provided by religious essentials. I have sought to explicate Mead's ambiguity in Gamwell 1995, chapter 6.

4. Another way to make this point is to note that Murray's proposal assumes a certain account of what can and what cannot be validated by natural reason. The answers to ultimate or spiritual questions (i.e., about the character of eternal reality) are said to transcend what our natural reason can comprehend, while it is said to be sufficient when the questions concern the temporal order—because natural reason can know the natural law. But this explication is itself an account of how knowledge open to reason and knowledge not open to reason are related. If we assume, with Murray, that religions differ with respect to a reality whose character reason cannot comprehend, it follows that religions may differ with respect to the capacities of natural reason—such that some religions may refuse to separate principles for the temporal order from their answers to spiritual questions. For this reason, Murray's proposal has been criticized as inseparable from a Roman Catholic understanding of how temporal human existence, bound by the natural law open to reason, relates to its eternal and suprarational ground. I have offered one expression of this critique in Gamwell 1995, chapter 4. For a reading of Jefferson as essentially at one with Murray, see Buckley.

5. I have presented a critical assessment of Rawls's solution in Gamwell 2000, 266–79.

6. The phrases "ultimate terms of political evaluation" and "terms for evaluating politics as such" are not meant to beg any relevant questions. If someone holds that politics as such has no single principle of evaluation but, rather, is constituted by two or more principles that must somehow be balanced, or, alternatively, holds that political evaluations are always in all respects dependent on the specific situation, then she or he takes the ultimate terms of political evaluation to involve more than one principle, or takes complete dependence on context to define how politics as such should be evaluated.

7. I will not seek here to engage the discussion of how religion should be defined and, instead, will simply assert my conviction that religions, strictly speaking, have a distinct function in human life: religion is the primary way in which we humans represent explicitly an answer to our abiding existential question of ultimate worth—and thus represent explicitly an understanding of the ultimate context and orientation of human life. On this understanding, a religion may or may not affirm a transcendent reality, but as the primary form of representing explicitly ourselves in relation to our ultimate context, religious beliefs are differentiated from philosophical beliefs that also represent explicitly an answer to our existential question; the latter do so through critical reflection or in a secondary way. The distinct function of religion, then, is so to explicate its answer in concepts and symbols, including symbolic practices, that attention to them or participation in them cultivates or mediates existential decision for the given understanding of our ultimate worth. But that strict sense of religion, as well as Jefferson's apparent reference, is extended by the proposed account of religious freedom.

8. This conclusion may seem to interpret the nonestablishment clause in the First Amendment to the US Constitution, and thus one might ask what the second or free exercise clause could mean. Once the extended sense of "religious" is in place, however, I am inclined to see both clauses as protection for any conviction about the ultimate terms of political evaluation. This is because "religious" and "religion" are so often assumed to designate in the conventional sense. If the first clause prohibits establishment in that sense, this clause by itself permits the state to teach or support the teaching of some nonreligious comprehensive assessment. The free exercise clause, then, denies such permission by asserting explicitly that religion is legitimate. Given the conventional meaning of "religion," in other words, the two clauses together simply prohibit the establishment of any comprehensive assessment or legitimize all convictions about justice as such—and thus underscore the sovereignty of the people. In this respect, I am inclined to endorse the US Supreme Court's decision in *Employment Division, Department of Human Resources of Oregon v. Smith* (1990).

In the history of US Constitutional interpretation, however, the free exercise clause has sometimes been read to have another meaning—which, roughly speaking, is this: religious practices cannot be substantially burdened by laws of general applicability unless so required by a compelling state interest that cannot be served in a less restrictive way. As the previous paragraph implies, I am not persuaded by this reading of the Constitution, at least if the First Amendment is understood to underscore popular sovereignty. But if not constitutional, special protection for comprehensive assessments might still be advocated as statutory law—as enacted, for instance, in the US Religious Freedom Restoration Act (1993). I will not seek here to assess whether religions or comprehensive assessments should be so protected.

9. Assuming that religious freedom legitimizes or protects any possible comprehensive assessment, one may wonder whether the Constitution thereby adds to its protection of free speech. Freedom to speak any political claim, it might be said, implies freedom to assess all political claims. Indeed, one may wonder whether protection of free speech adds anything politically to religious freedom. Freedom to evaluate all political claims, it might be said, implies freedom to speak any political claim. Even if both implications are correct, however, the stipulation of both constitutionally is, I judge, wise—because each makes explicit what is implicit in the other, thereby helping to avoid misinterpretation of either.

10. This is my reformulation of one argument advanced by Steven D. Smith, for whom every understanding of how government properly relates to religion implies certain "background beliefs" that include, in my terms, a comprehensive assessment—so that a principle of religious freedom is, for him, theoretically impossible (see Smith, chapter 6).

11. On the other hand, perhaps the context of popular sovereignty is not needed. Some thinkers have argued that any subject who makes any claim to validity—or, at least, any claim to moral validity—implies the right of any other subject to contest the claim and pledges, if the claim is contested, that reasons can be given commanding the assent of all subjects (see, e.g., Habermas 1984; Apel 1979; the argument in the text is dependent on both thinkers). Although I am inclined to think that something like this conclusion can be defended, I will not seek to establish it here (see Gamwell 2011, chapter 4, especially 122f.). It is sufficient for present purposes to show that, given popular sovereignty, anyone who makes a political claim pledges herself or himself to politics by the democratic way.

12. Some may note that applying these undeniable terms to specifically political decisions as such ("the ultimate terms of political evaluation" in the second sense mentioned in the text) involves some general facts about human life and community that are open to contestation on empirical grounds. If so, I take convictions about the relevant general facts to be included in what religious freedom protects.

13. Indeed, I doubt that a proper democratic constitution may stipulate that claims for ultimate terms of political evaluation answer a rational question. To the contrary, claims for comprehensive assessments on which that understanding of the question is denied are, however inconsistent they may be with the commitment made in so claiming, also legitimized by religious freedom. As far as I can see, therefore, what the constitution of popular sovereignty prescribes is adherence by all citizens to a) the rights each citizen has because that community of rights defines the people, together as equals in discourse, as the final ruling power, and b) the institutions of political decision making through which activities of the state are determined by "we the people."

14. On my accounting, Steven D. Smith's argument mentioned in n. 10 to this essay, which concludes that no principle of religious freedom is possible, fails to credit this distinction.

15. Even in this case, then, "the opinions of men are not the object of [democratic] civil government" (Jefferson, 391). Indeed, both constitutional and statutory legislation may be understood as stipulating imperatives, such that, in each case, what

the state properly teaches are the actions all citizens are bound to take or norms they are bound to observe. In promulgating its own constitution, the civil government teaches adherence to a political practice: all citizens should always act in accord with rights and procedures defining politics by the way of reason. In promulgating statutory law, the state teaches adherence to other practices: all relevant citizens should act or interact in specified ways. But neither teaching properly includes teaching any political opinion. Constitutional provisions require action explicitly neutral to all political differences, and statutory provisions should never teach anything about true or false comprehensive assessments by stipulating how any activity of the state ought to be evaluated.

16. Depending on precisely what diversity of convictions is said to overlap, a theory of religious freedom on which democracy *is* an overlapping consensus will, I believe, be either a religionist or a separationist theory. For an example of the former, see Murray; for an example of the latter, see Rawls 2005, 440–90.

CHAPTER TWO

1. This is the third of three reasons Strauss offers for the persistence of originalism. "The first is that there is something natural about originalism"; that is, "when we interpret a text, we think about how the authors of the text understood the words they used" (29). "The second . . . is that originalism is not actually a way of interpreting the Constitution. It is a rhetorical trope" (31). Strauss discusses each of these reasons (see 29–31).

2. As far as I can see, Strauss's use of "the living Constitution" does not always clearly include the written text. For instance, he writes: "the written Constitution is as important as the living Constitution of precedents and traditions" (101), and "our living Constitution is a common law constitution that restrains judges better than the alternatives" (118; see also 43). Perhaps these citations can be so read as to include the written text within the living Constitution. Still, the reader might well be excused for reading them to the contrary. Be that as it may, the book as a whole makes apparent that what lives is not simply a body of common law but, rather, includes the written text, which can be included precisely because its interpretation involves a body of common law. This is confirmed by Strauss's use of capital C in speaking of "the living Constitution," given that he has called the body of common law "the small-*c* constitution" (35).

3. I here use "hermeneutical" in a narrow sense to mean, not the broad theory inclusive of how to understand understanding as such but, rather, how to understand the meaning of another understanding or of some text. In this case, the hermeneutical question asks how to understand or interpret the US Constitution.

4. We should add, some might insist, "so long as the change occurs in an evolutionary way that is generally accepted by successive generations." Against the denial of any changeless meaning of our Constitution, however, this qualification asserts "Burkean ideology" as an abiding character of US politics. If any such character were denied, what Strauss calls "our constitutional culture" (103), marked by attitudes of humility and cautious empiricism, would itself be open to change without changing the Constitution.

5. As far as I can see, the denial of a changeless constitutional meaning reveals the self-refutation consequent on denying the distinction between hermeneutical and normative questions. The latter denial implies that definitions of good politics and, by implication, moral validity are contextual in all respects, given by a political tradition or historical location. But statements about a historical location imply other historical locations—and were moral validity anywhere contextual in all respects, moral validity everywhere would be contextual in all respects. A noncontextual moral principle absent anywhere is absent everywhere, and *that* implication is a noncontextual moral principle. Without a distinction between the character of any political tradition and the character of good politics, in other words, one implies a (self-refuting) principle of good politics on which it is defined by some tradition.

6. I have been educated by the discussion of authority in Ogden 1986, chapter 3.

7. If the question of US politics is distinguished from that of good politics, an argument for Burkean ideology as proper to the living Constitution might proceed as follows: a political tradition identified by some abiding character is inescapably involved with clarifying and applying that character in circumstances that could not have been anticipated by those who originally established its authority, and humility and cautious empiricism in doing so are prescribed because communal traditions typically cannot persist without the continuity that evolutionary change generally accepted over generations provides. I do not mean here to endorse that argument and thus to propose an approach to constitutional law—but, rather, to note how the hermeneutical question might be clarified by differentiating it from the normative question.

8. Richard T. DeGeorge distinguishes between executive authority, which "involves the right or the power to act in certain ways," and nonexecutive authority, for instance, epistemic authority or authority of competence. Executive authority may include the right to command others; nonexecutive authority never does (see DeGeorge, chapters 3 and 4; the citation is from 62). The Constitution's authority does not seem to fit into either side of this apparently exclusive distinction. The Constitution, on my accounting, has the right to prescribe—and, in that sense, to act or command—with respect to US politics. Still, its authority might be called or be said to include epistemic authority, because its right to prescribe is the right to define what should be believed by anyone who asks what the abiding character of US politics is.

9. The early United States apparently included a minority movement seeking to establish monarchical government, which was not completely defeated until Jefferson became president. Nonetheless, democratic or republican government, not monarchy, is what the Constitution constituted. "The monarchists . . . had been—and were—counting on the failure of the new government. Monarchy would then step into the breach" (Meachum, 311).

10. Notably, the Declaration of Independence was itself never submitted for popular approval. In this respect, the primary authority for democracy might seem deficiently democratic. To be sure, the Declaration did not seek to institutionalize democracy but, rather, simply to declare it. Nonetheless, the Continental Congress also declared independence as necessary for republican government, and the people

were never asked to approve this conclusion. Earlier in 1776, however, numerous associations in the colonies, both formal political bodies and informal assemblies, had already issued similar declarations (see Maier 1997). Moreover, Britain had already attacked the colonies militarily, and conflict with loyalists was pervasive, so that, under the resulting conditions, a deliberative referendum by the people might well have been out of the question (see Amar, 9). Be all that as it may, the act of declaring independence was, we might say, a declaration by the Continental Congress that events already under way were part of the Revolution, whose promise was republican government.

11. Clarity may be served by repeating that ratification could never confer more than *de facto* authority on the Constitution itself. If *de jure* authority is conferred on institutional details by ratification, this conferral occurs only because the Constitution is *de jure* authoritative in assigning sovereignty to "we the people." Continuing authority for the details is conferred by ratification only because something prior conferred authority on the Constitution of popular sovereignty.

12. Nondemocratic constitutional provisions are what I will subsequently call substantive constitutional prescriptions, and I will return later to the issue they pose for democratic citizens.

13. Constitutional authority for the political community, whether or not a provision is fully consistent with popular sovereignty, may counsel greater importance for original understandings of the text, if they are available, than Strauss might be read to allow. To be sure, some such understandings may be subject to change. Until such change occurs, however, provisions authoritative for political participation stipulate prescriptions to which US citizens are bound. If judicial decision alone effects a change, without formal amendment, it cannot be simply announced to citizens but, rather, requires good reasons—because the prescriptions to which US political participants are bound are now different. Judges, therefore, are called to determine, whenever and insofar as possible, what the text meant to its drafters and ratifiers because giving good reasons for difference entails clarifying the difference. Strauss himself clarifies such differences in making a case for his living Constitution—for instance, with respect to the free speech clause of the First Amendment. Still, he notes, apparently without criticism, how "the text of the Constitution plays," in most Supreme Court decisions, "at most a ceremonial role" (33). Whether this observation is or is not true, I wonder if it properly captures judicial responsibility.

14. Exercising a right to extra-constitutional action may but does not necessarily take the form of civil disobedience. All such action, I expect, seeks to present reasons justifying its course, but civil disobedience is also marked, on my understanding, by a willingness to suffer prescribed punishments and a commitment to nonviolence (see Habermas 2008, 256–57). Such marks might not have characterized, say, violations of the Constitution's fugitive slave provision or slave rebellions. But I am not in a position further to clarify this comparison.

15. Lincoln thereby honored a characterization of democracy used more than once before. In 1787, Wilson spoke of the several states "as made *for* the people, as well as by them" (Wilson, I, 214). In 1819, John Marshall's opinion in *McCulloch v. Maryland* spoke of "government of the people, . . . by them, . . . and for their benefit" (cited in Amar, 362).

16. Given these words, some may further object, the Revolution's promise cannot be the primal source authorizing the nation's political tradition because the Declaration claimed to be further authorized by nature and nature's God. But this objection confuses authorization of US politics with the authorization of good politics. Participants at Philadelphia in 1776 claimed moral authorization for the Revolution and its promise, and whether that claim is valid is (or is included in) the *normative* question about US politics. If that claim *is* valid, then we might distinguish the Revolution's promise as the explicit authorizing source of our political tradition from the moral law or the ultimate terms of political evaluation and their ground as the implicit authorizing source. Still, the present discussion seeks to focus on the explicit authorizing source because focused on the *hermeneutical* question about the Constitution.

17. Whether the Supreme Court's decisions have always had this effect—for instance, whether the recent rulings in *Citizens United v. Federal Election Commission* (2010), regarding campaign financing, or *Shelby County v. Holder* (2014), regarding the Voting Rights Act, cut back on rights of equal inclusion—is controversial.

18. This argument for popular sovereignty's implicit inconsistency with exclusion among the governed naturally raises the question of how children relate to the political process. I cannot here address this issue adequately. But there is, I assume, no serious contention that very young children should be included. Hence, the question is not *whether* all children should be members of "we the people" but, rather, *when* in the process of maturation those who have been excluded as political children become political adults. The Twenty-Sixth Amendment to the US Constitution stipulates eighteen years of age as the legal rule. The pertinent issue, then, is whether that rule is proper. In any event, we should note the following difference between this issue and the other exclusions that have in the past characterized (or yet characterize) our constitutional understanding: the exclusion of children is temporary and thus is not occasioned by some feature that does or even might mark them throughout life. Given their survival through maturation, all children will then become political participants. In contrast, the exclusion of others (e.g., women or African Americans or the poor) was (or is or could be) permanent, marking them throughout their mature lives.

19. Given affirmation of both consent of the governed and, say, free male suffrage, one might ask why the former, rather than the latter, is the original understanding to be worked out or perfected and thus is the abiding character of our Constitution. If the two are inconsistent, why should the resolution go to a given one of the two alternatives? The important response, I believe, was noted earlier: on the attestation of eighteenth-century Americans, the principal question to which the Revolution's promise was an answer concerned the assignment of sovereignty. Against assignment by inheritance or to something else other than consent of the governed, activities of the state should occur only through discussion and debate among the people, who are the final ruling power. With this overriding republican commitment, the limitations on political participation were inconsistent because they were, in their own way, political power by inheritance.

20. In this regard, I am indebted to the Honorable Stephen Breyer and, if I understand him rightly, am in substantial agreement with his argument in *Active Liberty: Interpreting Our Democratic Constitution* (see Breyer).

21. This is true even if they contest some constitutional provision as nondemocratic or inconsistent with popular sovereignty. Patriotic citizens can have, in the term William Sloane Coffin often applied to himself, a "lover's quarrel" (e.g., Coffin 2004, 84) with the US Constitution.

22. In other words, only formative prescriptions are those to which democratic citizens are required to adhere as political participants; such prescriptions define the process by which governmental activities are determined through full and free discourse. To be sure, the obligations of citizens include (setting aside here the possibility of civil disobedience or rebellion) adherence to substantive statutory laws, but never as political participants. Citizens are never bound to profess any law or policy. It follows that substantive laws ought to be expressly noncomprehensive, that is, should not include an explicit affirmation or denial of any ultimate terms of political evaluation, and expressly nonpolitical, that is should not explicitly prescribe any political claim citizens should profess. Religious freedom prohibits government from violating the sovereignty of each citizen over her or his evaluation of every political claim.

For completeness, I might mention that I do not consider the distinction between formative and substantive prescriptions equivalent to that between constitutional and statutory law, even if all constitutional prescriptions should be formative and all substantive prescriptions should be statutory. It remains that statutory law may also be formative, insofar as it rightly applies formative constitutional provisions to changing circumstances. I take this to occur, for instance, with rightly prescribed laws regulating fair access to public spaces for political advocacy—or, although the issues are complicated, rightly prescribed campaign finance laws, whose purpose is, I believe, to help protect the equality of political speech that, on my accounting, the constitutional provision for freedom of speech intends.

23. The US Constitution's Eighteenth Amendment, which established prohibition, was also a substantive provision. Whatever the merits or demerits of prohibition as statutory law, its stipulation constitutionally required all of the governed to adhere to it, not simply as members of the society but, rather, as political participants—and the only way so to adhere in one's act of political participation is to profess prohibition, so that any citizen who seeks to contest it contradicts herself or himself. The recently proposed constitutional amendment defining marriage would likewise introduce a substantive provision.

24. That democracy can and should be understood as politics by the way of reason, whereby a universal moral principle is implied, is, I am persuaded, the beginning of a sound argument for why democracy, at least given certain enabling conditions, is good. Given those conditions, the only alternative to a democratic community is one that defines good politics by appeal to authority, which implies that moral validity is circumscribed by historical context—and that understanding is, I think, self-refuting (see n. 5 to this essay). Nonetheless, completion of this argument requires explication of a universal moral principle or encompassing purpose that authorizes good politics and thus authorizes democracy. Whether such an explication can be defended and, if so, whether it implies metaphysical theism (i.e., an individual properly designated as "that than which nothing greater can be conceived") are, naturally, controversial—although I am inclined to credit both possibilities.

25. Naturally, one might seek to prevent change by stipulating governmental imposition of a certain account, for instance, Rawls's account of democracy as affirming the freedom and equality of all citizens. With that addition, however, it becomes apparent that both the question of a tradition's abiding character and the question of good politics are begged—because both are answered by stipulation. Perhaps that stipulation is present when Rawls speaks of "reasonable" comprehensive doctrines as those among which an overlapping consensus occurs; a reasonable such doctrine "does not reject the essentials of a democratic regime" (Rawls 2005, xvi). Absent governmental imposition, as far as I can see, nothing prevents US political culture from so evolving as to be dominated by an overlapping consensus among unreasonable comprehensive doctrines that prescribe a nondemocratic form of government.

CHAPTER THREE

1. If I understand rightly, the necessity for some or other conception of, which inevitably also betrays, "the *concept* of American liberty" is what Burt means by Lincoln's "tragic pragmatism."

2. It is apparent, I hope, that "popular sovereignty" is not used here in the sense Douglas used the term when he defended the Kansas-Nebraska Act but, rather, is used here in the sense Lincoln intended in calling self-government "absolutely and eternally right" (Lincoln, 303).

3. This was especially so following the death in February 1862, of Lincoln's son, Willy. The president's relationship with Gurley seems confirmed by the hours following Booth's shooting in Ford's Theatre; Gurley was summoned to Lincoln's deathbed and offered the final prayer (see Donald, 337, 599).

4. Whitehead is not alone in calling this constitutive or existential human decision religious (see, e.g., Niebuhr 1942, 44; Tillich 1957, 50). Others, however, reserve "religion" to designate cultural systems or traditions in terms of which a community or communities of people explicitly affirm and seek to mediate their understanding of the proper existential decision about life's ultimate meaning. In contrast, the existential decision itself may be called the decision of faith, so that a religion provides terms with which explicitly to express what its adherents take to be the authentic faith (see, e.g., Ogden 1992, chapter 1). Although I find the latter proposal more precise, I will not seek in this discussion to introduce the difference and, accordingly, will follow Whitehead's usage.

5. Why humans are pervasively tempted by false understandings and why we pervasively yield to temptation pose vexing problems for philosophical theology. I have sought to address them in Gamwell 2000, chapter 2.

6. On this reading, war was inevitable because Union without war would have required agreement by the South and, especially, the slave-owning aristocracy in the South that slavery was wrong, whereby the public mind could believe in its ultimate extinction. But that agreement was not possible for slaveholders, who could not persist with the institution they controlled without believing it to be a positive good, and given its contradiction to democracy, that belief required dominating or subverting democratic politics. Accordingly, the war came, and the Union, seeking to be a democratic political community, could not be preserved without abolition.

Whether war required the incredible loss of life and suffering that occurred is, I hope, debatable—but I am not competent to an opinion.

CHAPTER FOUR

1. On Habermas's account, both claims to truth and claims to rightness are claims to *universal* validity, although this is not the case with all validity claims. For his full analysis of communicative action, see Habermas 1984.

2. In his earlier work, Habermas could write, "conditions of validity . . . are," in the theory of communicative action, "interpreted in terms of reasons that can be advanced in discourse" (Habermas 1993, 29)—and this statement applied equally to both valid claims to truth and those to rightness. More recently, he has taken that account improperly to generalize the character of valid claims to rightness. Claims to truth, that is, for understandings of what is the case, are now said to have "a justification-transcendent point of reference," namely, an objective world that is "not made for us" and is "the same for everyone"—such that "no matter how carefully a consensus about a proposition is established and no matter how well the proposition is justified, it may nevertheless turn out to be false in light of new evidence" (Habermas, 257, 260, 257). Valid rightness claims are, indeed, the same for everyone but have no justification-transcendent reference. They are constructed: "Ideally warranted assertibility *is* what we mean by moral validity" (Habermas 2005, 258). But I will not pursue this difference that Habermas now asserts with respect to conditions of validity. Although it, too, is consequent on his commitment to postmetaphysical reasoning, the implications of the latter for how democracy relates to religion define the issue on which I will seek to focus.

3. At least beginning with *Between Facts and Norms* (1996), Habermas calls the discourse principle a more abstract principle for action norms that is specified in, on the one hand, the moral principle and, on the other, the principle of democracy. But attention to the meaning of this formulation is not, to the best of my reasoning, relevant to the present discussion (see 1996, 107; 2008, chapter 3).

4. On my understanding, a learning process in the sense relevant here is a process through which social life evolves because new forms of knowledge inform responses to cognitive challenges and thus contribute to the solution of problems (see 2013, 349, 362).

5. If I read him rightly, Habermas understands modern or postmetaphysical reason—"decentered" reasoning—to be the consequence of social evolution and thus of learning processes, through which new forms of knowledge inform responses to cognitive challenges and thus contribute to the solution of problems. Explicating these solutions to problems is at least part of what he calls "rational reconstruction," while "the *genealogical perspective* reveals the contingent historical constellations that made the actual learning processes possible" (2013, 362). In this evolution of postmetaphysical reason, the two singular moments are these: first, "the Axial Age revolution in worldviews" effected "the moralization of . . . propitious and unpropitious forces, which had hitherto appeared *within* the world, into a God or godhead who *transcends* the world," thereby universalizing morality, and second, "the separation between secular and religious thought in modern Europe," through which a "religious

consciousness that 'reformed' itself . . . and . . . postmetaphysical thinking . . . are in the final analysis *complementary* answers to *the same* cognitive challenges" (2013, 349, 351, 362). But further pursuit of Habermas's rational reconstruction or genealogy of reason is not needed for the present discussion.

6. That Habermas begins this assertion with the word "today" suggests two possible readings. On the one hand, he could mean that philosophy itself has a history, without which the postmetaphysical understanding of rationality we enjoy today would not have been possible—even while that understanding is, in truth, what any exercise of reasoning presupposes and, therefore, there is no alternative for us. Thereby, Habermas would assert a revised Kantian transcendental analysis of reason. On the other hand, he could mean that postmetaphysical rationality does not purport to be presupposed by reasoning as such but is, rather, the only alternative for us today, in distinction from other times past and future. The latter reading is, I think, the more plausible, in part because he avoids calling his account of communicative reason a transcendental one and, instead, writes the following:

> The rational structure of action oriented toward reaching understanding is reflected in the presuppositions actors *must* make if they are to engage in this practice at all. The necessity of this "must" has a Wittgensteinian rather than a Kantian character. . . . After the pragmatic deflation of the Kantian approach, "transcendental analysis" means the search for presumptively universal, but only *de facto* inescapable, conditions. (27)

This formulation seems to imply that postmetaphysical reasoning, although inescapable for us today, is one among many contingent (or *de facto*) understandings of rationality. On that accounting, if I understand rightly, he still intends that what is inescapable for us has become so through a history that can be rationally reconstructed.

To the best of my reasoning, his account on this latter reading is problematic. The assertion that forms of rationality, however inescapable, are always *de facto* or historical contingencies appears to require, in order to be valid, a kind of rationality that cannot belong to any such form. Reliance on a historically contingent form of reasoning allows, by implication, that some past or future form of rationality might establish a statement to the contrary. Thus, the assertion implies a form of rationality not included in what is said about all such forms. Similarly, the assertion that our form of rationality, as all such forms, is only *de facto* inescapable appears to be a statement that cannot be redeemed by a reconstruction of historical changes. "Inescapable" implies that our reasoning results from changes that are rational and thus implies a supposedly sound form of rationality presupposed by all others, absent which there is no rational reconstruction but, rather, mere description. Indeed, Habermas seems to concede this latter point: the rational reconstruction of these changes as learning processes depends, he says, on "the perspective of a specific normative self-understanding of modernity" (2008, 144)—which appears to imply that postmetaphysical reasoning must be posited in order to reason to its inescapability for us today.

In sum, if the "self-understanding of modernity," as forms of rationality generally, is said to be only *de facto*, this conclusion apparently counts as rational only if exempted from what is said, such that rationality is there the object but not the subject of the account (see Apel 1998, 164). Accordingly, Karl-Otto Apel, if I understand him rightly, speaks of the "self-appropriation" of reason, which entails a transcendental understanding of rationality from the perspective of which the history through which that understanding has become inescapable is rationally reconstructed (see Apel 1992). But I will not attempt to pursue further this issue between Habermas and Apel—because doing so is not required by the point I seek to make about democracy and religion.

7. In this context, it may be worth noting that our English term "translation," used to characterize how Habermas intends the truth contents of religion to enter formal political deliberation, may be misleading. Because what is said and what is meant are not identical, this term sometimes designates a process of stating or seeking to state the same meaning in a different formulation or different language. In this sense, political positions expressed in the symbolic language of a given religion may, in order to be duly considered, require translation into terms commonly understood in political discussion and debate. In the present context, however, that is not Habermas's intent, because the contents of religious contributions that pass through the institutional "filter" are to be defended by different arguments—namely, secular rather than religious ones or postmetaphysical ones rather than those dependent on metaphysics. If the claim to validity for a political prescription includes in its meaning the implied reasons for its supposed validity, the translation in question results in a different meaning. What is first advocated for reasons dependent on an ultimate order directing all human purposes is, following the translation, to be advocated for reasons that have no such dependence; what is first advocated because "the good enjoys epistemic primacy over the right" (263) is, through translation, now advocated independently of any such priority. Thus, a "form of faith," Habermas can say, "resists . . . any nimble switchover of religiously rooted political convictions onto a *different* cognitive basis" (127). It is worth noting that secular contributions in the best sense need no such translation—even if one or another nonreligious assertion and argument might be translated without change of meaning into, say, some more widely understandable expression. In any case, Habermas is thoroughly aware of what "translation," which might also be termed "transformation," means for him. That the burdens of tolerance on believers and unbelievers are not equal is an expression of this point. But he also makes the point directly:

> the inclusion condition . . . would be violated if the collectively binding decisions were not formulated *and justified* in a *universally accessible language*. Religious languages, in particular, would violate the condition because they involve *a category of reasons* (for example, revealed truths) that prima facie cannot claim universal acceptability outside the corresponding religious community. (2013, 384; last use of emphasis added)

8. Against this defense, on the other hand, Rawls also calls "the knowledge and desire on the part of citizens generally to follow public reason and to realize its ideal in their political context" one of "three essential elements of deliberative democracy" (Rawls 2005 448), thereby suggesting an ideal for citizens on which each herself or himself honors public reason "in due course."

9. As noted, Rawls sometimes speaks of a politically liberal community as including a "family of liberal political conceptions of justice," such that "to engage in public reason is to appeal to one of these" (Rawls 2005, 453), and perhaps he also intends that democracy is publicly justified and thus stable when the several reasonable comprehensive doctrines form an overlapping consensus on simply the freestanding character of justice.

10. This is because a moral principle said to be both universal to human activity and nonteleological implies that all conceptions of the good are person- or context-specific, and that implication *is* a universal conception of the good or, at least, something about the good universally. On that implication, the prescribed telos of human life is everywhere and always specific in all respects to person or context.

11. Some have, I recognize, appealed to the difference between justification and truth in order to defend a theory wherein justice, or at least democratic commitment, is defined by something like Rawls's overlapping consensus. On this distinction, justification, unlike truth, is dependent on specific epistemic situation. A belief is justified if supported by the intellectual resources available to the particular individual or group in question; in contrast, truth is universal or independent of any specific situation. Thus, the argument goes, principles of justice may be justified on differing grounds within differing comprehensive doctrines notwithstanding that each claims truth for its understanding. On my reasoning, this distinction could warrant the independence of justice from any given comprehensive doctrine only if adherents of any such doctrine could also claim truth for the following: justice is defined by principles independent of any but justified by all comprehensive doctrines. But a claim for this assertion contradicts the claim to truth for one's comprehensive doctrine—because the latter entails that morality and justice are defined only by principles that imply or depend on it.

As far as I can see, then, the claim to truth for a statement relativizing all comprehensive doctrines to epistemic situation cannot itself consistently be relativized; doing so cancels its claim to truth because the statement, by implication, both affirms and denies that a statement to the contrary in some other epistemic situation might be true (see Apel 1996, 178). Accordingly, the attempt to avoid politics dependent on a comprehensive doctrine yields, by implication, a universal assertion about politics and thus a (self-refuting) competitive doctrine on which all (other) comprehensive doctrines are denied. The merit on Habermas's side of his theoretical difference from Rawls is the recognition that a metaphysical (in Rawls's sense) account of democracy cannot be avoided. Although, for Habermas, political decisions are "impartially justified in light of generally accessible reasons" and thus "justified equally toward religious and nonreligious citizens" (122), he is nonetheless clear that so understanding democracy with religious freedom cannot be independent of what he calls the postsecular "self-understanding of modernity" (144). We can say, I think, that each thinker has a sound reason to criticize the other: Rawls can rightly criticize Habermas for asserting that all democratic citizens must explicitly accept a given comprehensive doctrine (in Rawls's sense), and Habermas can rightly criticize Rawls for purporting to be independent of any such doctrine (in Rawls's sense). Accordingly, neither can be convincing.

12. Here is, I think, another way to make this point: In *Political Liberalism*, Rawls formulates and explicates his basic distinction between a political conception and a comprehensive doctrine and thus between a conception of justice independent of any comprehensive doctrine and a conception of justice dependent on a comprehensive doctrine. If we ask about grounds for this distinction, he must intend that it, too, is formulated solely within the domain of the political because only so could the distinction itself be independent of any comprehensive doctrine. This response, however, only reasserts the distinction and thus assumes its own validity. But is it ever defended? To the best of my reading, Rawls's extensive development of political liberalism never includes an argument for the implied assertion that a conception of justice or the domain of the political *can be* independent of any comprehensive doctrine. Rather, that premise is posited by the proposal. Failure to defend the premise is problematic if the project intends to be one in political philosophy and thus a theory of democracy. To the best of my reasoning, moreover, Rawls could not defend the independence in question without making the distinction dependent on a particular account of human practices as such, that is, a universal theory of politics in relation to other human practices—a comprehensive doctrine. But positing the premise is surely permissible if the point is practical political in the sense of a counsel to democratic participants.

13. Perhaps someone will suggest taking Habermas's account also to be a "practical political" counsel to those who seek democratic political outcomes. But that interpretation is more difficult with Habermas because of his philosophical difference from Rawls. In Habermas's case, democracy as a political form is not simply taken for granted or posited. At least by implication, he holds that modern or fully critical moral and political rationality prescribes, at least wherever possible, government by way of (postmetaphysical) discourse. He defends democracy in the form of "Kantian republicanism" (102), that is, as the political expression of "the equalitarian individualism of modern natural law and universalistic morality" (137). Accordingly, the account of political decision based on secular reasons cannot be simply a procedural counsel to democratic citizens but is, rather, a postmetaphysical account of constitutional liberalism that is inconsistent with religious freedom.

14. I may here use the term "discourse" with a more inclusive meaning than does Habermas, at least typically. If, on his usage, discourse is the practice of argument, in which participants suspend other purposes in order to pursue solely the validation and invalidation of validity claims, I intend, in speaking of political discourse, to include all aspects of the public discussion and debate through which activities of the state are democratically determined. Accordingly, political discourse, in my sense, includes not only discourse in his strict sense but also what he calls communicative action. Still, the public discussion and debate always properly includes possible discourse in Habermas's strict sense—because every political claim pledges that, if contested, it can be validated by reasons.

15. Moreover, this reading is confirmed when, in his summary paragraph to "The Idea of Public Reason Revisited," Rawls formulates the question to which his proposal is addressed as follows: "How is it possible for those affirming a comprehensive doctrine, religious or nonreligious, and in particular doctrines based on religious authority, such as the Church or the Bible, also to hold a reasonable political conception of justice that supports a constitutional democratic society?" (Rawls

2005, 490). As far as I can see, the reference to beliefs based on religious authority intends the class of reasonable comprehensive doctrines to include some whose truth and falsity cannot be validated or invalidated by public reason. If so, the theory of democracy on which all reasonable comprehensive doctrines are legitimized must treat them all in like manner. If the true member of the protected class might be immune to reasoned validation, political principles determined through public reason cannot depend on which protected conviction is true—and, therefore, Rawls seeks a theory circumscribed by the domain of the political.

16. I do not imply that framers of the First Amendment to the US Constitution used "religious" in this sense. On my understanding, they meant by "religious" a more narrow class of convictions, namely, those conventional use of the term at the time singled out (most of which were Christian sects, although some popular uses may well have included all among, as we call them, the world religions). Perhaps this is why the First Amendment includes two clauses. Given that narrow meaning of "religious," the no establishment clause permits, by implication, the coercive imposition of a nonreligious or secularistic doctrine. Accordingly, the free exercise clause legitimizes what such a coercive imposition would delegitimize, namely, adherence to any religion. Coerced secularism is no less a violation of the Constitution than is an imposed religion. On that accounting, the two clauses together prohibit the state from establishing either a conventionally religious or a secularistic belief, that is, from teaching that any such belief is true or false. This is my point in proposing that "religious" in the principle of religious freedom, be understood broadly to include any explicit conviction about the ultimate terms of political evaluation—and on that meaning, the two clauses are, at least in this respect, redundant.

I recognize that, for some thinkers, the two clauses together do not, given the narrow meaning of religion, prevent the government from supporting "religion generally" and, therefore, teaching the falsity of or delegitimizing secularism. I doubt that such governmental teaching can be defended without appealing to a particular religious belief among those supported—so that it must be constitutionally imposed on all citizens. In any event, the view in question contradicts what I take to be the political importance of religious freedom, namely to constitute politics as a full and free discourse among all convictions about justice as such. For this reason, I propose using "religious" in the broad or extended sense.

17. Moreover, I expect, so to answer a question that one necessarily begs the question is, by implication, to call the question itself meaningless.

18. Accordingly, we may restate the critique of Rawls and Habermas: in each case, the theory becomes problematic because the account of public reason is not itself something about which the public as conceived in the theory may reason. Each theory imposes constraints on public reason—and does so, as mentioned previously, because the truth and falsity of religious beliefs, either in a strict or extended sense of "religious," is assumed to be immune to discursive assessment. Thereby, each theory proposes or entails a constitutional stipulation about the ultimate terms of political evaluation, namely, that they are, in the one case, freestanding and, in the other, postmetaphysical.

19. In an essay that contrasts his own "political liberalism" with Habermas's "Kantian republicanism," and wherein he calls the latter a comprehensive doctrine,

Rawls writes the following: "From what point of view are the two devices of representation to be discussed? And from what point of view does the debate between them take place? Always, we must be attentive to where we are and whence we speak. To all these questions the answer is the same: all discussions are from the point of view of citizens in the culture of civil society, which Habermas calls the *public sphere*" (Rawls 2005, 382). Some might read this last statement to intend, by implication, that a democratic constitution establishes nothing more or less than a full and free discourse within the public sphere, such that a democratic constitution is explicitly neutral to all conceptions of justice. Hence, political liberalism should not be constitutionally stipulated. If that is the point, the only argument I can find in Rawls for his proposal and thus against democratic theories dependent on a comprehensive doctrine turns on the following assertion: democratic options are exhausted by political liberalism and the constitutional imposition of a comprehensive doctrine. This assertion is, I speculate, why Rawls believes that civil society can debate differing conceptions of justice—and is also why he could ask for the better democratic solution. But the assertion implies either a) the freestanding character of justice should itself be constitutionally stipulated, or b) there is a third option, namely, a constitution that establishes nothing more and nothing less than a public debate among conceptions of justice. On this third alternative, the assertion and thus Rawls's argument for political liberalism are unconvincing. In other words, Rawls cannot deny a constitutional stipulation of political liberalism and simultaneously defend successfully the freestanding character of justice on the grounds that democratic options are exhausted by the two he asserts. If he continues to insist on a public debate, the defense of political liberalism would require an argument invalidating comprehensive conceptions of justice—and the conclusion of that argument is, against itself, a competitive comprehensive statement, equivalent to asserting that justice and, indeed, all moral prescriptions are everywhere and always dependent solely on conditions peculiar to historical location.

20. More often than not, Habermas speaks of moral and political discourses as concerned with the interests of affected individuals and groups, such that justice is explicated in terms of regulations equally in the interest of all or equally good for all (see, e.g., 1993, 5–8; 2005, 261–66). Moreover, the interests in question are not merely given "at the beginning" but, rather, are understood "at the end" of such discourses. Practical discourse depends, in other words, on each participant taking the perspective of the other or others, so that "equal consideration of everyone's interests" defines the interests from a "first-person plural perspective" (2005, 267, 268). Hence, "the worthiness of norms to be recognized is based not on an objectively determined agreement of interests that are given, but on the participants' interpreting and evaluating interests" (2005, 268). But it remains, as far as I can see, that moral principles or norms assume the goodness of fulfilling human interests, and those interests, following the cooperative interpretation and evaluation of them, are said to be morally indifferent—so that another principle of evaluation, on which moral indifference means equally good, is, against the nonteleological theory, implied. The implication becomes the more apparent when Habermas insists that his account does not contradict "the assumption that some of our needs are deeply rooted in our anthropology" and thus constitute "a core of what we take for

granted morally" as something "we encounter in all cultures" (2005, 268). What is taken for granted is the equal goodness of fulfilling those needs. Perhaps "the moral language game cannot be maintained intact in any other way under the conditions of postmetaphysical thinking" (2005, 275). But if, given postmetaphysical thinking, nonteleology alone remains, the implied self-indictment I have sought to identify is a negative argument against the denial of metaphysics.

CHAPTER FIVE

1. Some wish to distinguish between a denial and a refusal of universal moral principles. At least, this is one reading of Richard Rorty's point in proposing simply to "drop . . . the vocabulary" (Rorty 1988, 268) or "change the subject" (Rorty 1982, xiv). As far as I can see, however, a refusal here *is* a denial. To assert that moral theory may be valid while simply refusing claims to universal validity is to assert, by implication, that such theory requires no universal principle. But the latter assertion denies what every theory based on some universal moral principle or principles affirms, namely, that no moral prescription can be valid that does not imply the universal principle or principles in question.

2. I recognize that some moral theorists, for instance, some utilitarians, assert universal principles that do not claim to be a priori. I will briefly discuss those theories subsequent to a consideration of the two challenges mentioned here. At that point, I will be in a better position to explain why, in my judgment, universality without a priori status is not tenable.

3. On my usage, "ethical" is synonymous with "moral." I do not distinguish the two designations as does, for instance, Jürgen Habermas or Ronald Dworkin (see Habermas 1993; Dworkin 2011).

4. It may seem that Kant thereby defined "metaphysics" in what I earlier called its broad sense. But that formulation would be at least misleading. Kant's meaning purports to be independent of metaphysics in the strict sense, that is, of critical thought about existence as such—an independence expressed theoretically in his distinction between things-in-themselves and things-as-they-appear to humans. On my understanding, metaphysics in the broad sense implies but is not implied by metaphysics in the strict sense.

5. I should, perhaps, underscore that one or more thinkers may, in the case of each label mentioned, embrace the name and yet be an exception to what this summary statement alleges. For instance, John B. Cobb, Jr. and David Ray Griffin use the term "postmodern" to designate a metaphysical proposal and its importance for both science and morality that contrast with some distinctive features of modern thought (see, e.g., Cobb; Griffin).

6. This assertion, I recognize, implies the failure of arguments by Kant and every other Kantian for a supreme moral principle that is nonteleological. If any such argument is successful, some may hold, it thereby shows why alternatives for purpose in respects other than those designated by the principle are morally indifferent—namely, because those alternatives in those respects are neither morally good nor morally bad, both such evaluations being properly identified by the successfully established principle. As far as I can see, however, this line of thought presupposes

what needs to be established, namely, that moral and immoral characterize alternatives for purpose in some but not all respects. In other words, argument for moral evaluation of purposes in some respects would not be a successful argument for nonteleology unless the moral theorist in question could also show why comparing alternatives for purpose only in these respects is *sufficient* to moral evaluation. To the best of my knowledge, no such argument can be convincing, precisely because one would thereby evaluate purposes in all other respects as morally indifferent. That a partial comparison is sufficient to moral evaluation cannot, in other words, be derived from a nonteleological principle previously established; rather, it is a necessary condition of validating such a principle and, therefore, requires another principle by which alternative purposes are morally compared in all respects. Accordingly, arguments for supreme moral principles that are nonteleological cannot, I believe, be successful—and I have sought to criticize not only Kant (see Gamwell 1990, chapter 2) but also the revisions of Kant found in Karl-Otto Apel (see Gamwell 1990, chapter 5) and Alan Gewirth (see Gamwell 2000, chapter 5).

To be sure, Kant himself sought to define good action as such independently of *any* reference to ends humans pursue. Hence, every rational being as an objective end in itself "can be conceived only negatively, that is, as that which we must never act against" (Kant 1949, 54). In Kant, we might say, the partialist fallacy becomes complete; that is, purposes in all respects are said to be morally indifferent, notwithstanding a moral constraint on them that is "conceived only negatively." In the end, I doubt that Kant's theory provides any distinction between moral and immoral decision, and for this reason, recent Kantians (e.g., Apel and Gewirth) have sought other formulations of nonteleology. But it is not necessary to argue for that conclusion here.

7. Kantian conceptions of morality, we can conclude, are finally self-destructive in a way similar to separationist democratic theories on which the explicit meaning of religious freedom includes principles of justice separated from inclusive conceptions of the good. Each separationist account contradicts religious freedom because it stipulates in the political constitution a moral theory and thus denies or delegitimizes all religious convictions inconsistent with it. In a similar way, a nonteleological principle purporting to be universal contradicts its supposed separation because it implies its own inclusive conception of the good and, thereby, denies all others inconsistent with it.

8. The Kantian denial of an inclusive good, we might also conjecture, contributed more generally to the subsequent critique of universal subjectivity. Making a claim to meaning or truth is itself a purpose or aspect of a purpose; if the inclusive evaluation of purposes is in all respects dependent on location within the human adventure, then so, too, is evaluation of the validity or invalidity of any claim.

9. I have pursued an extended argument against alternatives and for metaphysical teleology in Gamwell 2011.

10. In this discussion, I intend to reserve "comprehensive good" to designate a good defined by the character of reality as such and thus a metaphysical good, so that "comprehensive purpose" designates pursuit of this good. But elsewhere, I have spoken of comprehensive assessments, just as Rawls speaks of comprehensive doctrines. In accord with this latter usage, one might well assume that a comprehen-

sive good is affirmed by any comprehensive assessment whose fundamental principle is teleological, whether or not the good thereby affirmed is metaphysical. On that meaning, "comprehensive good" and "inclusive good" are synonymous. The ambiguity in meaning is, perhaps, occasioned by my conviction that Kant, as discussed in the previous paragraph, was correct in this: an inclusive moral good by which all decision with understanding is directed can only be a metaphysical good. In any event, neither understanding of "comprehensive good" will cause one to misunderstand my subsequent discussion, given only the recognition that some affirmations of an inclusive good assert, as does the neoclassical metaphysics I will appropriate, a metaphysical good.

11. Given the necessity of these discriminations to subjectivity as such, I take the primitive understanding of "self, others, and the whole" to include the particular self in question, subjectivity as such, concrete reality as such, and the difference between all-inclusive and fragmentary relativity as such.

12. The good defined metaphysically is, moreover, exemplified in the subjective pursuit of it, such that a given human activity maximizes its own creativity when it decides in accord with the comprehensive purpose. Some neoclassical thinkers have argued to the contrary, taking the moral law to require some balance between present realization and contribution to future realization of unity-in-diversity. Given the focus here on activities as concrete singulars, that view is, I think, untenable. If the required aim at maximal good includes some balance between present and future creativity, what should be pursued for future activities, when they become present, would not be creativity but, rather, the right balance of their then present and the then future creativity. The good would be realized, in other words, not insofar as creativity is realized but, rather, insofar as pursuit of creativity in the right balance between present and future is realized. But this conclusion refutes itself: there would be no reason to seek a balance between present and future creativity unless the realization of creativity (not the realization of this balance) defines the good. Moreover, I doubt that a present human activity can decide with understanding its own measure of the good if this is distinct from deciding what future end or state of affairs to pursue. Choosing the latter *is* choosing what to be or become. Still, nothing said here denies that moral activity may sacrifice the future good of the human individual in question, even if service to the future as such also can be substantially coincident with service to the individual's own future good. Rather, original decision for maximal creativity in the future as such maximizes creativity *in the present activity*; the aim at maximal future good *is* realization of maximal present good.

13. Strictly speaking, I believe, the phrase here should be "whatever the other consequences." All human decisions, I am persuaded, aim at consequences, including those that decide in accord with the deontological norms of social practices. For instance, to keep a promise is so to decide that, in consequence, whatever one has promised occurs—even if, in conforming to the norm of promise making as a social practice, one does so whatever the other consequences of one's action. One pays the financial debt as owed, say, whatever might be the other consequences of so using one's money. Thus, "other consequences" designates what one would be obligated to assess with respect to maximizing the good were one to apply the comprehensive purpose directly to one's action.

Also, "whatever the (other) consequences" does not mean that norms of social practices are unexceptionable. But the definition of exceptional circumstances must be specific; for instance, many promises are not morally binding if acting to the contrary is required to save a life. What is proscribed is a *nonspecific* definition of circumstances, which would prescribe an appeal to the value of consequences overall. For more extended discussions, see Gamwell 2000, 182f.; 2011, 115f.

14. I do not imply that Barry would agree with my use of his argument.

15. I am not sure whether Apel in fact uses this name. Still, it clearly summarizes, as far as I can see, the meta-norm for which he repeatedly argues.

CHAPTER SIX

1. On my reading, Niebuhr is not entirely clear whether his "negative proof of Christian truth" includes a sound argument against classical as well as secularistic alternatives. In the summary introduction to his Gifford Lectures, a refutation of secularism alone seems possible: "The conviction that man stands too completely outside of both nature and reason to understand himself in terms of either without misunderstanding himself, belongs to general revelation in the sense that any astute analysis of the human situation must lead to it. But if man lacks a further revelation of the divine he . . . will end by seeking absorption in a divine reality which is at once all and nothing" (I, 15). Nonetheless, the human situation, on Niebuhr's account, includes our participation in nature as well as our self-consciousness, and a later chapter makes clear that human decisions or actions relate something unique to totality as a realm of meaning: "Human consciousness involves the sharp distinction between the self and the totality of the world. Self-knowledge is thus the basis of discrete individuality . . . and thereby of the uniqueness of the individual" (I, 55). Given this analysis, both classicism and secularism are, for any astute reasoning, incoherent as explications of the human situation. "From the standpoint of human thought," Niebuhr writes, "this unconditioned ground of existence, this God, can be defined only negatively" (I, 14). On his strongest position, as far as I can see, reflection on our common existential experience is sufficient to negate both alternatives to authentic theism, even if, for Niebuhr, human thought cannot provide a positive validation of Christian truth—and henceforth, I will assume this stronger account.

2. Niebuhr's use of the term "religion" is not consistent throughout his writings. At the least, one may identify two different meanings. Narrowly used, the term designates the affirmation that some reality beyond or transcendent to the world is the source of meaning—in which case, "secularism" is used in contrast to "religion" (see, e.g., 1944, especially chapter 1). Broadly used, "religion" designates any conviction regarding the source of meaning—in which case, secularism is a religious type. To repeat the point, "religion" (narrowly used) designates the theistic type of "religion" (broadly used). This essay uses the term in Niebuhr's broad sense.

3. For Niebuhr, every answer to the religious question (what is the source of meaning for human life?) implies and is implied by some answer to the ethical question (what is the norm of human existence?). In terms somewhat foreign to him, there is, for Niebuhr, no fundamental separation between fact and value; to the contrary, religious beliefs in one way or another understand the totality of things as

a realm of *meaning*. Because politics is included within the totality, every political theory, at least in some basic respect, implies and is implied by some answer to the ethical question.

4. To my knowledge, Daniel Day Williams was the first to point this out. If "'the highest unity is a harmony of love in which the self relates itself in its freedom to other selves in their freedom under the will of God,' where is the 'ultimate contradiction' between the self-assertion of the human life and the divine *agape*?" (Williams 1949, 75–76).

5. Or, again: "The real fact is that the absolute character of the ethic of Jesus conforms to the actual constitution of man and history, that is, to the transcendent freedom of man over the contingencies of nature and the necessities of time, so that only a final harmony of life with life in love can be the ultimate norm of his existence" (II, 50–51).

6. As these last two citations suggest, the terms "justice" and "harmony"—and now, by implication, "imperfect harmony"—appear to be, at least for the most part, Niebuhrian synonyms for the reciprocity sought by "mutual love." It is true that Niebuhr's writings sometimes suggest a distinction between the aims at justice and at mutual love. "The will to do justice is a form of love, for the interests of the neighbor are affirmed. Mutual love . . . is also a form of love, for the life of the other is enhanced" (1953a, 160). The difference implicit here is probably that between seeking reciprocity among a large number of individuals in a society (justice) and seeking reciprocity among a small number of individuals, such as those included in family or friendship relations (mutual love). On Niebuhr's account, as is well known, the possibilities for "harmony with other interests and vitalities" (II, 74) are greater in the latter (see, e.g., 1932; I, 208–19; 1949, 185). Insofar as "justice" and "mutual love" are distinguished in this way, "imperfect harmony" appears to be the inclusive term for what both, each in its own context, seek, designating reciprocity whatever the number of individuals in question. But even if these differences are observed, all three terms have the following in common: each refers to an activity in which "the self regards itself as an equal, but not as a specially privileged, member of a group" (1953b, 160). It is this characteristic that, as we shall see, is critical to the argument Niebuhr offers for his ethic. Thus, we may, as he does more often than not, ignore the distinctions.

7. In 1932, Niebuhr published *Moral Man and Immoral Society: A Study in Ethics and Politics*, from which the religious and political publics first recognized the presence of an original and compelling mind. The title, Niebuhr wrote in 1965, should have been: "Not So Moral Man and Even More Immoral Society" (1965a, 22).

8. In Niebuhr's text, this description is used to characterize the Marxist "version of perfection," which, along with many other secularistic views, regards "the transcendent norm as a simple possibility" (II, 86). But Niebuhr, in the succeeding paragraph, calls this Marxist view "a significant secular vision of the 'Kingdom of God,' where even the highest form of equal justice is transcended in an uncoerced and perfect mutuality" (II, 87).

9. Or, again: "His [Jesus's] ethical doctrine contains an uncompromising insistence upon conformity to God's will without reference to the relativities and

contingencies of historical situations" (II, 73; see f.). If conformity to God's will were the pursuit of a transcendent telos, it would not ignore "reference to the relativities and contingencies of historical situations."

10. If the norm of mutual love is indeed theistic in presupposition, there is no need to read the dictum as Niebuhr apparently does. To the contrary, it may assert that loving God with all one's heart and soul and mind and strength, and thus loving the neighbor as oneself (i.e., acting for maximal mutuality in the world and in the long run), is losing the duplicity of trust in oneself and finding one's integrity by trusting in God alone.

11. Thus, the word "seems" in the previous paragraph's citation from *The Nature and Destiny of Man* is not added to suggest some rational conceivability in spite of initial appearances. Rather, Niebuhr asserts that eternity inclusive of time is literally incoherent but nonetheless ultimately coherent because it is the ground of ultimate meaning. See also Niebuhr's essay, "Mystery and Meaning" (1958a, 123–145).

12. On defining God negatively, see n. 1 to this essay.

13. Niebuhr was familiar with at least some of Whitehead's works. To the best of my understanding, however, Niebuhr never entertained the neoclassical concept of the divine reality because he read Whitehead through the assumption that, in speaking of God, "eternity" must be the inclusive designation. This seems confirmed when, in *Faith and History*, Whitehead's concept of God is apparently equated with Hegel's necessary process in or through which the inclusively eternal God achieves "self-conscious freedom" (see 1949, 43), and both are said to assert that "the true *nature* of God can be understood only in terms of the end as well as the genesis of the temporal process" (1949, 43, emphasis added). To be sure, Niebuhr's discussion does not explicitly identify Whitehead with Hegel's view. Still, Niebuhr never suggests that Whitehead's account advances quite a different concept, requiring an independent assessment.

Niebuhr was also familiar with Hartshorne's proposal, and a footnote in *The Nature and Destiny of Man* even suggests an affirmation of God's temporality. Hartshorne, Niebuhr writes, "gives a very profound analysis of this problem [that is, God's relation to history through suffering love] and presents the thesis that God's perfection must be defined primarily in terms of . . . His self-surpassing character" (II, 71, n. 1). But this appreciation of Hartshorne's thesis is appropriated within Niebuhr's own account of eternity and time, as becomes apparent in the final chapter of Niebuhr's Gifford Lectures:

> the freedom of man . . . in direct relation to eternity . . . would seem to justify . . . [the] dictum that each moment of time and history is equidistant from eternity. But the dictum is only partially justified, for it leaves the other dimension of history out of account . . . Insofar as every act and event, every personality and historical construction is immersed in an historical continuum it takes its meaning from the whole process. If we look at history only from 'above' we obscure the meaning of its 'self-surpassing' growth. (II, 300–01)

Taken out of context, Niebuhr's meaning here may not be entirely clear; but any ambiguity is removed, as far as I can see, by noting that this citation comes from the discussion where eternity above and at the end of time is said to be in all respects the same, so that God's character is suprarational because eternity includes time.

14. Given the general revelation of God's character "as redeemer as well as judge," one might wonder why sin occurs at all. Even if duplicity or inauthenticity is always an alternative because humans are self-consciously free, why would any human allow that possibility any credence, given her or his ever-present awareness that God's redemption is the source of worth or meaning? I have sought to address this question, which I take to formulate a vexing problem in theological anthropology, in Gamwell 2000, chapter 2. Our temptation to duplicity can be, I propose, explained by our fragmentary consciousness—and because the world is as necessary to God as God is to the world, it is senseless to call the fragmentariness of all worldly things and thus the temptation present in all human existence conditions for which God is responsible.

CHAPTER SEVEN

1. The argument, it may be objected, has concerned itself with completely negative *metaphysical* statements rather than all statements about reality, so that the conclusion about all statements is unwarranted. But any statement about reality that is completely negative implies a completely negative metaphysical statement, because metaphysical conditions are the conditions of possibility as such. Hence, if all valid metaphysical statements are at least partially positive, no valid statement about reality can be completely negative.

2. I have sought to formulate an extended argument against the logical possibility of statements that designate by complete negation in Gamwell 2011, chapter 1.

CONCLUSION

1. Here, as throughout the volume, I use "metaphysics," unless otherwise noted, in the strict sense, that is, to designate critical thought about reality or existence as such, so that "metaphysical" may also designate the characteristics or features common to strictly all things.

2. I do not include in this book essays that engage Kantian or post-Enlightenment alternatives because I have previously criticized representatives of each—for instance, Alan Gewirth and Karl-Otto Apel, in the one case, and John Rawls and Jeffrey Stout, in the other. See, for instance, Gamwell 2000, especially chapter 5, and Gamwell 2011, especially chapters 5 and 6.

3. Summarily stated, then, the humanitarian ideal backed by neoclassical theism is advocated against theories of moral and political principles said to be nonuniversal (post-Enlightenment), universal but nontranscendental (e.g., utilitarianism), transcendental but nonteleological (Kantian), metaphysical but nontheistic (Murdoch) and classically theistic (Niebuhr).

WORKS CITED

Alley, Robert S., editor. 1985. *James Madison on Religious Liberty*. Buffalo, NY: Prometheus Books.
Amar, Akhil Reed. 2005. *America's Constitution: A Biography*. New York: Random House.
Apel, Karl-Otto. 1979. "Types of Rationality Today: The Continuum of Reason between Science and Ethics." In *Rationality Today*, edited by Theodore Gereats. Ottowa: University Press, 307–40.
———. 1980. *Toward a Transformation of Philosophy*. London: Routledge and Kegan Paul.
———. 1992. "Normatively Grounding 'Critical Theory' through Recourse to the Lifeworld? A Transcendental-Pragmatic Attempt to Think with Habermas against Habermas." In *Philosophical Interventions in the Unfinished Project of Enlightenment*, edited by Axel Honneth, Thomas McCarthy, Claus Offe, and Albrecht Wellmer. Cambridge, MA: MIT Press, 125–70.
———. 1996. *Selected Essays, Volume Two: Ethics and the Theory of Rationality*. Atlantic Highlands, NJ: Humanities Press.
———. 1998. *From a Transcendental-semiotic Point of View*. Manchester and New York: Manchester University Press.
Aquinas, St. Thomas. 1948. *Introduction to St. Thomas Aquinas*, edited by Anton C. Pegis. New York: Modern Library.
Audi, Robert and Wolterstorff, Nicholas. 1997. *Religion in the Pubic Square: The Place of Religious Convictions in Political Debate*. New York: Rowan and Littlefield.
Barry, Brian. 1995. *Justice as Impartiality*. Oxford, UK: Clarenden Press.
Beer, Samuel H. 1993. *To Make a Nation: The Rediscovery of American Federalism*. Cambridge, MA: Harvard University Press, 1993.
Bellah, Robert. 1974. "Civil Religion in America." In *American Civil Religion*, edited by Russell E. Richey and Donald G. Jones. New York: Harper & Row, 21–44.
Benn, Stanley I. 1963. "Authority." In *The Encyclopedia or Philosophy*, edited by Paul Edwards. New York: Macmillan Publishing Co., 215–18.
Bennett, Lerone Jr. 2000. *Forced into Glory: Abraham Lincoln's White Dream*. Chicago: Johnson Publishing Co.
Bernstein, R. B. 2003. *Thomas Jefferson*. New York: Oxford University Press.
Breyer, Stephen. 2005. *Active Liberty: Interpreting our Democratic Constitution*. New York: Random House (Vintage Books).
Buckley, Thomas E., S. J. 1988. "The Political Theory of Thomas Jefferson." In *The Virginia Statute for Religious Freedom*, edited by Merrill D. Peterson and Robert C. Vaughan. New York: Cambridge University Press, 75–107.

Burt, John. 2013. *Lincoln's Tragic Pragmatism: Lincoln, Douglas, and Moral Conflict.* Cambridge, MA: The Belknap Press of Harvard University Press.

Carwardine, Richard. 2006. *Lincoln: A Life of Purpose and Power.* New York: Alfred A. Knopf.

Cobb, John B. Jr. 2002. *Postmodernism and Public Policy: Reframing Religion, Culture, Sexuality, Class, Race, Politics, and the Economy.* Albany, NY: State University of New York Press.

Coffin, William Sloane. 2004. *Credo.* Louisville, KY: Westminster John Knox Press.

DeGeorge, Richard T. 1985. *The Nature and Limits of Authority.* Lawrence, KS: University Press of Kansas.

Donald, David Herbert. 1995. *Lincoln.* New York: Simon & Schuster.

Dworkin, Ronald. 2006. *Is Democracy Possible Here? Principles for a New Political Debate.* Princeton, NJ: Princeton University Press.

———. 2011. *Justice for Hedgehogs.* Cambridge, MA: The Belknap Press of Harvard University Press.

Eberle, Christopher J. 2002. *Religious Convictions in Liberal Politics.* New York: Cambridge University Press.

Foner, Eric. 2010. *The Fiery Trail: Abraham Lincoln and American Slavery.* New York: W. W. Norton.

Fox, Richard. 1985. *Reinhold Niebuhr: A Biography.* New York: Pantheon Books.

Gamwell, Franklin I. 1990. *The Divine Good: Modern Moral Theory and the Necessity of God.* San Francisco: HarperCollins.

———. 1995. *The Meaning of Religious Freedom: The Modern Political Problematic and Its Democratic Resolution.* Albany, NY: State University of New York Press.

———. 2000. *Democracy on Purpose: Justice and the Reality of God.* Washington, DC: Georgetown University Press.

———. 2011. *Existence and the Good: Metaphysical Necessity in Morals and Politics.* Albany, NY: State University of New York Press.

Gaustad, Edwin S. 1996. *Sworn on the Altar of God: A Religious Biography of Thomas Jefferson.* Grand Rapids, MI: William B. Eerdmans.

Greenawalt, Kent. 1988. *Religious Convictions and Political Choices.* New York: Oxford University Press.

Griffin, David Ray. 2007. *Whitehead's Radically Different Postmodern Philosophy: An Argument for Its Contemporary Relevance.* Albany, NY: State University of New York Press.

Habermas, Jürgen. 1984. *The Theory of Communicative Action, Volume 1: Reason and the Rationalization of Society.* Boston: Beacon Press.

———. 1987. *The Theory of Communicative Action, Volume 2: Lifeworld and System: A Critique of Functionalist Reason.* Boston: Beacon Press.

———. 1990. *Moral Consciousness and Communicative Action.* Cambridge, MA: MIT Press.

———. 1992. *Postmetaphysical Thinking: Philosophical Essays.* Cambridge, MA: MIT Press.

———. 1993. *Justification and Application: Remarks on Discourse Ethics.* Cambridge, MA: MIT Press.

———. 1996. *Between Facts and Norms: Contributions to a Discourse Theory of Law and Democracy*. Cambridge, MA: MIT Press.

———. 2003. *The Future of Human Nature*. Cambridge, UK: Polity Press.

———. 2005. *Truth and Justification*. Cambridge, MA: MIT Press.

———. 2008. *Between Naturalism and Religion*. Cambridge, UK: Polity Press.

———. 2013. "Reply to My Critics." In *Habermas and Religion*, edited by Craig Calhoun, Eduardo Mendieta, and Jonathan VanAntwerpen. Cambridge, UK: Polity Press, 347–90.

Habermas, Jürgen et al. 2010. *An Awareness of What is Missing: Faith and Reason in a Post-Secular Age*. Cambridge, UK: Polity Press.

Hamilton, Alexander, Madison, James, and Jay, John. 2003. *The Federalist with Letters of "Brutus,"* edited by Terence Ball. New York: Cambridge University Press.

Hammond, Phillip E. 1998. *With Liberty for All: Freedom of Religion in the United States*. Louisville, KY: Westminster John Knox.

Hartshorne, Charles. 1948. *The Divine Relativity: A Social Conception of God*. New Haven, CT: Yale University Press.

———. 1962. *The Logic of Perfection and Other Essays in Neo-classical Metaphysics*. LaSalle, IL: Open Court.

Hofstadter, Richard. 1973. *The American Political Tradition*. New York: Alfred A. Knopf.

Hume, David. 1975. *Enquiries Concerning Human Understanding and Concerning the Principles of Morals*. Oxford: Clarendon Press. (Original publications 1748 and 1751)

Jaffa, Harry. 1982. *Crisis of the House Divided: An Interpretation of the Issues in the Lincoln-Douglas Debates*. Chicago: The University of Chicago Press. (Original publication 1959)

———. 2000. *A New Birth of Freedom: Abraham Lincoln and the Coming of the Civil War*. Lanham, MD: Rowan & Littlefield Publishers.

Jefferson, Thomas. 1999. *Political Writings*, edited by Joyce Appleby and Terence Ball. New York: Cambridge University Press.

Jefferson, Thomas. *The Papers of Thomas Jefferson*. http//avalon.law.yale.edu/subject_menus/jeffpap.asp.

Kant, Immanuel. 1934. *Religion within the Limits of Reason Alone*. LaSalle, IL: Open Court. (Original publication 1793)

———. 1949. *Fundamental Principles of the Metaphysic of Morals*. Indianapolis: Bobbs-Merrill. (Original publication 1785)

———. 1956. *Critique of Practical Reason*. Indianapolis: Bobbs-Merrill. (Original publication 1788)

———. 1965. *Critique of Pure Reason*. New York: St. Martin's Press. (Original publication 1781, 1787)

Lincoln, Abraham. 1946. *Abraham Lincoln: His Speeches and Writings*, edited by Roy P. Basler. Cleveland, OH: World Publishing Co.

Lincoln, Abraham and Douglas, Stephen A. 2004. *The Lincoln-Douglas Debates*. Mineola, New York: Dover Publications, Inc.

MacIntyre, Alasdair. 1984. *After Virtue*. Notre Dame: University of Notre Dame Press.
Maier, Pauline. 1997. *American Scripture: Making the Declaration of Independence*. New York: Random House.
———. 2010. *Ratification: The People Debate the Constitution, 1778–1788*. New York: Simon & Schuster.
Marty, Martin E. 1988. "The Virginia Statute Two Hundred Years Later." In *The Virginia Statute for Religious Freedom*, edited by Merrill D. Peterson and Robert C. Vaughan. New York: Cambridge University Press, 1–21.
McPherson, James. 1991. *Abraham Lincoln and the Second American Revolution*. New York: Oxford University Press.
Meacham, Jon. 2012. *Thomas Jefferson: The Art of Power*. New York: Random House.
Mead, Sidney E. 1963. *The Lively Experiment: The Shaping of Christianity in America*. New York: Harper & Row.
Miller, William Lee. 2008. *President Lincoln: The Duty of a Statesman*. New York: Alfred A. Knopf.
Murdoch, Iris. 1970. *The Sovereignty of Good*. New York: Routledge.
———. 1993. *Metaphysics as a Guide to Morals*. New York: Allen Lane/Penguin Press.
Murray, John Courtney, S. J. 1960. *We Hold These Truths: Catholic Reflections on the American Proposition*. Kansas City, MO: Sheed and Ward.
Niebuhr, Reinhold. 1932. *Moral Man and Immoral Society: A Study in Ethics and Politics*. New York: Charles Scribner's Sons.
———. 1935. *An Interpretation of Christian Ethics*. New York: Harper & Bros.
———. 1937. *Beyond Tragedy: Essays on the Christian Interpretation of History*. New York: Charles Scribner's Sons.
———. 1938. "Christian Faith and the Common Life." In *Christian Faith and Common Life*, edited by Nils Ehrenström, M. F. Dibelius, William Temple [and others]. Chicago: Willett Clark & Co., 69–97.
———. 1940. *Christianity and Power Politics*. New York: Charles Scribner's Sons.
———. 1941–43. *The Nature and Destiny of Man*, 2 volumes. New York: Charles Scribner's Sons.
———. 1942. "Religion and Action." In *Science and Man*, edited by Ruth Nada Anshen. New York: Harcourt Brace & Co., 44–64.
———. 1944. *The Children of Light and the Children of Darkness: A Vindication of Democracy and a Critique of Its Traditional Defense*. New York: Charles Scribner's Sons.
———. 1949. *Faith and History: A Comparison of Christian and Modern Views of History*. New York: Charles Scribner's Sons.
———. 1952. *The Irony of American History*. New York: Charles Scribner's Sons (republished Chicago: The University of Chicago Press, 2008).
———. 1953a "Christian Faith and Social Action." In *Christian Faith and Social Action*, edited by John H. Hutchinson. New York: Charles Scribner's Sons, 225–42.
———. 1953b. *Christian Realism and Political Problems: Essays on Political, Social, Ethical, and Theological Themes*. New York: Charles Scribner's Sons.
———. 1955. *The Self and the Dramas of History*. New York: Charles Scribner's Sons.

———. 1958a. *Pious and Secular America*. New York: Charles Scribner's Sons.

———. 1958b. "Reply to Interpretation and Criticism." In *Reinhold Niebuhr: His Religious, Social, and Political Thought*, edited by Charles W. Kegley and Robert W. Bretall. New York: Macmillan Co.

———. 1965a. *Man's Nature and His Communities: Essays on the Dynamics and Enigmas of Man's Personal and Social Existence*. New York: Charles Scribner's Sons.

———. 1965b. "The Religion of Abraham Lincoln." *Christian Century* 82 (February 10): 172–75.

Ogden, Schubert M. 1966. *The Reality of God*. New York: Harper & Row.

———. 1986. *On Theology*. San Francisco: Harper Row.

———. 1992. *Is There Only One True Religion or Are There Many?* Dallas: Southern Methodist University Press.

Rawls, John. 1971. *A Theory of Justice*. Cambridge, MA: The Belknap Press of Harvard University Press.

———. 1985. "Justice as Fairness: Political not Metaphysical." *Philosophy and Public Affairs*, 14: 223–51.

———. 2005. *Political Liberalism*, expanded edition. New York: Columbia University Press. (Original publication 1993)

Rorty, Richard. 1982. *Consequences of Pragmatism*. Minneapolis: University of Minnesota Press.

———. 1988. "The Priority of Democracy to Philosophy." In *The Virginia Statute for Religious Freedom: Its Evolution and Consequences in American History*, edited by Merrill D. Peterson and Robert C. Vaughn. New York: Cambridge University Press, 257–88.

Searle, John R. 1983. *Intentionality: An Essay in the Philosophy of Mind*. New York: Cambridge University Press.

———. 1992. *The Rediscovery of the Mind*. Cambridge, MA: MIT Press.

Smith, Steven D. 1995. *Foreordained Failure: The Quest for a Constitutional Principle of Religious Freedom*. New York: Oxford University Press.

Staloff, Darren. 2005. *Hamilton, Adams, Jefferson: The Politics of Enlightenment and the American Founding*. New York: Hill and Wang.

Stout, Jeffrey. 2004. *Democracy and Tradition*. Princeton, NJ: Princeton University Press.

Stone, Ronald H. 1972. *Reinhold Niebuhr: Prophet to Politicians*. Nashville, TN: Abingdon Press.

Strauss, David. 2010. *The Living Constitution*. New York: Oxford University Press.

Sunstein, Cass R. 1996. *Legal Reasoning and Political Conflict*. New York: Oxford University Press.

Taylor, Charles. 1995. *Philosophical Arguments*. Cambridge, MA: Harvard University Press.

Tillich, Paul. 1952. *The Courage to Be*. New Haven: Yale University Press.

———. 1957. *Systematic Theology*, vol. 1. Chicago: The University of Chicago Press.

White, Morton. 1978. *The Philosophy of the American Revolution*. New York: Oxford University Press.

Whitehead, Alfred North. 1925. *Science and the Modern World*. New York: Mentor Books/Macmillan.

———. 1926. *Religion in the Making.* New York: The MacMillan Company.
———. 1938. *Modes of Thought.* New York: Capricorn Books.
———. 1941. "Immortality." In *The Philosophy of Alfred North Whitehead*, edited by Paul A. Schilpp. Evanston, IL: Northwestern University Press, 682–700.
———. 1961. *Adventures of Ideas.* New York: The Free Press. (Original publication 1933)
———. 1978. *Process and Reality: An Essay in Cosmology*, corrected edition, edited by David Ray Griffin and Donald W. Sherburne. New York: The Free Press. (Original publication 1929)
Williams, Daniel Day. 1949. *God's Grace and Man's Hope.* New York: Harper & Bros.
Wills, Gary. 2002. *Inventing America: Jefferson's Declaration of Independence.* Boston: Houghton Mifflin.
Wilson, James. 2007. *Collected Works of James Wilson*, 2 vols, edited by Kermit L. Hall and Mark David Hall. Indianapolis: Liberty Fund.

INDEX

Active Liberty: Interpreting our Democratic Constitution (Breyer), 207n20
Adventures of Ideas (Whitehead), xii, 121, 195
Amar, Akil Reed, 53
American Colonization Society, 66
Anselm, 189
Apel, Karl-Otto, 211–12n6, 217–18n6, 220n15, 223n2 (conclusion)
   moral theory of, 126–27, 141
   post-Enlightenment, his critique of, 124–26
Aquinas, Thomas, 183
aristocracy, 25, 39, 45, 53, 131, 209–10n6
Aristotle, 106, 127, 131
Articles of Confederation, 40, 46
authority, 205n6, 205n8
   de facto and *de jure*, 42–43, 48, 206n11
   domain of, 44, 51–52
   primal source of, 43, 51
Axial Age, 210–11n5

Bacon, Francis, 23
Barry, Brian, 140, 220n14
Barth, Karl, 147
Beer, Samuel, 45
Bellah, Robert, 6
Bentham, Jeremy, 11, 122
Between Facts and Norms (Habermas), 210n3
Between Naturalism and Religion (Habermas), 94
Bill for Establishing Religious Freedom in Virginia. *See* Jefferson, Thomas: Virginia Bill of

Blair, Montgomery, 66
Breyer, Stephen, 207n20
Brown v. Board of Education, 32, 35, 55
Buchanan, James, 80
Buckley, Thomas E., 201n4
Burke, Edmund, 35
Burkean ideology, 40, 204n4, 205n7
   defined, 35
Burlamaqui, Jean Jacques, 11
Burt, John
   concepts and conceptions in, 64
   conversation with, 68–86 passim
   Kant in, 71
   Lincoln and colonization in, 66
   Lincoln's implicit intentions in, 64–68, 71–72, 79, 84
   Lincoln's racism in, 66
   Lincoln's Tragic Pragmatism, xi, 64
   Lincoln's tragic pragmatism, meaning of, 70, 209n1
   Rawls in, 68–70, 71
   "self-evident" in, 70

Calhoun, John C., 61, 75
Calvinism, 76, 77, 78
campaign finance laws, 208n22
children, 207n18
children of light and of darkness, 148–49, 158
Citizens United v. Federal Election Commission, 207n17
civil disobedience, 206n14, 208n22
Civil Rights Movement, 37, 55, 156
Civil War, 32, 37, 49, 75, 209–10n6
Clay, Henry, 66
Cobb, John B. Jr., 217n5

Coffin, William Sloane, 208n21
"Coherence, Incoherence, and the Christian Faith" (Niebuhr), 170
command theory of law, 34
common human experience, 28, 143–45, 197
  defined, 116–17
common humanity, defined, 139
common law constitution, explained, 34–35
  See also Strauss, David: living Constitution of
communicative respect, 126, 141–42, 197, 198, 220n15
community of human rights, 141, 197
complete negation, 127–28, 192, 223n1 (chapter 7), 223n2 (chapter 7)
  defined, 186
comprehensive assessment, 18–28 passim, 202–03n8, 203n9, 203n10, 203n13, 203–04n15, 218–19n10
  defined, 18
  systematic ambiguity of, 25
comprehensive good. *See* comprehensive purpose
comprehensive purpose, 131, 137–46 passim, 197, 198
  direct and indirect application of, 139–43
  present activity and, 219n12
  telos of, defined, 136, 218–19n10
comprehensive teleology, defined, 107
  See also metaphysical teleology
Comte, Auguste, 122
Constitution, US. *See* US Constitution
Constitutional Convention, 27, 45–47, 52, 63
Continental Congress, 3, 43, 44, 47, 51, 52, 53, 60, 61, 205–06n10, 207n16
Conway, Maria, 10
creativity, category of, 136–46 passim
  defined, 136
Critique of Practical Reason (Kant), 128
Critique of Pure Reason (Kant), 128
critique of universal subjectivity, 124–26, 133, 136, 146, 198

de facto and *de jure* authority, 42–43, 48, 206n11
Declaration of Independence, xi, 4, 23, 60, 195
  laws of nature and of nature's God in, 13, 28–29, 50–52, 70, 76, 201n2, 207n16
  as primary authority, 43–47, 49, 51, 52, 73, 85, 87, 205–06n10
  ratification of, 205–06n10
  the Revolution and, 43–47
  See also Lincoln, Abraham: Declaration and
DeGeorge, Richard T., 205n8
democracy
  as human right, 141–42
  question of, 73
  as telos, 142–43
  See also popular sovereignty; way of reason
democratic constitution
  explicit and implicit meanings of, 25, 56–57, 203n13
  hermeneutical and normative questions about, 56–57
  as self-democratizing, 57
  See also popular sovereignty; way of reason
democratic motivation, 99–100, 115–19
deontology, 197, 219–20n13
  human rights and, 139–42
  nonteleology and, 139–42
Dewey, John, 131, 186
divine good, ix, x, 138, 143, 175, 177, 190, 200
divine purpose, ix, xii, 29, 198
  Lincoln and, 81, 88
  Murdoch and, 190
  Niebuhr and, 177
Douglas, Stephen, 61–62, 67, 68, 80, 209n2
  See also Lincoln-Douglas debates
dramas of history, 148
Dred Scott decision, 62, 64
Dworkin, Ronald, 217n3

Eighteenth Amendment, 208n23
Eighth Amendment, 32, 33
Einstein, Albert, 67
Emancipation Proclamation, 66, 67, 79, 85
emotivism, 129
Employment Division, Department of Human Resources of Oregon v. Smith, 202n8
Enlightenment project, 181
Equal Rights Amendment, 37
ethics of citizenship, 5–26 passim, 48, 58, 73
  defined, 4
  explicit and implicit understandings, 132–34, 136
  humanitarian ideal and, 144–45

fairness or good policy, 34, 35, 39, 56, 59
Faith and History (Niebuhr), 222–23n13
Federalist Papers (Hamilton, Madison, Jay), 44, 45
Fifteenth Amendment, 37
First Amendment, 22
  free speech clause, 35, 55, 203n9, 206n13, 208n22
  religion clauses, 18, 36, 50, 202–03n8, 203n9, 215n16
formative prescriptions
  constitutional, 57, 58, 73, 74, 89, 208n22
  rights as, 73, 74
  statutory, 208n22
  substantive prescriptions and, 57, 74, 89, 208n22
Fort Sumter, 63, 75
Fourteenth Amendment, 32, 33, 55
Fox, Richard, 147
Franklin, Benjamin, 6, 14, 63
freedom of speech, 35, 55, 203n9, 206n13, 208n22

Gaunilo, 189
genealogy of reason, 98
  explained, 210–11n5

Gettysburg Address, 62, 71, 83, 87
Gewirth, Alan, 217–18n6, 223n2 (conclusion)
Gifford Lectures
  Murdoch's, 179
  Niebuhr's, 163, 165, 169, 175, 220n1, 222–23n13
global lifeworld, 145
good, the, and the right. *See* right, the, and the good
Griffin, David Ray, 217n5
Gurley, Phineas D., 78, 209n3

Habermas, Jürgen, xi–xii, 195, 214n14
  Apel and, 211–12n6
  Between Facts and Norms, 210n3
  Between Naturalism and Religion, 94
  conversation with, 91–119
  democratic motivation and, 99–100, 115–19
  epistemic attitudes in, 96–98, 103
  equalitarian universalism in, 96, 97, 98–99, 105, 214n13
  faith and knowledge in, 101, 110
  genealogy of reason in, 98, 210–11n5
  institutional translation proviso in, 96, 103
  Kant and, 91–93, 94, 99, 101–02, 106, 114, 117
  Kantian republicanism and, 94, 114, 214n13, 215–16n19
  learning processes in, 96–98, 101–04, 109, 115, 210n4, 210–11n5, 211–12n6
  lifeworld in, 132
  "metaphysical baggage" in, 101, 102
  metaphysics, the meaning of, in, 106–07
  morality and ethics in, 98–99, 101, 102, 104, 107, 216–17n20
  motivational deficiency in, 99, 117
  nonteleology and, 93, 98, 99, 107, 127, 216–17n20
  political deficiency in, 100, 118
  postmetaphysical, explained by, 91–92, 98, 101, 210–11n5, 211–12n6

Habermas, Jürgen (continued)
  postsecular consciousness in, 98, 213n11
  practical political and, 214n13
  project of, 91–93
  rational reconstruction in, 210–11n5, 211–12n6
  Rawls and, xi–xii, 94–96, 105–09, 213n11, 215n18, 215–16n19
  religion in, 92, 95–101, 102
  "Religion in the Public Sphere," 94, 100
  religious freedom in, 12, 93–109
  religious teleology in, 102, 105
  secularism in, 92–94, 98, 103
  Theory of Communicative Action, The, 91
  translation, his meaning of, 96, 97, 103–04, 212n7
  universalization principle in, 93
  validity claims in, 91–92, 210n1, 210n2
  way of reason and, 113–15
Hammond, Phillip, 6
Hart, H. L. A., 64
Hartshorne, Charles, xiii, 174, 195, 199, 222–23n13
  ontological argument and, 189–92
  See also neoclassical metaphysics; neoclassical theism
Hegel, George Wilhelm Friedrich, 190, 222–23n13
Heidegger, Martin, 124–25
hermeneutical question
  defined, 37, 204n3
  normative question and, 37–41, 56, 58–60, 205n5, 205n7, 207n16, 209n25
hermeneutical turn, 124, 132, 133
Herndon, William, 76, 77
Hodges, Albert G., 78
Hofstadter, Richard, 65, 83
"house divided," xi
  Lincoln's use of, 80–85
  New Testament meaning of, 80–81, 83
  radical sense of, 81

human flourishing, 122, 142, 143, 146, 175, 197–98
  defined, 138–39
human rights, 27, 123, 127
  community of, 141, 197
  Habermas on, 97
  Kantian account of, 139–41
  Lincoln on, 72
  neoclassical metaphysics and, 139–43
  nonteleology and, 130
  teleology and, 139–43, 197
humanitarian ideal, xii, 131, 136, 197–198, 223n3 (conclusion)
  explicit affirmation of, 143–46
  Kantian alternative and, 123, 126–30
  post-Enlightenment alternative and, 124–26
  twofold sense of, 122, 143
  Whitehead on, 121–22
Hume, David, 9, 10, 122, 128–29, 130
Hutcheson, Francis, 11

"Idea of Public Reason Revisited, The" (Rawls), 214–15n15
ideals, pursued and illustrated, 166–67, 168–69, 173, 177
implicit understandings, 132–35, 143
  as necessary, 133
  See also original understandings
inclusive good, defined, 218–19n10
Independence Hall, 61
institutional translation proviso, 96, 103, 104
Interpretation of Christian Ethics, An (Niebuhr), 163, 165
Irony of American History, The (Niebuhr), 147

Jaffa, Harry, 65, 71, 72, 74
Jefferson, Thomas, x–xi, xiii, 64–66, 195, 201n2, 201n4, 202n7, 205n9
  autobiography, 4
  bill of rights and, 3, 17
  colonization in, 66
  conversation with, 1–29
  Declaration and, 4, 11, 12, 23, 70

"democratical" government in, 45
eloquence of, 2
   First Inaugural, 5, 26
legacy of, 28–29
"Life and Morals of Jesus," 6
moral sense theory and, 8–12
Notes on the State of Virginia, 10
"Philosophy of Jesus," 6
privacy of religious beliefs in, 9
racial views of, 10
rationalism of, 13–15, 20, 22–23, 28, 29
religion, his meaning of, 5–6
religionist account of, 5–8, 19
religious freedom in, 1–15, 19, 20–26, 28–29
"self-evident" in, 11–12, 23, 70
separationist account of, 8–12, 19
theism of, 3, 9, 12, 13, 17, 28–29
tribunal of reason and, 13–14, 20, 23, 24, 26, 29, 195
Virginia Bill of, 2–4, 12, 13, 14–15, 17, 28, 50, 90
Virginia Constitution, draft of, 3–4
See also Lincoln, Abraham: Jefferson and

Jefferson's problem, 33, 36
   as heremenutical and normative, 38, 58–59
Jefferson's question, 33, 35, 48
   as hermeneutical and normative, 38, 40
justification and truth, 213n11

Kansas-Nebraska Act, 65, 209n2
Kant, Immanuel, 164, 175, 192, 223n3 (conclusion)
   basic moral options in, 118
   Burt on, 71
   complete negation in, 186
   critique of Hume by, 129
   Critique of Practical Reason, 128
   Critique of Pure Reason, 128
   Habermas on, 91–93, 94, 99, 101–02, 106, 114, 117
   insight of, 129–30
   metaphysics and, 123–31, 217n4
   moral theory of, 123–31, 136, 137, 139, 146, 199, 217–18n6, 218–19n10
   Murdoch on, 180–89 passim
   ontological argument in, 189
   original decision in, 137
   radical evil in, 137
   reason in, 71, 92–93, 123, 128–31, 181, 187, 211n6
   Religion within the Limits of Reason Alone, 137
   teleology in, 131
Kantian alternative, 123, 126–28, 131, 136, 199
   criticized, 128–30, 198
Kantian moral theory, 126–31, 136, 146, 183, 199, 218n8, 223n3 (conclusion)
   criticized, 128–30, 198, 213n10, 216–17n20, 217–18n6, 218n7
   Enlightenment project and, 181
   human rights and, 139–41
Kantian nonteleology. *See* Kantian moral theory
Kant's insight, 129–30

laws of nature and of nature's God, 13, 28–29, 50–52, 70, 76, 201n2, 207n16
learning process, 96–98, 101–04, 109, 115, 211–12n6
   explained, 210n4, 210–11n5
Leibniz, Gottfried Wilhelm von, 189
"Life and Morals of Jesus" (Jefferson), 6
lifeworld, defined, 124
Lincoln, Abraham, x, xiii, 195, 209n1, 209n2, 209n3
   ancient faith of, 68, 76, 80, 85, 86, 195
   Bible and, 77, 80, 86
   Bloomington Convention and, 85
   Clay and, 66
   colonization in, 66
   conversation with, 61–90
   Declaration and, 61–87 passim
   emancipation and, 63, 65, 66, 67, 79, 85

Lincoln, Abraham *(continued)*
  explicit commitments of, 65–66, 68, 74
  First Inaugural, 71, 75, 84
  formative/substantive distinction and, 74–75
  Gettysburg Address, 62, 83, 87
  government by and of the people in, 71, 74, 83, 96, 206n15
  "house divided" metaphor in, 80–85
  implicit commitments of, 64–68, 71–72, 74, 79, 84
  Jefferson and, 70–71, 76, 90
  legacy of, 86–90
  natural law in, 70, 76
  popular government in, 83
  public mind in, 84, 87, 209–10n6
  racism of, 66
  Rawls and, 68–71
  religious beliefs of, 76–79, 81–82, 86–88
  religious freedom and, 89–90
  Second Inaugural, 76, 78, 79, 86, 87, 133, 136
  slavery and, 52–53, 61–90 passim
  substantive justice in, 74
  Thirteenth Amendment and, 63, 87
  US Constitution and, 63
Lincoln, Mary, 76
Lincoln, Robert, 78
Lincoln, Willy, 209n3
Lincoln-Douglas debates, 61, 62, 63, 66, 68, 69
Lincoln's Tragic Pragmatism (Burt), xi, 64
linguistic turn, 124, 132, 133
Living Constitution, The (Strauss), xi, 31, 34, 37. 39
living Constitution. *See* Strauss, David: living Constitution of
Locke, John, 11, 23

MacIntyre, Alasdair, 181
Madison, James, 2, 5, 14, 17, 33, 44, 45, 48, 63
Marshall, John, 206n15
Marx, Karl, 77, 221n8

maximal common humanity, 139–46 passim, 198
maximal creativity. *See* comprehensive purpose
McClellan, George, 84
McCulloch v. Maryland, 206n15
Mead, Sidney E., 6–7, 201n3
meta-ethical
  as analogous to promising, 21, 22
  as pragmatic feature, 21
  See also pledge of political claims
metaphysical good. *See* comprehensive purpose
metaphysical teleology, 93, 102, 103, 109, 130–31, 137–46 passim, 218n9
  deontology and, 139–43
  divine individual and, 118
metaphysical theism, ix, xii, 208n24
  See also neoclassical theism
metaphysics, 219n12
  book's meaning of, x, 107, 123, 223n1 (conclusion)
  broad and strict meanings of, x, 180–81
  Habermas on, 106–07
  Kantian, 123–31, 217n4
  Murdoch on, 179–81, 188, 192
  Platonic, 124
  Rawls on, 106–07
  systematic ambiguity of, x, 123
  See also neoclassical metaphysics
Metaphysics as a Guide to Morals (Murdoch), mentioned, 179
Missouri Compromise, 65, 70
modus vivendi, 99, 196, 201n1
monarchy, 25, 45, 46, 53, 56, 205n9
Moral Man and Immoral Society (Niebuhr), 221n7
moral sense theory, 8–13, 28
motivational deficiency, 99, 117
Murdoch, Iris, xiii, 199, 223n3 (conclusion)
  conversation with, 179–93
  demythologization in, 184
  egoism in, 182
  emphatic moral realism of, 179–85, 186, 189, 193

Gifford Lectures, 179
God, her view of, 179, 184–85, 187, 189–93
  the Good in, 183–91, passim
  Hartshorne and, 189–92
  Hegel and, 190
  Kant and, 180–92 passim
  life without telos in, 187
  loss of theism in, 184, 185, 189
  metaphysics in, 179–81, 188, 192
  Metaphysics as a Guide to Morals, mentioned, 179
  ontological argument in, 179, 183, 184, 189
  perfection in, 183–86, 189, 191, 192
  pilgrimage in, 182, 183, 187, 190, 191
  Plato and, 180–92 passim
  pragmatism of, 185–89
  religion in, defined, 183
  remythologization in, 185
  as reserved friend, xiii, 179, 193
  Sovereignty of Good, The, 185, 187
  theism and, 179, 184, 187, 189
  Tillich and, 183, 184, 185, 189, 191
  ubiquity of value in, 181, 186, 193
Murray, John Courtney, 73–74
  religionist account of, 7–8, 16, 201n4, 204n16
  We Hold These Truths, 73
mutual love as theistic norm, 168, 177, 222n10
  See also Niebuhr, Reinhold: mutual love in
"Mystery and Meaning" (Niebuhr), 222n11

Nature and Destiny of Man, The (Niebuhr), 147, 222n11, 222–23n13
Nazi Germany, 166
negation. *See* complete negation
negative apologetic, 148, 172–73, 220n1
neoclassical metaphysics, xii, 121–46 passim, 195–96, 200
  democracy and, ix–x, 141–42
  final real things in, 135–36
  good defined by, 136, 137
  human rights and, 139–41
  humanitarian ideal and, 123, 143–44, 197–99
  Kant and, 127–28
  the moral law and, 136–38
  religion and, 144
  See also metaphysics
neoclassical theism, 134–36, 138, 196, 197, 199
  arguments for, 88–89, 137–38
  Niebuhr and, 172–77
  sin and, 223n14
New York and Pennsylvania, 5
New Zealand, 33
Newton, Isaac, 23
Niebuhr, H. Richard, 147
Niebuhr, Reinhold, xii, 223n3 (conclusion)
  agape in, 152–54, 159, 160, 163
  Biblical symbols in, 170–71, 175
  Burt's use of, 86
  children of light and of darkness in, 148–49
  classicism in, defined, 150
  "Coherence, Incoherence, and the Christian Faith," 170
  conversation with, 147–77
  democracy in, 27
  existential decision in, 148–50, 172–73, 175–76, 220n1
  Faith and History, 222–23n13
  forgiveness in, 160–61, 172
  general resurrection in, 161, 174
  Gifford Lectures, 163, 165, 169, 175, 220n1, 222–23n13
  God, his view of, 150–51, 169, 170–72, 174, 175–76, 199, 222n12, 222–23n13
  harmony in, 151–72 passim, 221n5
  Hartshorne and, 222–23n13
  ideals pursued and illustrated and, 166–67, 168–69, 173, 177
  imperfect harmony in, 221n6
  "impossible possibility" in, 163
  indeterminate love in, 159, 163, 165, 166, 167

Niebuhr, Reinhold *(continued)*
　Interpretation of Christian Ethics, An, 163, 165
　Irony of American History, The, 147
　Jesus Christ, his view of, 152, 155, 159, 171, 172, 176, 221n5, 221–22n9
　justice and love in, 160, 163
　justification in, 154–56, 159–61, 163, 167–68, 174–75, 177
　Kingdom of God in, 158–60, 161, 163, 166, 169, 174, 175, 221n8
　law of love in, 153
　Lincoln and, 86–87
　Marxist perfection in, 221n8
　Moral Man and Immoral Society, 221n7
　mutual love in, 154–58, 174, 221n6, 222n10
　"Mystery and Meaning," 222n11
　Nature and Destiny of Man, The, 147, 222n11, 222–23n13
　negative apologetic of, 148, 172–73, 220n1
　project of, 147–51
　realism in, xiii, 27, 158, 173, 176
　religion, his use of, 148–51, 220n2, 220–21n3
　revelation in, 171, 172, 175–76, 220n1
　sacrificial love in, 151–72 passim, 174, 221n5
　secularism in, defined, 149–50
　sin in, 157–58, 163–65, 176, 223n14
　as systematic theist, 148, 171, 174
　Union and, 147–48
　Whitehead and, 222–23n13
nonteleology, 198, 218n8
　criticized, 128–30, 198, 213n10, 216–17n20, 217–18n6, 218n7
　defined, 127
　deontology and, 139–42
　desire and, 117
　Habermas on, 93, 98, 99, 107, 127, 216–17n20
　way of reason and, 113–15
　See also Kant: moral theory of; Kantian moral theory

normative question
　defined, 38
　hermeneutical question and, 37–41, 56, 58–60, 205n5, 205n7, 207n16, 209n25
Notes on the State of Virginia (Jefferson), 10

Obama, Barack, 147
Ogden, Schubert M., 173, 188, 205n6
omnipresence of value. *See* ubiquity of value
ontological argument, 179, 189–93
original decision, 81, 137, 144, 209n4, 219n12
original understandings, 28, 81, 118, 144, 145, 197
　moral principle and, 116–17, 136–37
　See also primitive understanding
originalism, xi, 34, 37–38, 42, 43, 47, 204n1, 206n13
　moderate form, 33
　rigorous form, 31–33
ought implies can, 24, 95, 117, 137, 141, 163, 164

pacifism, 152, 166, 169
Paine, Thomas, 77
partialist fallacy, 128, 139, 217–18n6
patriotic citizen, 51, 208n21
　defined, 38, 57
　extra-constitutional action and, 49
Pennsylvania, 46
　New York and, 5
permanence of worth, 88–89, 177, 187–88, 190
Phenomenology of Mind (Hegel), 190
"Philosophy of Jesus" (Jefferson), 6
Pierce, Franklin, 80
Plato, 121, 124
　Murdoch on, 180–92 passim
Platonic pragmatist, 186–87
pledge of political claims, 24, 25–26, 92, 141–42, 196, 203n11, 214n14
　as analogous to promising, 20–22
　as pragmatic, 21, 111
Plessy v. Ferguson, 35, 55

political deficiency, 100, 118
Political Liberalism (Rawls), 12, 68, 214n12
political respect, 26, 141–42, 198
popular sovereignty, xi, 15–27, 44–59, 196, 202–03n8, 203n11, 206n11, 209n2
  adherence to and profession of, 26, 56–58, 72–74, 208n22
  children and, 207n18
  constitutional authority and, 41–59 passim
  defense of, 208n24
  defined, 15–16, 73
  exclusions and, 45, 52–58, 208n21
  explicit constitutional meaning of, 56–57, 203n13, 203–04n15
  inclusiveness of, 53–56
  Lincoln and, 72–75, 89
  pledge to argument and, 20–21
  ratification and, 46–49
  religious freedom and, 16–17, 50
  republican government and, 44–46, 48–50, 51, 53, 55, 58, 207n19
  way of reason and, 20–27, 54–58
  See also religious freedom, way of reason
post-Enlightenment, 130, 132, 146, 223n2 (conclusion), 223n3 (conclusion)
  as alternative, xii, 123–25, 131, 136, 199
  criticized, 125–26, 198
postmetaphysical, xii, 91–119 passim, 210–11n5, 211–12n6
  Habermas's definition of, 92
postmodern, 124, 217n5
postsecular, 98, 213n11
pragmatic necessity, 24, 28, 29, 70, 116, 125–26, 136, 137, 141
  See also original understandings; original decision
pragmatic self-evidence, 24, 70, 71–72
pragmatism, 185–89, 192
  See also tragic pragmatism
precept of avoidance, 108, 110

primitive understanding, 134, 136, 219n11
  See also original understandings
promise of the Revolution. *See* Revolution, promise of
Proslogion (Anselm), 189
public mind, 84, 87, 209–10n6

question of democracy, 73

ratification
  as authoritative, 48–49, 206n11
  Declaration and, 205–06n10
  as nonauthoritative, 42–43, 46–48
  opposition to, 48
rational reconstruction, 210–11n5, 211–12n6
Rawls, John, 201n5, 209n25, 218–19n10, 223n2 (conclusion)
  argument for political liberalism, 109–10, 215–16n19
  Burt on, 68–70, 71
  democracy in, 72–73
  family of political conceptions in, 213n9
  Habermas and, xi–xii, 94–96, 105–09, 213n11, 214n13, 215n18, 215–16n19
  "Idea of Public Reason Revisited, The," 214–15n15
  ideal for citizens of, 212n8
  metaphysics, the meaning of, in 106
  Political Liberalism, 12, 68, 214n12
  political liberalism in, 12, 59–60, 70, 94, 105, 106, 108–09, 214n12, 215–16n19
  as practical political, 108, 214n12
  precept of avoidance in, 108, 110, 214–15n15
  proviso of, 95, 96, 105–06
  religious freedom and, 12, 94, 110
  separationism of, 12, 204n16
  Theory of Justice, A, 12, 68
  way of reason and, 113–15
reality presupposes understanding, 125, 132

reality prior to understanding, 132
reason's tribunal. *See* tribunal of reason
religion. *See* religious, the meaning of
religion clauses, 18, 36, 50, 202–03n8, 203n9, 215n16
"Religion in the Public Sphere" (Habermas), 94, 100
Religion within the Limits of Reason Alone (Kant), 137
religionist account, 6–8, 13, 16, 19, 201n4, 204n16, 215n16
religious
   conventional meaning of, 18, 19, 23, 28, 96, 110–11, 115, 117, 119, 202n8, 215n16
   extended meaning of, 17, 18, 23, 28, 110, 117, 202n8, 215n16
   as rational or not rational, 21–22, 23, 111–12, 196–97
   strict meaning of, 110, 111, 144, 202n7
religious freedom
   constitutional authority and, 50–51
   constructive account of, 15–29, 109–19
   explicit and implicit meanings of, 21, 25, 112, 119
   extended sense of, 17–18, 118
   First Amendment and, 18, 36, 50, 202–03n8, 203n9, 215n16
   Habermas on, 12, 93–109
   Habermas and Rawls on, 105–109
   hopeless idealism and, 27
   Jefferson on, 1–15, 19, 20–26, 28–29
   Lincoln and, 89–90
   motivational implications of, 115–19
   Murray on, 7–8
   neoclassical metaphysics and, 195–200
   Rawls on, 12, 59–60, 105–109
   religious intransigence and, 26
   US history and, 195
   See also popular sovereignty; way of reason
Religious Freedom Restoration Act, 202–03n8

religious reservation, 86, 87, 117, 118, 119
republican government. *See* popular sovereignty: republican government and
Revolution, promise of, xi, 11, 43–52 passim, 205–6n10, 207n16, 207n19
right, the, and the good, 102, 104, 105, 113–14, 115, 212n7
   See also Habermas, Jürgen: morality and ethics in
Robert's Rules of Order, 3
Rorty, Richard, 186, 217n1

Second Amendment, 32, 55
Second Great Awakening, 78
senseless agencies, 121, 122, 145
separationist account, 10–13, 19, 204n16
Seventeenth Amendment, 37
Shelby County v. Holder, 207n17
slave rebellions, 49, 206n14
slavery, 49, 52–53, 209–10n6
   See also Lincoln, Abraham: slavery and
Smith, Steven D., 203n10, 203n14
social practices, 139–43, 197, 219–20n13
   argument for, 141
   democracy as, 141–43
   as universal, 140–41
solipsism, 125
Sovereignty of Good, The (Murdoch), 185, 187
sovereignty of the people. *See* popular sovereignty
statutory law, 3, 18, 57, 74, 203–04n15, 208n22, 208n23
Stephens, Alexander, 75
Stout, Jeffrey, 223n2 (conclusion)
Strauss, David, 195, 204n4
   Brown v. Board of Education in, 32, 35, 55
   Burkean ideology in, 35, 36, 40, 204n4
   commerce clause in, 32–33
   conversation with, 31–60
   Eighth Amendment in, 32, 33
   Fifteenth Amendment in, 36
   First Amendment in, 35, 36

Fourteenth Amendment in, 32, 33, 36, 55
freedom of speech in, 35, 55
Jefferson's problem and, 32, 36, 38–40
Jefferson's question and, 33, 35, 40, 48
Living Constitution, The, xi, 31, 34, 37, 39, 204n1
living Constitution of, 31–43 passim, 54–56, 204n2, 205n7, 206n13
originalism and, xi, 31–33, 34, 37–38, 42, 43, 47
popular sovereignty and, 41–59 passim
religion clauses in, 36
Second Amendment in, 32, 55
small-c constitution of, 34, 204n2
Thirteenth Amendment in, 37
written Constitution of, 31–40 passim, 54–55, 60, 204n2
subjective turn, 124
substantive prescriptions
  as constitutional, 57–58, 206n12, 208n23
  formative prescriptions and, 57, 74, 89, 208n22
  as religious conviction, 144
  as statutory, 208n22, 208n23
  as theory, 89
Sunstein, Cass, 108
Supreme Court, 32, 34, 55, 80, 202n8, 206n13, 207n17

Taney, Roger B., 62, 80
teleology
  defined, 98
  direct and indirect application of, 139–43
  as nonmetaphysical, 131
  See also comprehensive purpose; metaphysical teleology
Theory of Communicative Action, The (Habermas), 91
Theory of Justice, A (Rawls), 12, 68
Thirteenth Amendment, 37, 63, 87
Tillich, Paul, 147, 183, 184, 185, 191
  ontological argument and, 189

tragic pragmatism, 70, 209n1. See also *Lincoln's Tragic Pragmatism*
tribunal of reason, 13–14, 20, 23, 24, 26, 29, 195
Twenty-Sixth Amendment, 207n18

ubiquity of value, 181, 186, 193
ultimate terms of political evaluation
  defined, 15–16
  systematic ambiguity of, 25, 203n2
undeniable truths, 11, 23, 24–25, 70, 116, 203n12
understandings, implicit, 132–35, 143
  See also original understandings
Union Theological Seminary, 147
Unitarianism, 14
universal social practice, 140–41
universalization principle, 93
US Constitution, xi, 31–59 passim, 204n4
  abiding character of, 39–58, 207n19
  adherence to and profession of, 26, 56–58, 72–74, 208n22
  Article V, 42, 46, 47
  Article VI, 42, 50
  Article VII, 46, 47
  authority of, 41–59 passim, 205n7, 205n8, 206n11, 206n13
  commerce clause, 32–33, 55
  Eighteenth Amendment, 208n23
  Eighth Amendment, 32, 33
  Fifteenth Amendment, 37
  First Amendment, 18, 22, 35, 36, 50, 55, 202–03n8, 203n9, 206n13, 208n22, 215n16
  Fourteenth Amendment, 32, 33, 55
  free speech clause, 35, 55, 203n9, 206n13, 208n22
  fugitive slave provision, 49, 206n14
  hermeneutical question about, 37–41
  normative question about, 38–41
  Preamble, 49, 51, 63
  religion clauses, 18, 36, 50, 202–03n8, 203n9, 215n16
  Second Amendment, 32, 55
  Thirteenth Amendment, 37, 63, 87

utilitarianism, 131, 199, 217n2, 223n3 (conclusion)

von Hügel, Baron, 170
Voting Rights Act, 207n17

Washington, George, 63
way of reason, the, 11–12, 197–200, 203–04n15, 208n24
   adherence to and profession of, 26, 56–58, 72–74, 208n22
   as better solution, 109–15
   as coherent alternative, 20–27
   democratic motivation and, 115–19
   nonteleology and, 113–15
   See also popular sovereignty; religious freedom
We Hold These Truths (Murray), 73
we the people. *See* popular sovereignty
Weber, Max, 93
White, Morton, 11–12, 23, 70
Whitehead, Alfred North, xiii, 174, 181, 199, 222–23n13
   Adventures of Ideas, xii, 121, 195
   adventures of ideas and, 195
   appeal to reason in, 145
   consciousness and experience in, 132
   creativity in, 136
   democracy's justification in, 122, 146
   final real things in, 135, 136, 140
   God, his view of, 134
   humanitarian ideal in, xii, 121–22
   individuals in, 135
   metaphysical compliments in, 191
   morality without metaphysics in, 122, 131
   permanence of worth in, 88, 177, 188, 190
   primitive discrimination in, 134
   reality and understanding in, 132
   religion and, 80, 82, 209n4
Williams, Daniel Day, 221n4
Williamsburg, 3
Wilson, James, 41, 45–47, 63, 206n15
Wittgenstein, Ludwig, 124–25, 126
world religions, 5, 215n16
written Constitution. *See* Strauss, David: written Constitution of

Zeus, 185